Alexander Kalinin

Fabiano Caruana

His Amazing Story and His Most Instructive Chess Games

New In Chess 2018

© 2018 New In Chess

Published by New In Chess, Alkmaar, The Netherlands
www.newinchess.com

All photos New In Chess except page 10 (Tony Cortizas, Jr) and 178 and 194
(both Lennart Ootes).

Cover design: Buro Blikgoed
Translated and updated from *Fabiano Caruana. Shakhmatniye uroky* (Russian
Chess House, 2018)
Translation: Steve Giddins
Supervision: Peter Boel
Proofreading: Maaike Keetman
Editing and typesetting: Peter Boel
Production: Anton Schermer

Have you found any errors in this book?
Please send your remarks to editors@newinchess.com. We will
collect all relevant corrections on the Errata page of our website
www.newinchess.com and implement them in a possible next edition.

ISBN: 978-90-5691-813-2

Fabiano Caruana

Contents

Explanation of symbols

The chessboard
with its coordinates:

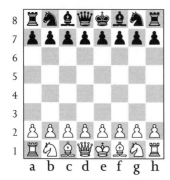

±	White stands slightly better
∓	Black stands slightly better
±	White stands better
∓	Black stands better
+−	White has a decisive advantage
−+	Black has a decisive advantage
=	balanced position
!	good move
!!	excellent move
?	bad move
??	blunder
!?	interesting move
?!	dubious move
N	novelty

❑ White to move
■ Black to move
♔ King
♕ Queen
♖ Rook
♗ Bishop
♘ Knight

Introduction

His brilliant result at the St Louis super-tournament in 2014, with the remarkable score of 8.5/10 (including, in the first seven rounds, the Fischeresque score of seven victories), propelled 22-year old Fabiano Caruana into the small group of challengers to the World Champion.

In the 2016 Candidates' tournament in Moscow, Caruana was regarded as one of the favourites. This is how he was described in pre-tournament prognostications by grandmaster Emil Sutovsky:

> 'Fabiano Caruana was somewhat surprisingly regarded as favourite by almost half of the survey respondents. Despite the fact that eighteen months have passed since his legendary performance at St Louis, people understand that the Italian-American is capable of achieving something similar again. However, I personally am mystified that a whole series of appearances at the highest level since then has seen him drop sharply, from his cosmic rating of 2844 to a more modest 2794. Why did the qualitative leap in his play, which was noticed in the summer-autumn of 2014, turn out to be so short-lived? I do not know. But honestly, I would very much like to see that Caruana again – his play was the sort of chess that I personally consider ideal. An extraordinary degree of principle in the opening, a "wholeness" in his formulation of the game, deep strategic plans based on tactical subtleties, and, to the delight of the fans, numerous victories in games against the "Berliners" (including Carlsen). It was chess that was a symbiosis of science, game and sport, rather than the Carlsen approach, which can be described as purely chess-as-a-game. Can Caruana again combine these ingredient and shine? Definitely!'

In that Moscow Candidates tournament, Caruana was close to qualifying for the 'match of his life', but after losing a dramatic game in the final round against Sergey Karjakin, he was forced to settle for 'only' second place. He then followed up with a convincing win in the US Championship and a gold medal with the American team at the Olympiad (Baku 2016), all of which showed that he was ready for a new step forward.

In the January 2017 FIDE rating list, Caruana (2827) occupied second place, only 13 points behind Magnus Carlsen (2840).

Two years after Moscow, Caruana did make the final jump. After a highly convincing win in the Berlin Candidates Tournament in March 2018 (despite losing to Karjakin again!) the American grandmaster is up for his greatest challenge to date. In November he will be playing his World Championship match with Magnus Carlsen. Experts predict that this match will be very close and tense. Will it be the culmination of the amazing story of Fabiano Caruana?

Alexander Kalinin
Moscow, July 2018

Note: In several games I have cited a few comments by Fabiano Caruana himself or by other (grand-)masters. Most of these comments appeared earlier in New In Chess Magazine or on ChessBase.

PART I

The rise of an American chess star

Fabiano Caruana, 2003, New England (Photo: Tony Cortizas, Jr)

CHAPTER 1

A running start

Fabiano Caruana was born on 20 July 1992 in Miami. He was the third child in a large Italian family, significantly younger than his brother and sister.

Fabiano showed exceptional chess ability early on, and his father took the five-year-old to the Brooklyn Chess Club (at the time, the family had moved to Brooklyn), the same club where the legendary Bobby Fischer had begun his career! Fabiano loved to read chess books and later said:

'At first, I studied by myself, from books and magazines, and spent many hours at the board every day. I think this was a very important step, as I acquired the habit of working hard.'

Soon the youngster began working with the popular American children's trainer, Bruce Pandolfini.

'I started working with Fabiano when he was only five,' recalls Pandolfini, 'and it was obvious that he had a rare intuition, was brave in attack and was one of the five most talented players of his age, whom I had seen.'

Then, between the ages of eight and twelve, Caruana trained with grandmaster Miron Sher.

As expected in this age, the boy plunged into the atmosphere of numerous chess battles with his peers. The habit of playing a lot is one which has remained with Fabiano to this day, and he remains notable for it among his colleagues and to the surprise of experts.

Here are some extracts from an interview which Caruana gave to journalist Evgeny Atarov for the Russian website Chess Pro in 2012:

E.A. 'You feel a need to play and work constantly?'

F.C.: 'Most of all, to play! I can greatly enjoy the feeling of battle. Nowadays study means hours and hours of working with the computer, in which you have to be the creator. The computer is excellent at refuting stuff, but you have to come up with the ideas yourself. I prefer the process of play, because here we are in equal conditions with the opponent: he invents something, then I invent something...'

EA.: 'What aim do you set yourself when you sit at the board: do you want to get pleasure from the game, or just to win and score a point in the tournament table?'

FC.: 'For me, chess is a battle. Most of all, I want to win. Of course, I enjoy it when I manage to create something special on the board, a beautiful idea or something that I can recall with pleasure afterwards...'

EA.: 'Many children fall madly in love with chess when they first start to play, but gradually, when they have to work at it, this love dissipates and gives way to necessity. Haven't you lost your love of chess over the years of work?'

FC.: 'Undoubtedly, it is hard to retain all your life that initial feeling of wonder. I have the same story, but I have never come to hate chess... over the years, I have come to like some aspects of chess more and some less, but every time, I find something special. Chess opens before one a mass of tempting possibilities, such as the chance to see the world.'

EA.: 'So the love remains, all the same?'

FC.: 'Hmm. Probably, yes... I have never thought about this, but now you ask, I have to say probably yes. I get enormous pleasure every time I sit at the board. Every time!'

EA.: 'What does a professional chess player need, so as constantly to improve?'

FC.: 'First and foremost, never relax your demands on yourself. One must constantly work, not give oneself pauses and indulgences. It is also very important, in my opinion, to constantly maintain one's form, i.e. all the time to be involved in the game. You have to be constantly engaged in chess, and if you are not sitting directly at the board, you should be engaged, looking at what is happening around you... you must constantly improve, find and identify for yourself what is new. If you are talented and do all this, you will constantly grow. I don't think there is any other method of self-perfection.'

EA.: 'Looking at yourself, do you sometimes ask yourself where you get the energy to work and play so much? Do you have problems with energy?'

FC.: 'Yes, chess requires a lot of energy. After a seven-hour game, one often finds it hard to stand up, one is so tired. But it's not a problem for me. I don't get so tired during a game as others do. I don't know the explanation – maybe it is just my physiology. I recover my strength quickly.'

EA.: 'Do you do sport or anything? Gymnastics or maybe jogging?'

FC: 'None of these things at all. I walk a lot...'

EA.: 'We understand that you can play 20 or more games in a month. But do you enjoy it, when you play so much?'

FC.: 'Not always. You can't play every game with the same degree of pleasure. Sometimes you just feel tired. But I try to get pleasure from the process of playing, from every game, and do not think about the fact that

I played yesterday, and the day before, and will play again tomorrow. After all, this is my job and I should try to do it properly.'

In 2002 and 2003, Caruana won the Pan-American Championship (under 10) and achieved the FIDE Master title. At this same period, he scored his first victory against a GM in a one-to-one game. In the first round of September's Manhattan Chess Club tournament, his victim was the experienced Alexander Wojtkiewicz.

Game 1 Sicilian Defence B27
Fabiano Caruana
Alexander Wojtkiewicz
New York 2002

1.e4 c5 2.♘f3 g6 3.d4 ♗g7 4.♗e3 ♘f6 5.♘c3 cxd4 6.♗xd4 ♘c6 7.♗b5 ♘xd4 8.♕xd4 0-0 9.e5 ♘e8 10.0-0-0 d6 11.♕d2?!

He could keep the initiative with 11.♕h4!. Now the advantage passes to Black.

11...♗g4 12.♗xe8 ♖xe8 13.exd6 exd6 14.♕xd6 ♗xc3 15.♕xd8 ♗xb2+ 16.♔xb2 ♖axd8 17.♖xd8 ♖xd8 18.♘e5 ♗f5 19.g4 ♗e6 20.♖e1

The endgame favours Black, thanks to his strong bishop and superior pawn structure. Now 20...♖d6 is tempting, planning to attack with the queenside pawns, or 20...

g5, fixing the g4-pawn on a light square.

20...♖d2?
The rook will be attacked on the d2-square. It is hard to say exactly what the grandmaster overlooked, but almost every one of his next few moves looks doubtful.

21.♘d3 ♗xg4 22.h3

22...♗f3
As soon becomes apparent, Black is ready to sacrifice the exchange. But why not do so whilst picking up the h3-pawn: 22...♗xh3 23.♔c3 ♖xd3+ 24.cxd3 ?

23.♖e3 ♗c6?
The other bishop retreat, 23...♗h5 leads to a draw by repetition after 24.♖e7 ♗f3 25.♖e3, Perhaps the GM was working on the principle that it was better to lose than to draw!

24.♔c1 ♖xd3 25.♖xd3

Stronger was 25.cxd3, creating a passed pawn.

25...♔g7 26.♔d2 ♔f6 27.♔e3 ♔g5 28.♔d4 ♔h4 29.♖g3 f5 30.♔e5 ♗e4 31.c4 g5 32.♖b3 ♗g2 33.♔xf5 h6

34.♔g6 h5 35.♔h6 g4 36.hxg4 hxg4 37.♔g6 ♗f3 38.♔f5 ♔h3 39.♔f4 ♔g2 40.♖b2 a6 41.c5 ♔h2 42.a4 ♔g2 43.a5 ♔h2 44.♖b3 ♔g2 45.♖xf3

Black resigned.

Of course, the game is far from being a masterpiece, but the sensationalist Americans claimed that, by winning this game at the age of 10 years and 61 days (!), Caruana had become the youngest player ever to defeat a grandmaster in an official game. This is probably true, although one should remember that in 1922, the wunderkind Sammy Reshevsky, also aged 10, defeated the great David Janowski at the New York tournament of American masters.

In 2002 and 2003, Fabiano took part in the World Junior Championships (at U-10 and U-12 respectively), but without any special success. On neither occasion did he even get in the top three medallists. Luckily, in chess, as well as sporting success, there are also creative criteria, by which one can judge the potential of a young player.

Once again, we turn to the 2012 interview with Atarov:

EA.: 'How would you describe your chess style? Are you a tactician or a strategist?'

FC.: 'I would not measure in such categories. It seems to me that I'm a good fighter. It gives me pleasure to play different positions, both tactical and strategic. I cannot say that I avoid anything. I can attack with a full board of pieces or manoeuvre about in a roughly equal position, I have nothing against the endgame.'

EA: 'Do you now understand how you played as a child?'

FC.: 'Oh, then I preferred to attack all the time. I loved to sacrifice pieces and break through to the enemy king. I was like that for a long time, but eventually, as I got stronger, I understood that winning by a direct attack is not always possible... I had to become more universal, learn to manoeuvre, defend, etc.'

Maybe the young Fabiano really did sacrifice pieces right and left, but those games that have come down to the database present a quite different picture! Sacrifices are extremely rare and instead, one is astonished at the ten year-old's ability to harmonise his pieces and find possibilities for continually strengthening his position. One sees combinations in his games, but modest ones, which arise out of the logical demands of the position.

The following two games are very characteristic.

Game 2 Dzindzi-Indian A40
Levan Bregadze
Fabiano Caruana   2103
Heraklion Wch U-10 2002 (5)

1.d4 g6 2.c4 ♗g7 3.♘c3 c5 4.d5 ♗xc3+ 5.bxc3 f5 6.h4 ♘f6 7.♘h3 ♘e4 8.♕c2 ♕a5 9.♗d2 d6 10.♘g5 ♘xd2 11.♕xd2 h6 12.♘f3
More flexible is 12.♘h3 followed by ♘f4.
12...♘d7 13.e3 ♘f6 14.♖c1 ♗d7 15.♗d3 0-0-0 16.♕b2 e5 17.dxe6 ♗xe6 18.0-0

18...♗d7!
As a result of the bishop's transfer to c6 and the appearance of the king's rook on e8, the black pieces occupy ideal positions.
19.♘d2 ♗c6 20.♖fe1 ♖he8 21.f3 ♕c7 22.♘f1 h5 23.♕c2 ♘d7!
The black knight was splendidly placed, but an even better square awaits it.
24.♕f2 ♘e5 25.♗e2 ♕a5 26.♖ed1 ♕a3 27.♕e1 ♔b8 28.♔h1 f4!
A small tactic. On 29.exf4 there follows 29...♘xc4.

29.e4

All the black pieces are ideally placed. Is there anything further one can perfect in this composition?
29...♕a5!
The queen heads on a journey around the whole board, so as to support the kingside attack!
30.♘h2 ♕c7 31.♕f2 ♕e7 32.♖g1 g5 33.hxg5 ♕xg5 34.g3 fxg3 35.♕xg3 ♕e3 36.♕e1 ♘g4!
Again a tactical trick!
37.♘f1 ♕f4
Admittedly, here it was possible to win quite simply – 37...♘f2+ 38.♔h2 ♕f4+ 39.♖g3 h4.
38.♖g2 ♘e5 39.♕d2 ♕f7 40.♖f2 ♗xe4 41.♘g3 ♗c6
White resigned.

Game 3 Scandinavian Defence A00
Fabiano Caruana   2137
Vaclac Svoboda   2048
Halkidiki 2003 Wch U-12 (4)

1.e4 d5 2.♘c3 d4 3.♘ce2 c5 4.c3 ♘c6 5.d3 e5 6.f4 ♗d6

7.f5 ♘f6

The game immediately assumes a closed character. Fabiano goes on to show that he is fully acquainted with the language of such blocked positions.

8.♘g3 0-0 9.♘f3 ♕c7 10.♗g5 ♗e7 11.♗e2 h6 12.♗d2 ♖d8 13.c4 a6 14.0-0 b5 15.b3 ♖b8 16.h3 bxc4 17.bxc4 a5 18.♘h2 ♗a6 19.♘h5 ♔h7 20.♘xf6+ ♗xf6 21.♘g4 ♕e7

22.♕c1!

It is a rare quality to be able to see the whole board. It may appear that the text move is made solely with the aim of a blow on h6.

22...♖d6 23.♕a3!

It turns out that Black has problems with the defence of the c5-pawn.

23...♖d7 24.h4!

And again White switches back to the kingside!

24...♖db7

After 24...♗xh4 White develops his initiative by means of 25.f6 ♗xf6 26.♘xf6+ gxf6 27.♖f5 ♖db7 28.♖af1 ♖b1 29.♗c1 ♔g7 30.♖h5 with advantage.

25.♕c1 ♖b2

So which white piece would you think about here, dear reader?

26.♗d1! ♖2b6 27.a3 ♔g8 28.g3 ♕d8 29.♗a4 ♖8b7 30.♔g2 ♖a7 31.♖h1 ♗b7 32.♕c2 ♕d6 33.♖af1 ♘e7 34.♘xf6+ ♕xf6 35.g4 ♕d6 36.♕d1 ♗c6 37.g5 ♗xa4 38.♕xa4 ♕c6 39.♕d1 ♔h7 40.gxh6 gxh6 41.♕h5 ♘g8 42.f6 ♕e8 43.♖h3 ♖aa6 44.♗g5 ♕f8 45.♖hf3 ♖e6 46.♔h1!

A subtle move, freeing the g-file for the attack.

46...♖ac6 47.♖f5 ♖b6

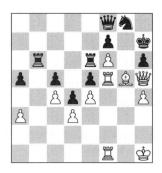

48.♖g1!

By sacrificing the f6-pawn, White achieves a combinational breakthrough.

48...♘xf6

If 48...a4 White decides with 49.♗xh6! ♘xh6 50.♖g7+.

49.♗xh6! ♕xh6 50.♕xf7+ ♔h8 51.♖h5! 1-0

With every day, chess captivated the youngster more and more and Fabiano gradually formed the firm intention to become a professional player.

FC.: 'At first, I played just for pleasure, but then things started going better and better for me and I started thinking: why not?'

Sher advised his pupil to go to Europe, believing that the opportunity to play in numerous tournaments would quickly develop the youngster's talent. This idea was fully supported by his family and in November 2004, the 12-year old Fabiano, together with his parents (the older children remained behind in the USA), moved to Spain.

FC.: 'My parents always supported me, in whatever I did. For them, the main thing was that their children should be happy, and what they ended up doing was not so important. They accepted it quite normally when I said I wanted to be a professional chess player.'

In Madrid, on Sher's recommendation, Caruana began studying with international master Boris Zlotnik, a well-known trainer and brilliant methodologist, who did a great deal for junior chess training in Moscow.

Boris Zlotnik: 'I had never come across such vision of the board and a veritable avalanche of variations before. He was a kid, 12 years old and rated 2180, but it was clear that a great player was in the making...

When I learned that Fabiano wanted to become a professional player, I spoke to his father and the following scheme was adopted. Firstly, practical play, with at least one tournament per month. When he wasn't playing, we worked together twice a week. But of course, at home he worked a great deal by himself. He did all homework exercises with great interest. As well as great talent, he has a tremendous capacity to work, and so results came quite quickly and within two and a half years, his rating was 2530.

In principle, I think this was the right course: every month, a tournament. There was always fresh material for analysis, and of course we used books, which he always analysed scrupulously at home, finding many mistakes even in books by the most well-known authors.'

The resulting creative union brought quick results. In April 2006, the 13-year-old Fabiano became an international master. The following two games were played on the way to this achievement.

Game 4 Sicilian Defence B33
Sandor Farago 2262
Fabiano Caruana 2255
Budapest 2005 (2)

1.e4 c5 2.♘f3 ♘c6 3.d4 cxd4 4.♘xd4 ♘f6 5.♘c3 e5 6.♘db5 d6 7.a4 ♗e7 8.♗e2 0-0 9.g4 a6 10.♘a3 ♘d4 11.g5 ♘e8 12.h4

White has played too adventurously. With three pawn breaks (...b7-b5, ...d6-d5 and ...f7-f5) Fabiano opens the position and gets into the rear of the enemy camp!
12...b5! 13.axb5 axb5 14.♗xb5 ♘xb5 15.♘cxb5 ♗b7 16.♘c3 f5! 17.gxf6 ♘xf6 18.♖g1 d5! 19.exd5 ♗c5 20.♗e3 ♗xe3 21.fxe3 ♘xd5 22.♕g4 ♕e7 23.♘xd5 ♗xd5 24.♕g5 ♕c7 25.0-0-0
The white king is finally evacuated from the centre, but goes from the frying-pan into the fire.
25...♗e4 26.♖d2 g6 27.♕g4

27...♕c4!
An elegant development of the attack! The black queen gets into a2.
28.h5 ♖xa3! 29.bxa3 ♕a2 30.♖h2 ♖d8! 0-1
Fabiano conducted the attack very energetically!

Game 5 Grünfeld Indian Defence D04
Dimo Werner 2376
Fabiano Caruana 2373
Budapest 2005 (1)

1.d4 ♘f6 2.♘f3 g6 3.e3 ♗g7 4.♘bd2 d5 5.♗d3 0-0 6.0-0 b6 7.e4 dxe4 8.♘xe4 ♗b7 9.♕e2 ♘c6 10.c3 ♖e8 11.♖e1 ♕d7 12.♗f4

Having placed his forces harmoniously, Caruana goes over to active operations in the centre.

12...♘h5! 13.♗e3 e5!

Fully in the style of the Grünfeld. It turns out that Black's fianchettoed bishops are better prepared for a battle in the centre than the opponent's 'centralised' army!

14.dxe5 ♘xe5 15.♘xe5 ♖xe5
16.♕c2 c5 17.♘g3 ♘xg3 18.hxg3
♖ae8 19.♗f1

19...h5!

All in accordance with the classical canons of chess strategy – having seized the initiative in the centre, Black shifts the offensive to the kingside.

20.♖ad1 ♕g4 21.♗e2?

In trying to drive the black queen from its dominating position, White commits the decisive mistake.

21...♖xe3!

A beautiful blow!

22.♗xg4

The main line of the combination is 22.fxe3 ♕xg3 23.♗b5 ♗e5! 24.♕f2 (24.♗xe8 ♕h2+ 25.♔f1 ♕h1+ 26.♔e2 ♕xg2+ 27.♔d3 ♗e4+) 24...♕h2+ 25.♔f1 ♗g3 (also good is 25...♖e6) 26.♕g1 ♕h4 27.♗xe8 ♗a6+ 28.♖e2 ♕f6+ with mate.

22...♖xe1+ 23.♔h2 hxg4 24.♖xe1 ♖xe1

And Black soon realised his large material advantage.

Caruana's purposeful play in this example makes a strong impression – the young player did not make a single superfluous move!

A great role in Fabiano's sporting career has been played by his father Luigi. He took his son to all tournaments, located trainers and dealt with financial issues. As a result of the youngster's great successes, a sponsor was found (still anonymous to this day) and in February 2006, Fabiano transferred to the Italian Chess Federation. At the same time, he continued living in Madrid, working with Zlotnik.

In May, Fabiano took part in the Vani Somov Memorial in Kirishi. The main organiser Gennady Nesis listened to the advice of his old friend Boris Zlotnik and invited the talented young master to the tournament called 'Young Stars of the World'. In the company of his talented contemporaries (future GMs Popov, Nepomniachtchi, Linchevsky, Safarli and Sjugirov), Caruana made a solid impression and shared 3rd-5th places with 7/11.

Game 6 Italian Game C54
Fabiano Caruana   2421
Srinath Narayanan   2170
Kirishi 2006 (9)

1.e4 e5 2.♗c4 ♘f6 3.d3 ♗c5 4.♘f3 ♘c6 5.c3 a6 6.0-0 ♗a7 7.♖e1 d6 8.♘bd2

Of course, he should have preserved the Italian bishop from exchange by means of 8.♗b3.

8...0-0 9.♘f1 ♘a5 10.♘g3 ♘xc4 11.dxc4

White tries to make capital out of the exchange, exploiting his doubled pawns in the fight for the centre.

11...♔h8

More energetic was 11...b5!.

12.♗e3 ♘g4?! 13.♗xa7 ♖xa7 14.h3 ♘h6

15.c5!

His opponent's inaccurate play has allowed White to obtain the advantage. Black will have a backward pawn on d6.

15...f6 16.cxd6 cxd6 17.♕d3 b5?!

This pawn push only leads to the creation of weaknesses on the queenside.

18.a4! bxa4 19.♖xa4 ♘f7 20.♘f1!

The knight hurries to the weak square d5.

20...♖d7 21.♘e3 ♗b7 22.♘d5 ♗xd5 23.♕xd5 ♕b6 24.♖b4 ♕c5 25.♖d1 ♖c7 26.♕a2! ♕a7 27.♖d5 ♖b7 28.♖a4 ♕b6 29.b4 ♕c6 30.c4 ♖b6

31.c5!

Transformation of the advantage. In removing the opponent's weakness on d6, White obtains a strong passed pawn on the c-file and the possibility of breaking in along the opened lines.

31...dxc5 32.bxc5 ♖b1+ 33.♕xb1 ♕xa4 34.♕b7 h6 35.c6 ♕c4 36.c7 ♕c1+ 37.♔h2 ♕f4+ 38.♔h1 ♕c1+ 39.♘g1 ♕c4 40.♖d7 ♔g8 41.♖xf7! Black resigned.

A simple game, but typical of Caruana's style – determined play for centralisation, and the continual improvement of the position of his pieces is crowned by a short tactical assault.

In September 2006 Caruana played for the Italian team in the Mitropa Cup, whilst in December he played in the 66th Italian Championship. The 14-year old succeeded in sharing 1st-2nd places with the experienced GM Michele Godena. Admittedly, at his first attempt, the title eluded him, as the grandmaster triumphed in the rapid and blitz playoff. But silver in the national championship was a great success for such a young player.

Fabiano entered 2007 with great hopes...

Amsterdam 2008

CHAPTER 2

Vertical takeoff

Three years of purposeful work brought its rewards, and in 2007, Fabiano achieved great successes. After winning three First Saturday tournaments (March, April and June) in Budapest, on 15 July 2007, at 14 years, 11 months and 15 days, Caruana became the youngest GM in Italian history and one of the youngest in the world.

At the same time, he began to work with a new trainer – Alexander Chernin, who lived in Budapest. The young player's family again moved, this time to the Hungarian capital.

Working with Chernin, who also brought in Yuri Razuvaev and Alexander Beliavsky to work with the youngster, brought Caruana's potential to new heights.

From an interview with Razuvaev on the Chess Pro website:

'I asked Chernin what potential Caruana had, and he replied: "I am lucky; before me, the boy worked with Boris Zlotnik". Fabiano fell into the hands of an experienced methodologist, who taught him all the chess classics. What separates a weak player from a real one? The weak player simply replays the moves on the board, whereas the real player retains the ideas of the best games in his head, like on a hard disk, and he "lives" them, not even needing to commit them to memory. This is construction material of a very high quality, on the basis of which the player can build plans and find correct decisions. Caruana already had such a base, and on its foundations, one could work on calculating variations, methods of seeking plans, and the overall conduct of the battle. If one lacks such a base, working is significantly harder. In addition, a good knowledge of the classics allows one to develop a very subtle evaluation function. The positioning of the pieces, their cooperation, pawn structures, etc. – all of this goes through an evaluation function, and without a knowledge of the classics, one's assessments will be much cruder.'

In August 2007, Caruana won the small open in Vlissingen, and in December, at the end of a good year for himself, he became Italian Champion!

The following principled encounter was played in the 2007 Italian Championship.

Game 7 Sicilian Defence B51

Michele Godena 2535

Fabiano Caruana 2594

Martina Franca ch-ITA 2007 (8)

1.e4 c5 2.♘f3 d6 3.♗b5+ ♘c6 4.0-0 ♗d7 5.♖e1 ♘f6 6.c3 a6 7.♗a4 b5 8.♗c2 ♗g4 9.d3 e6 10.♘bd2 ♗e7 11.h3 ♗h5 12.♘f1 0-0 13.♘g3 ♗g6 14.♘h4 d5

'I prepared this variation before the tournament, especially for Godena' – Caruana on ChessBase.

15.exd5

'A very solid continuation, leading to an absolutely equal position. In the majority of cases with this exchange on d5, the players quickly agree a draw. However, I know from experience that even the most equal positions conceal a great deal of play and many opportunities to outplay a weaker opponent.

In this game, I succeeded after numerous small mistakes by White.' – Caruana.

A more complicated game results from 15.e5 ♘d7 16.♘xg6 hxg6 17.d4 b4 18.♘e2 ♖b8 or 15.f4!?.

15...♕xd5 16.♘xg6 hxg6 17.♕e2 ♖fd8 18.a3

Weakening the square b3.

18...♖ac8 19.♗e3

More accurate was 19.♗f4.

19...♕e5!

A good consolidating manoeuvre. The black queen evacuates the centre, freeing d5 for the knight.

20.♕f3 ♕c7 21.♗f4 ♗d6 22.♗g5

Godena wants to keep the bishop pair. More solid was 22.♗xd6 ♕xd6 23.♖ad1.

22...♗xg3

23.♕xg3?

'And this is already a real mistake! After 23.fxg3 I would prefer Black, but maybe this is compensated by the computer's liking of White. In any case, the game remains roughly equal. For example, 23...♖d5 24.♗f4 (24.♗xf6? ♖f5 25.♕e3 gxf6 is in Black's favour) 24...e5 (24...♕d7

25.g4) 25.♗e3 c4!? 26.dxc4 bxc4
with mutual chances' – Caruana.
An interesting note, which shows
the respect the modern GM has for
the computer's assessments. If one
approaches the assessment of the
position after move 23 from general
principles, then one can note the
two bishops – the presence of
queens on the board allows White
to retain dynamic compensation for
his inferior pawn structure.

**23...♕xg3 24.fxg3 ♖d5 25.♗e3 ♘e5
26.♖ed1**

Black is favoured by the variation
26.♗xc5 ♘xd3 27.♗xd3 ♖xd3
28.♗e3 ♖cd8 29.a4 ♘d5.

26...c4! 27.d4

The continuation 27.dxc4 ♘xc4
28.♗c1 (28.♖xd5 exd5! 29.♗c1 a5∓)
28...a5 (28...♘e4!?) 29.a4 b4 30.cxb4
(30.b3? ♘e3! 31.♗xe3 ♖xc3∓) 30...
axb4 31.♗b3 ♘e4 Caruana also
assesses as better for Black.

27...♘c6

The position has blockading
features, which determines the
superiority of Black's knights over
the white bishops.

**28.g4 ♖d7 29.♖e1 ♘d5 30.♗d2 ♘a5
31.♖ad1 ♘b3**

32.♗e3?!

Caruana points out the inaccuracy
of this move, recommending
32.♖e2! (with the idea of keeping
the bishop on the e1-a5 diagonal,
which makes the break ...b5-b4
harder).

**32...a5 33.♗e4 b4 34.axb4 axb4
35.♗xd5 ♖xd5 36.♗f2 ♖a8 37.♖e2
bxc3 38.bxc3 ♖da5 39.♗e1 ♖a1
40.♖xa1 ♖xa1**

Black has gradually seized all the
important points in the position,
whilst his knight is stronger than
the white bishop.

41.♔h2

41...♔h7?!

Black misses the chance to set up
an ideal pawn structure with 41...
g5!. The more experienced Caruana
would never have committed this
inaccuracy!

42.g5!
Now the battle becomes more complicated. Even so, the young player manages to overcome his opponent's tenacious resistance. **42...♘c1 43.♖c2 ♘d3 44.♗g3 ♔g8 45.♗d6 ♖a6 46.♗e7 ♔h7 47.♔g3**

♖a5 48.h4 ♔g8 49.♗d6 f6 50.gxf6 gxf6 51.♔h3 ♖a1 52.g4 ♔f7 53.h5 g5 54.h6? ♔g6 55.♗f8 ♖c1 56.♖a2 ♖xc3 57.♖a7 ♘f4+ 58.♔h2 ♖h3+ 59.♔g1 ♖g3+! 60.♔f2 ♖xg4 61.h7 ♖h4 62.♖g7+ ♔f5 63.♖c7 ♘d5
White resigned.

From the interview with Atarov: 'Probably, the strongest impressions on me were made by Fischer and Kasparov. I consider them the two greatest players in history. I still remember many of their games by heart and always look with pleasure at new games by them.'

Fabiano followed one of his heroes not only on the chessboard. After becoming a grandmaster, he quit school, without even obtaining an average level of education! We will not pass judgement on this decision, with all its plusses and obvious minuses, but will follow our hero on his next tournament outing.

In January 2008, Fabiano had his first real international success – he won the C-group at the traditional festival at Wijk aan Zee.

Game 8 Sicilian Defence B66
Fabiano Caruana   2598
John van der Wiel   2490
Wijk aan Zee 2008 (9)

1.e4 c5 2.♘f3 d6 3.d4 cxd4 4.♘xd4 ♘f6 5.♘c3 ♘c6 6.♗g5 e6 7.♕d2 a6 8.0-0-0 ♗d7 9.f3 b5 10.♔b1 h6 11.♗e3 ♘e5 12.♗d3 ♖b8 13.g4

13...♘xd3?!
'A serious inaccuracy. Maybe my opponent underestimated the strength of the idea of the knight retreat to b3. He should have played 13...g6! 14.h4 ♗g7 with mutual chances' – Caruana on ChessBase.
14.cxd3 a5 15.h4 g6

Preventing the advance g4-g5-g6.
16.♘b3!

Caruana: 'I think this is a good demonstration of where the computer is weaker than the human. On seeing the move 16.♘b3, the assessment of Fritz 11 drops sharply and one might think that White has committed some sort of oversight!

In actual fact, this is the start of an excellent regrouping, which allows White to place his knights ideally. Let us look more closely at this idea. White has to prepare d3-d4, but the retreat 16.♘c2 fails to 16...b4 followed by ...b4-b3, opening up the white queenside. On the other hand, the square e2 needs to be reserved for the ♘c3, in the event of ...b5-b4.

After 16.♘b3 Black can also advance the queenside pawns, but this cannot be considered a gain of time, because the white knights get the excellent posts e2 and d3'.

16...a4 17.♘c1 b4 18.♘3e2

'The white queenside is completely safe – on ...a4-a3 there follows b2-b3, and on ...b4-b3 there is a2-a3. Thus, White is left with a huge superiority in the centre, with a complete lack of any sort of counterplay for the opponent' – Caruana.

18...♗g7 19.d4 h5?!

As the lesser evil, Caruana recommends 19...♗b5!?, preparing for the knight the march to f6 and then d7-b6.

20.g5 ♘g8 21.d5! e5 22.♘d3 b3 23.a3 ♘e7

'Alexander Chernin once told me that the square e7 is a very bad one for the knight in the King's Indian. This is especially noticeable in this position, where the knight has no mobility at all because of the blocked pawn structure' – Caruana.

24.f4

White's ideal piece set-up guarantees the success of the attack that now begins.

24...exf4 25.♗d4! 0-0 26.♗f6 ♗g4?

As Van der Wiel pointed out, it was essential to play 26...♔h7! 27.♕xf4 ♗g4 28.♖de1 ♗xf6! 29.gxf6 ♘g8 30.♖hf1 ♗xe2 31.♖xe2 ♘h6, returning the knight to life. However, even in this case, White would have a serious advantage. For example, he could play 32.♘b4, aiming at the weak square c6.

27.♖df1 ♖e8 28.♘d4 ♕b6 29.♕xf4 ♗f8 30.♘b4 ♖b7 31.♘dc6

The white pieces dominate the entire board!

31...♘xc6 32.dxc6 ♖a7 33.♘d5 ♕a6 34.♗c3 ♖e5 35.♘f6+ ♔g7 36.♗xe5 dxe5 37.♕xe5 ♕d3+ 38.♔a1 ♖e7 39.♘xh5+ ♔g8 40.♘f6+ ♔g7 41.♕b8 ♗e2 42.h5 gxh5

43.♖c1

'Nigel Short told me that he expected the variation 43.♖xh5 ♗xf1 (43...♗xh5 44.♘xh5+) 44.♕xf8+! ♔xf8 45.♖h8+ ♔g7 46.♖g8#. But more elegant is 43.♕h2! ♗xf1 44.♕xh5' – Caruana.

43...♖xe4 44.c7

Black resigned.

A wonderful game, demonstrating Caruana's progress in chess strategy!

In November of the same year, Caruana took part for the first time in the Olympiad, heading the Italian team. After losing his first two games, which can fairly be attributed to nerves, Fabiano demonstrated remarkable psychological stability and in the end, scored 7,5 out of 11!

The following game against one of the world's strongest players was especially memorable.

Game 9 French Defence C03
Michael Adams 2734
Fabiano Caruana 2640

Dresden ol 2008 (5)

1.e4 e6

The inclusion of the French Defence in the youngster's repertoire is a clear sign of the influence of Zlotnik, a noted connoisseur of this opening.

2.d4 d5 3.♘d2 ♗e7 4.♘gf3 ♘f6 5.e5 ♘fd7 6.♗d3 c5 7.c3 b6 8.♕e2 a5

Black insists on the exchange of the 'bad' French bishop. However, this does not come free of charge, in view of the poor prospects of the ♘b8.

9.a4 ♗a6

10.♗xa6

A good alternative was 10.♗b5. If 10...♗xb5 11.axb5 the pawns on b5 and e5 limit the scope of the black knights to the maximum.

10...♘xa6 11.0-0 ♘c7 12.♖e1 ♘b8

Black's foremost task is to improve the position of the ♘d7. Incidentally, a black knight on d7 in the French is the mirror of the aforementioned ♘e7 in the King's Indian!

13.♘b3!?

White wants to provoke the advance ...c5-c4, since releasing the pressure on the centre would free his hands for operations on the kingside.

Caruana was preparing to meet the manoeuvre 13.♘f1 ♘c6 14.♘g3 with 14...h5.

13...♘c6 14.♗e3 c4 15.♘c1 b5?!

An incorrect move, after which Black gets an unpleasant position. More accurate was 15...♛b8!, preparing, after ...b6-b5, the capture on b5 with the queen.

16.axb5 ♘xb5 17.♛c2

'At this moment, I understood that my position was worse. The black knights are awkwardly placed to create counterplay on the queenside, whilst White's plan is clear – he intends the manoeuvre

♘c1-e2-f4, to create pressure on the kingside' – Caruana on ChessBase.

17...♘ba7!

'The correct idea. The knight goes to b6, to support ...a5-a4' – Caruana.

18.g3 ♘c8 19.h4 h6 20.♘e2 ♘b6 21.h5 a4?!

A mistake, analogous to 15...b5?!. There was no need to hurry, but instead Black should prepare for the break f4-f5 by means of 21...♔d7! 22.♘h2 ♛g8 23.f4 ♛h7.

22.♘h2

22...♔d7

Typical (as in the manoeuvre ...♛d8-g8-h7 indicated above) for such positions – the black king evacuates the danger zone.

23.f4 ♔c7 24.f5

More accurate is 24.♖f1!. In Caruana's opinion, the English GM underestimated Black's 25th move.

24...♗g5 25.♘f4 ♘e7! 26.fxe6

Similar consequences follow 26.g4 ♛c8.

26...♗xf4 27.♗xf4 fxe6 28.♖f1

White still retains the initiative, but Black's position is solid.

28...♛d7 29.♖f2 ♖af8 30.♖af1 ♛e8 31.♛e2 ♖f5 32.g4 ♖f7 33.♗c1 ♖hf8 34.♘f3 ♘d7 35.♛c2 ♘b6

36.♔g2?!

Caruana considers that after 36.♘h4 ♖xf2 37.♖xf2 ♖xf2 38.♔xf2 Black would face a difficult defence.

36...♕b5

This move is possible, thanks to the fact that with the king on g2, there is not the move ♘f3-g5.

37.♘h4?

After this mistake, it is White who must fight for a draw!

The continuation 37.♔g3 ♔d7! (meeting the threat of ♘g5) leads to an approximately equal position, since now the queen has managed to jump out to b5, Black has ensured himself counterplay.

37...♕b3!

Maybe Adams had missed this move.

38.♕h7?

A second mistake, after which White's game cannot be saved! As Caruana pointed out, with accurate play, White could hold the position: 38.♕d2! (if 38.♕xb3? ♖xf2+ 39.♖xf2 ♖xf2+ 40.♔xf2 cxb3 we reach an endgame which is lost for White) 38...♖xf2+ 39.♖xf2 ♖xf2+ 40.♕xf2 (40.♔xf2? a3 41.bxa3 ♘a4−+) 40...a3 41.bxa3 ♕xc3 42.♕f7 (42.♗e3 ♘d7∓) 42...♘bc8 43.♗f4 ♕xd4 44.♘g6 ♕b2+ 45.♔h3 ♕xa3+

46.♔h4 c3 47.♕xg7 c2 48.♕xh6, and the outcome of the battle is unclear.

38...♖xf2+ 39.♖xf2 ♖xf2+ 40.♔xf2 ♔d7 41.♘f3

He loses after 41.♕xg7 ♕c2+ 42.♔g3 ♕xc1 43.♘g6 ♘bc8 or 41.♘g6 ♕c2+.

41...a3 42.bxa3 ♘a4!

The breaking up of the white pawn structure leads to a decisive advantage. The black knight is aiming for e4!

43.♗d2 ♘xc3 44.♗xc3 ♕xc3

The passed pawn on c4 will cost White a piece. The position remains sharp, but White no longer has realistic chances of saving the game.

45.♕b1 ♔c7 46.a4 ♘c6 47.♕g6 ♕b2+ 48.♔g3 c3 49.♘e1 ♕e2 50.♘c2 ♔b6 51.a5+ ♔xa5 52.♕xe6 ♕d3+! 53.♔f4 ♕e4+ 54.♔g3 ♕d3+ 55.♔f4

55...♕xc2 56.♕xd5+
Or 56.♕xc6 ♕f2#!.
56...♔b4 57.♕c5+
If 57.♕xc6 ♕f2+ 58.♔e4 ♕g2+
White loses the queen.
**57...♔b3 58.♕d5+ ♔b2 59.♕b5+
♕b3 60.♕xc6 c2 61.♕g2 ♔b4
62.♔f5 ♕xd4 63.♕e2 ♔c3 64.♕e1+
♕d2 65.♕a1+ ♔b3 0-1**
A difficult, sharp and, at the same
time, grand battle, in which one
can definitely detect the hand of
Zlotnik. I first became acquainted
with many of the ideas used by
Caruana in this game when I
studied with Boris Anatolievich as
a junior.

On the subject of the French
Defence, let us look at another of
Fabiano's games with it:

Game 10 French Defence C03
Stefan Kristiansson 2476
Fabiano Caruana 2598
Reykjavik 2008 (9)

1.e4 e6 2.d4 d5 3.♘d2 ♗e7

This continuation came into
modern practice largely through
the efforts of GM Oleg Romanishin.

**4.♗d3 c5 5.dxc5 ♘f6 6.♕e2 0-0
7.♘gf3 a5 8.0-0 ♘a6 9.e5 ♘d7 10.c3
♘axc5 11.♗c2 b6 12.♖e1 ♗a6
13.♕e3 f6 14.b4**

14...fxe5!
Such 'clearance' operations in the
centre are characteristic of a correct
handling of the French.
**15.♘xe5 ♘xe5 16.bxc5 ♗xc5!
17.♕xe5 ♗xf2+ 18.♔h1 ♗xe1
19.♕xe6+ ♔h8 20.♕xe1**

White has two pieces for rook and
pawn, and if these pieces 'wake up',
then Black will be in trouble.
20...d4!
Decisively opening lines for the
rooks! Caruana used a similar idea
in a later game against Bologan
(Game 44).
21.♗b2?

White cannot withstand the opponent's pressure and defends badly. The calm 21.cxd4 ♕xd4 22.♕e4 ♕xe4 23.♗xe4 ♖ad8 24.♔g1 ♖fe8 25.♖b1 leads to an equal game.

21...d3 22.♗d1 ♕g5 23.♘f3 ♖ae8 24.♕f2 d2 25.♗a4 ♖e2 26.♕g1 ♕e7 27.c4 ♗b7 28.♖f1 ♖e1 29.♗d1 ♖xf3 30.gxf3 ♖xd1

White resigned.

Caruana ended 2008 with victory in the Italian Championship (December), thus becoming two-time national champion.

In January 2009, he again won at Wijk aan Zee, this time in the B-group, obtaining the right to play in the top group the following year.

It should be noted that no other player has yet managed to win the C- and B-groups at Wijk in consecutive years!

Caruana and his father,
Amsterdam 2009

CHAPTER 3

The calm before the storm

But in July's double-round tournament of six players at Biel, Caruana shared last place with Gelfand, scoring 4/10. The young GM's winning run thus came to an end. But this is not surprising. The higher one goes, the harder each new step becomes, as the resistance of one's opponents becomes ever more tenacious.

Among significant tournaments in 2009, we should mention our hero's performance in the World Cup, held in November in Khanty-Mansiysk. After defeating in succession GMs Bruzon (Cuba), Dominguez (Cuba) and Alekseev (Russia), Caruana reached the last eight, where he lost on tie-break against Azeri GM Vugar Gashimov.

His performance in the main group at Wijk aan Zee in 2010 did not bring Caruana any prizes, as he finished only 10th, with 5.5/13. At the same time, though, none of Anand, Kramnik or Carlsen succeeded in beating him. Caruana was gradually getting closer to the best players in the world.

The following game was Caruana's only victory at Wijk aan Zee 2010.

Game 11 Scandinavian Defence B01
Fabiano Caruana   2675
Sergei Tiviakov   2662
Wijk aan Zee 2010 (8)

1.e4 d5 2.exd5 ♕xd5 3.♘c3 ♕d6 4.d4 ♘f6 5.♘f3 c6

'The Scandinavian is just a good Caro-Kann!' said Danish GM Bent

Larsen. This is the idea brought to this old defence by modern GMs.
6.g3 ♗g4 7.♗g2 e6 8.0-0 ♗e7 9.h3 ♗xf3 10.♗xf3 0-0 11.♘e2 ♘bd7 12.♗g2

White has played the opening modestly and, from a 'Caro-Kann' viewpoint, Black has no problems.
12...e5

Given that the opponent has the bishop pair, Black could refrain from hurrying with the opening of the game. The alternative was the consolidating 12...♕c7.

13.c3! ♖ad8 14.♕b3 ♕c7 15.dxe5 ♘xe5 16.♗e3

The chances are roughly equal – although White has the two bishops, Black's position has no weaknesses. Even so, such positions are easier for White to play, since he has clear ideas. For example, if we remove all the major pieces, then the significance of the bishop pair grows. Black, in his turn, has to look more for concrete ideas.

16...♘fd7 17.♖ad1 ♘c5 18.♕c2 ♘c4 19.♗f4 ♗d6 20.♗g5 ♗e7 21.♗f4 ♗d6 22.♗c1 ♖fe8 23.b3 ♘b6 24.♘d4 ♘e6 25.♘xe6 ♖xe6 26.♖fe1 ♖xe1+ 27.♖xe1 ♘d5

The position has slightly simplified, which suits White. Now he begins to prepare to drive the black knight out of the centre.

28.a3! ♕c8 29.b4 ♖e8 30.♖xe8+ ♕xe8 31.c4 ♘c7 32.♕d3! ♕e1+ 33.♔h2 ♕e7 34.♗g5 ♕e6 35.h4

The white bishops gradually become more dangerous, which is the usual tendency in positions with an open centre and pawns on both wings.

35...g6 36.♕d4 a6 37.♗h3 f5 38.♕a7 ♕c8 39.♕d4 ♗f8 40.♗f6 ♘e6 41.♕e5 ♔f7 42.c5

Now all the black pawns are fixed on light squares and in the future may become potential victims of the ♗h3.

This means that even if dark-squared bishops are exchanged, the remaining white bishop will be significantly stronger than the black knight.

42...♕c7 43.♕c3 ♗g7 44.♗xg7 ♘xg7

45.♗f1!

Confirmation of the old adage that 'the advantage of the two bishops lies in the possibility of exchanging one of them off'. Now the light-squared bishop comes into its own!

45...f4 46.♗c4+ ♔e8 47.g4 ♕e7
48.♔g1 h5 49.♕d3 ♕f6 50.g5 ♕f5
51.♕d6 f3 52.♕b8+ ♔e7 53.♕d6+
♔e8 54.♗d3 ♕g4+ 55.♔f1 ♕g2+
56.♔e1 ♕g1+ 57.♔d2 ♕xf2+
58.♔d1 ♕g1+ 59.♔c2 ♕f2+ 60.♔b3

♕e3 61.♔a4 ♕e7 62.♗xg6+
♔f8 63.♕b8+ ♘e8 64.♕f4+ ♔g8
65.♗xh5 ♘c7 66.♗xf3 ♘b5 67.g6 a5
68.h5 axb4 69.h6 1-0

A classic example of exploiting the two bishops!

In September 2010, Caruana once again led the Italian team at the Olympiad in Khanty-Mansiysk. His result of 5.5/10 looks modest. In the match Italy-Russia, he once again met Kramnik and the game was again drawn.

However, Caruana was not without a victory in 2010. In July, he took first place in the round-robin event at Biel (admittedly, the field was less strong than the previous year and was 'only' Category 17), whilst in December, he scored his now customary victory in the Italian Championship.

However, in the new year event at Reggio Emilia, the host representative had to settle for only 50%. Evidently, his dissatisfaction with his results led him to change trainers. He began to work with Vladimir Chuchelov and his family moved yet again, this time to the Swiss city of Lugano.

Fabiano continued to be inconsistent in 2011. Thus, after winning in June in New Delhi (Category 17), he flopped at Biel (Category 19) a month later, taking last place. Caruana raised his rating over 2700, but further advance stalled. At the end of the year, he played in his last Italian Championship, winning the title for the fourth time, and then in the new year event at Reggio Emilia 2011/12 in a Category 20 event, he shared fourth place with 5.5/10.

USA $12.99 EUROPE €11.99   2018#3   WWW.NEWINCHESS.COM

NEW IN CHESS

READ BY CLUB PLAYERS IN 116 COUNTRIES

The Blitz Whisperer
Maxim Dlugy

Matthew Sadler
My all-time hero

Louis Paulsen
Forgotten chess
innovator

'Superman' Adhiban:
My win in Reykjavik

Opening Surprise
Aronian's 'Patzer
move'

Nigel Short
Why Twitter?

Judit Polgar
Breaking
strategic
rules

**Just
Checking**
Lawrence
Trent

It's Fabiano Caruana vs Magnus Carlsen!

Berlin Candidates
- The drama
- The games
- The winner speaks

ISBN 978-90-5691-782-1

9 789056 917821

51299

CHAPTER 4

The ascent to Mount Olympus

By the start of 2012, Caruana was firmly established at the foot of Mount Olympus (in the January rating list, he was 17th in the world, with a rating of 2736), at the head of which were the 'gods' – the 2800 club of Carlsen, Kramnik, Anand and Aronian.

In the course of 2012-2014 the upcoming GM managed to cross the gap and join this elite group at the top of modern chess. Caruana, as we have already said, played a great deal, sometimes exceeding 20 games per month! Along with round-robin tournaments, he also played Swiss tournaments, not worrying about the risk of losing rating points. Consequently, from now on, we will concentrate only on tournaments which were significant in terms of his sporting biography.

His advance started at Wijk aan Zee in January 2012. In a Category 21 tournament, Caruana scored 8/13 and shared 2nd-4th places with Carlsen. His next super-tournament was the Tal Memorial in Moscow. Caruana scored 5/9 and shared 2nd-3rd places with Radjabov, only half a point behind Carlsen. At the same event, Fabiano scored his first win against Kramnik, which was especially memorable for him.

In July, together with Karjakin, Fabiano came equal first at Dortmund (6/9) and again defeated Kramnik!

Game 12 Ruy Lopez C65
Fabiano Caruana 2775
Vladimir Kramnik 2799
Dortmund 2012 (8)

1.e4 e5 2.♘f3 ♘c6 3.♗b5 ♘f6 4.d3 ♗c5 5.0-0 d6 6.c3 0-0 7.♘bd2 ♘e7 8.d4

White needs to take the initiative in the centre, else, by playing ...c7-c6 and ...♘g6, the opponent will obtain a comfortable position.

8...exd4 9.cxd4 ♗b6 10.b3 d5

Breaking up the white centre. Now the game enters a forcing stage.

11.e5 ♘e4 12.♗d3 ♗f5 13.♕e2 ♘c6 14.♗b2 ♘xd2 15.♕xd2 ♗e4 16.♗e2!?

Aiming for complicated play. The alternative 16.♕e3 ♗xf3 17.♕xf3 ♗xd4 18.♗xd4 ♘xd4 19.♗xh7+ ♔xh7 20.♕d3+ ♔g8 21.♕xd4 leads to quiet equality.

16...f6

17.b4!

'This was my idea when I played 16.♗e2. Now Black will be forced to reckon with the possibility of b4-b5 on each move. In addition, I prevent ...♗a5' – Caruana in New In Chess 2012/6.

17...fxe5 18.dxe5

18...♔h8?!

'This move doesn't meet the demands of the position. Black had two viable options, one aggressive and one prophylactic.

I was expecting 18...h6, which prevents ♘g5, and I wasn't sure how the position should be assessed after 19.b5 ♘a5 20.♖ae1. Here, the

computer points out a strong idea: 20...c6, undermining the b5-pawn, with a satisfactory position.

The other possibility, which I hadn't taken seriously during the game, is 18...d4!?, immediately starting aggressive counterplay. The positions after this move are incredibly complex, with variations branching out after every move. A possible continuation out of many is 19.♖ae1 ♗d5 20.b5 ♗a5 21.♕d1 ♗xe1 22.♖xe1 and the machine estimates this as roughly equal, although it's not clear to me exactly what's going on at first sight!' – Caruana.

19.b5 ♘e7 20.♘g5 ♘g6

21.g3!

An excellent prophylactic move. Now the ♘g6 does not reach f4, whilst White can strengthen his position by means of e5-e6 and h2-h4-h5. Black also must constantly reckon with the exchange of the bishop on e4. I would add that winning the exchange here would be a serious mistake: 21.♘e6? ♕h4 22.♘xf8 ♖xf8 with an irresistible attack for Black.

21...♕e7 22.e6 ♖f5 23.♘xe4

A good moment for this exchange, as the white queen penetrates to d7.

23...dxe4 24.♕d7 ♖af8 25.♕xe7
In the endgame, the passed pawn
on e6, supported by the two
bishops, will be a great strength.
25...♘xe7 26.♗a3 ♖e8 27.♖ad1

27...h5?
'The idea behind this move is to
prevent g3-g4, but it's too slow.
Black should have gone for the
exchange sacrifice with 27...♘d5
28.g4 ♖e5 29.♗b2 ♖8xe6 30.♗c4 c6
31.bxc6 bxc6 32.♗xe5 ♖xe5, with
good drawing chances' – Caruana.
28.♖d7 ♘d5 29.♖f7 ♘f6 30.♗c4
♗c5 31.♗b2 ♖e7 32.♗d4 ♗d6
33.♖e1 b6 34.♖f8+ ♔h7 35.♖xe4
White adds an extra pawn to his
positional advantage. Kramnik tries
his last chance, which unexpectedly
succeeds...

35...♖xf2!? 36.♔xf2?

A serious mistake in time-trouble,
which places the win in question.
After the calm 36.♖e1! ♖d2 (36...♖f3
37.♔g2) 37.♗e3 ♗c5 38.♗xc5 bxc5
39.♖f7 Black loses.
36...♘xe4+ 37.♔g2 ♘c5 38.♖a8

38...♘xe6?
A mistake in return. After 38...♔g6
Black should make a draw.
39.♗d3+
Now the black king comes under
attack.
39...♔h6 40.h4 g6 41.♖h8+ ♔h7
42.♖g8

Forcing Black to give up the
exchange, which decides the game.
42...♖g7 43.♗xg7+ ♔h7 44.♖e8
♘xg7 45.♖e3 ♔h6 46.a4 46...♔h7
47.♔h3 ♔h6 48.♗c2 ♔h7 49.g4
hxg4+ 50.♔xg4 ♔h6 51.♖e2 ♗b4
52.♖e5 ♘h5 53.♖e6 1-0

In September, at the double-round super-tournament at Sao Paulo/Bilbao, Caruana and Carlsen triumphed with 6.5/10, with Caruana taking first on tie-break! In their own micro-match, the two winners exchanged victories and ended 1-1.

At the Wijk aan Zee event in January 2013, Caruana experienced a real disaster – 12th place (5/13). There is nothing surprising about this – he was simply physically unable to continue playing at such a high level in all tournaments in a row! But already in March, Caruana took revenge, winning a small super-tournament (four players, double round) in Zurich with 4/6. Here he scored his first victory over Anand!

In June, Caruana shared 3rd-5th places in the next Tal Memorial in Moscow (5/9), including wins as Black against both Carlsen and Anand! Remarkably, the last two places in the tournament were occupied by Anand and Kramnik.

One could not help recalling the words spoken by the world's oldest GM, Yuri Averbakh: 'Chess shows in the most open way what happens secretly in life: the battle of the generations. Look at the tournament tables over the course of 10-15 years and you will see how the generations battle one another and how they change places. The rising generations gradually move to the top, whilst the older generation, alas, slips down.'

Game 13 Ruy Lopez C88
Viswanathan Anand 2786
Fabiano Caruana 2774

Moscow 2013 (1)

1.e4 e5 2.♘f3 ♘c6 3.♗b5 a6 4.♗a4 ♘f6 5.0-0 ♗e7 6.♖e1 b5 7.♗b3 0-0 8.h3 ♗b7 9.d3

9...d5!?

Despite the fact that White has played the anti-Marshall, Black nonetheless carries out the idea of the legendary American grandmaster! After 9...d5 10.exd5 ♘xd5 11.♘xe5 Black usually chooses between 11...♘d4, keeping the two bishops to compensate for the pawn, and 11...♘xe5 12.♖xe5 ♕d6. In the present game, Anand declines the gambit, preferring to exert positional pressure against the enemy centre.

10.exd5 ♘xd5 11.♘bd2 f6 12.c3
The main discussion in this variation centres around 12.c4.
12...♔h8
'I spent a long time deciding between this move and the

principled 12...♞a5. As usual, probably I made the wrong choice' wrote Caruana in New In Chess 2013/5.

13.♗c2

'This move may look passive, but it has a purpose: White is planning ♞b3 and d3-d4, when he can recapture on d4 with a piece. During the game I was most worried about 13.d4 exd4 14.cxd4'.

13...♛d7 14.♞b3 a5

Directed against d3-d4.

15.a4 bxa4 16.♖xa4

16...♞cb4

'For the pawn I eliminated White's bishop, and I was happy my king would finally feel secure.

I couldn't afford to allow White's rook to h4: 16...♞b6 17.♖h4! f5, and here I stopped calculating when I saw 18.♞g5, with what seemed to be a tremendous attack. Instead, the machine suggests 18.d4!?, a move which, to put it mildly, I find shocking. Since I don't understand much in this position, I'll trust Houdini and say White has an advantage' – Caruana in New In Chess.

17.♖xa5 ♞xc2 18.♛xc2 ♞b6

In Caruana's opinion, more energetic was 18...g5.

19.♖xa8 ♖xa8 20.♞bd2 g5

21.♞h2?!

'In hindsight this looks like a mistake, but during the game it was the move I expected.

It seems risky for White to play 21.d4 and aloow 21...g4 22.hxg4 ♛xg4, and I felt like I would have a strong attack here, but White has more than sufficient defensive resources. A possible variation is 23.♞e4 ♖g8 24.♞g3 h5 25.♞xe5 fxe5 26.♖xe5 ♗g5 27.♗xg5 ♖xg5, and White has a perpetual with 28.♖e8+ ♖g8 29.♖e5, but no more' – Caruana.

21...♖d8 22.d4 exd4 23.cxd4 ♗b4 24.♖e2 ♛xd4 25.♞df1?

This is Vishy's first veryserious mistake, and after it he is on the verge of losing.

Although it looks risky, White should bite the bullet with 25.♛xc7, when he will probably survive. For example, 25...♛d5 26.♞hf3 ♞a8 27.♛c2 ♖c8 28.♛d1, and White has got over the worst of it' – Caruana.

25...♛c5 26.♛xc5 ♗xc5 27.♖c2 ♗d6 28.♞g4 ♔g7 29.♗d2

29...♔g6
White does not even have an extra pawn and the endgame is very difficult for him. In an open position, White simply has nothing with which to oppose the enemy's powerful bishops.
With his last move, Black prepares a pawn offensive on the kingside.
30.♘ge3 f5 31.♘c4 ♗xc4 32.♖xc4 ♖a8 33.♖c1 f4 34.♗c3 h5 35.♘d2 ♗d5 36.f3?!
Allowing the decisive penetration of the enemy bishop to e3, but there was already no way to save the game. After the inevitable ...g5-g4 Black's territorial advantage on the kingside turns into a direct attack on the white king.

36...♗c5+ 37.♔f1 ♗e3 38.♔e2 ♗c4+ 39.♔e1 ♖e8

40.♔d1
'During the game I started to get worried by the clever 40.♗e5!?, which would have been a great last chance. After 40...♗b5 41.♗xc7, I would have to find the study-like 41...♖e7!!, and the bishop on c7 is trapped! (Instead, something like 41...♗b6+? 42.♘e4 gives Black nothing.) Now 42.♗d8 (42.♔d1 ♗a4+ 43.b3 ♗xb3+ 44.♘xb3 ♗xc1, ed.) 42...♖d7 43.♗a5 ♗xd2+ 44.♗xd2 ♖e7+ and White is completely dominated' – Caruana.
40...♗xd2 41.♔xd2 ♖e2+ 42.♔d1 ♖xg2 43.♗d4 ♗e2+ 44.♔e1 ♗xf3 45.♖xc7 ♖e2+ 46.♔f1 ♖h2 47.♖g7+ ♔f5 0-1

Below are several extracts from an interview Caruana gave to Evgeny Atarov straight after the tournament.

Caruana: 'The last two years, during which I have been working with Chuchelov, have been a real breakthrough for me and I am very grateful to my trainer.'
Atarov: 'Does he travel to tournaments with you?'
FC.: 'Yes, we go together to all the most important tournaments. I understood how important his support can be a year ago, when we went together to the Tal Memorial. We have managed to find a very successful system of working together, which has brought me excellent results... I

consider him one of the best trainers in the world, and for me personally, Vladimir is simply the best.'

EA.: 'During your travels around Europe, you have worked with Chernin, Razuvaev and Beliavsky, and before that, you were with the excellent methodologist Boris Zlotnik. Can one describe you as the product of the Soviet school of chess?'

FC.: 'I think that would be an exaggeration. But I learnt a lot from them and will always remember the lessons and what I learned. One can never know too much.'

When the smoke of battle had cleared, it turned out that in the July 2013 FIDE rating list, Caruana was up to third place in the world!

In July, he was at the board again, at the super-tournament in Dortmund. The result was modest – 4/9 and a share of 5th-8th places. I recall my own youth, when the doctor of medical science Viktor Borisovich Malkin explained to us chess students that, after a successful tournament appearance, one should on no account immediately play another – the peak of one's sporting form has passed and the chance of a failure grows appreciably. As we have seen, throughout his career, Caruana has broken this rule. One cannot say that he has refuted Malkin's principle, but it is clear that regularly playing tournaments is his natural habit!

In October Caruana shared first place with Gelfand (7/11) in the final stage of the FIDE Grand Prix in Paris. In the overall series, Caruana finished third, but there were only two qualifying places in the 2014 Candidates tournament, which were taken by Topalov and Mamedyarov.

Out of this Grand Prix series, we present this game, in which one of the world's most famous GMs was outplayed by outwardly simple strategic means.

Game 14 Ruy Lopez C76
Fabiano Caruana 2774
Vasily Ivanchuk 2755
Thessaloniki 2013 (2)

1.e4 e5 2.♘f3 ♘c6 3.♗b5 a6 4.♗a4 d6 5.c3 g6 6.d4 ♗d7 7.0-0 ♗g7

In choosing the Deferred Steinitz Defence, Black tries to give the game King's Indian features.

8.h3 h6 9.♗e3 ♘ge7 10.♘bd2 0-0 11.dxe5

This pawn exchange in the centre allows White to restrict to a maximum the ♗g7.

11...dxe5

12.♗c5

A typical manoeuvre. The white bishops exert unpleasant pressure on the black queenside.

12...♖e8 13.♖e1 b6 14.♗a3 ♘a7 15.♗xd7 ♕xd7 16.♘c4 ♕e6 17.♘e3

Black's camp has vulnerable light squares, whilst his ♗g7 is currently not playing. The attempt to consolidate the position with 17...c5 18.c4 leads to a small, but stable advantage for White.

17...♘b5 18.♗xe7 ♖xe7 19.♕a4

The loose black queenside becomes a target for the white queen.

19...♘d6 20.♕c6 ♖c8 21.♖ad1 ♔h7 22.♖d2 ♘e8 23.♕b7 ♘d6

24.♖xd6!

This positional exchange sacrifice aims at establishing light-square domination.

24...cxd6 25.♕xa6 ♖cc7?!

A significant inaccuracy. It would have been much harder for White to fix his positional advantage after 25...♖ee8!. For example, 26.♘d5 f5 27.c4 fxe4 28.♘d2 b5! 29.♕xb5 ♖b8 with counterplay (as pointed out by GM Mikhail Golubev).

26.♘d5 ♖a7 27.♕b5 ♖eb7 28.a4 f5 29.♘d2 ♗f6 30.♕e8 ♗e7 31.c4 ♕g8 32.♕c6

The black rooks do not have open lines and are worth significantly less than the white cavalry.

32...♕d8 33.b3 ♕d7 34.♕xd7 ♖xd7 35.♘xb6 ♖db7 36.♘c8 ♖a6 37.♘xe7 ♖xe7

Having given up the b6-pawn, Black takes play into an endgame, but this does not bring him significant relief. White's plan is clear: transfer the king to the queenside and then advance the passed pawns.

38.♖e3 ♔g7 39.♖d3 ♖b7 40.♔f1 ♖ab6 41.♔e2 ♔f6

The assessment of the position is not changed after 41...fxe4 42.♖d5.

42.♔d1 ♔e6 43.♔c2 h5 44.f3 ♔f6 45.♔c3 ♖a6 46.♖d5 ♔g5 47.a5 ♔f4

This desperate attempt at counterplay by Black proves insufficient to save the game, as the white pawns advance too quickly to the desired eighth rank.

48.b4 ♔g3 49.♘b3 ♔xg2 50.b5 ♖a8 51.♖xd6 ♔xf3 52.a6 ♖g7 53.♘c5 fxe4 54.b6 e3 55.♖f6+ 1-0

Caruana became the real star of 2014. If in the first half of the year his results were stable, but somewhat modest (e.g. 2nd place in the Gashimov Memorial in Baku, with 5.5/10, a point behind Carlsen), then in the second half of the year, he had a real breakthrough!

In July, he was first at Dortmund (5.5/7, one and a half points ahead of second prize winner Leko). This victory allowed Caruana finally to break the magic 2800 rating barrier!

In August at the Olympiad, Fabiano showed an excellent result on top board – 7.5 points out of 9. At the end of the same month, he started in the super-tournament Sinquefield Cup in St Louis, where he was to score the most famous victory of his chess career: first prize with 8.5/10! He was three points clear of second prize winner Carlsen!

Game 15 Slav Defence D11

Hikaru Nakamura	2787
Fabiano Caruana	2801

St Louis 2014 (5)

1.d4 d5 2.c4 c6 3.♘f3 ♘f6 4.♘bd2 ♗f5 5.♘h4 ♗e4 6.f3 ♗g6 7.e3 e6 8.g3 ♗e7 9.a3 ♘bd7 10.cxd5 cxd5 11.♘xg6 hxg6 12.♗d3

12...e5!

Nakamura's refusal to adopt a principled line in the opening has allowed Black to equalise easily.

13.0-0 0-0 14.♕b3

Going into a position with an isolated queen's pawn on d5 (14. dxe5 ♘xe5 15.♘b3) is unfavourable for White, because of the looseness of his pawn structure on the kingside.

14...♕c8 15.♘b1!

The transfer of the knight to c3 will improve White's position.

15...exd4 16.exd4

16...♘b8!

If White can do it, well so can Black!

Caruana correctly realises that with the fixed central pawn position, his knights will be in no way inferior to the white bishops.

17.♘c3 ♘c6 18.♗e3

If 18.♘xd5 ♘xd5 19.♕xd5 ♘xd4 Black has good chances of seizing the initiative.

18...♕d7 19.♖ad1 ♖fd8 20.♖fe1

The position looks absolutely equal, but Caruana feels so at home in it that he gradually outplays his opponent.

20...♘e8!

With the given pawn structure, Black's knights are more active than White's bishops. Now the king's knight is aiming at e6 and after the bishop comes to f6, the pawn on d4 will not be smiling.

21.♗f2 ♘c7 22.♗f1

Intending to parry the knight's appearance on e6 by the move ♗h3.

22...♗f6 23.♕a2?!

He needed to prevent his opponent's next move, by playing 23.f4.

23...g5!

Seizing space on the kingside.

24.b4 g6

Black improves his position further – after ...♔g7 the transfer of the rook to the h-file will be on the agenda.

**25.♕d2 ♔g7 26.b5 ♘e7 27.♗e3 ♘e6
28.♗h3 ♘f5 29.♗xf5 gxf5 30.f4?**
Now the weakness of the light
squares and the bad ♗e3 render
White's position strategically
hopeless.

It is understandable that Nakamura
did not like 30.♕d3 f4 31.♗f2 fxg3
32.hxg3 ♖h8 with a powerful attack
on the kingside. But 30.♘e2! (with
the idea of 30...♕xb5 31.♕c2) allows
the black initiative to be contained
without a catastrophic weakening
of the white position.

30...g4 31.♕d3 ♖ac8 32.♖c1

32...♖c4!
Occupying the light squares
and setting a small tactical trap:
33.♕xf5? ♘xd4 34.♕xd7 ♘f3+
35.♔f2 ♖xd7, winning.

33.♘e2 ♘c7 34.♘c3
White's position is not eased by
34.♖xc4 dxc4 35.♕xc4 ♘xb5.

34...♖c8 35.h3
Striving for some sort of
counterplay. After 35.a4 ♗d8 the
black bishop aims for a5 and the
♘c7 comes via e8 and f6 to e4.

**35...gxh3 36.♔h2 ♘xb5 37.♘xb5
♕xb5 38.♔xh3 ♕d7 39.♔g2 b5
40.♖b1 a6 41.♖bc1 ♕e6**

In principle, the coming exchange
of queen for two rooks was not
strictly necessary. Black can win
without any great complications by
means of 41...♖8c6 with the idea of
...♕e6-d7-c8.

42.♗f2
On 42.♗d2 there follows 42...♖xd4.

42...♖xc1 43.♖xe6 fxe6 44.g4

44...fxg4?!
Missing a chance to end the game
nicely: 44...♗h4!! 45.♗xh4 ♖8c3!,
and the white queen is suddenly
trapped!

**45.♕e2 ♔f7 46.♕d3 ♖1c2 47.♕h7+
♔e8 48.f5?**
Losing at once – Black simply takes
the bishop and it turns out that
White does not have a perpetual.
He could have prolonged his
resistance with 48.♔f1.

**48...♗xd4 49.♕g6+ ♔d8 50.♕xe6
♖xf2+ 51.♔g3 ♖c3+ 52.♔xg4 ♖g2+
53.♔f4 ♖f2+ 54.♔g4 ♔c7 55.♕e7+
♔b6 56.♕d8+ ♖c7 57.♕xd5 ♗c5
58.♕d8 ♔b7 59.f6 ♗xa3 60.♕d5+
♔b6 61.♕d8 ♗c5 62.♕b8+ ♖b7
63.♕d8+ ♔a7 64.♕d5 ♗b6
65.♔g5 ♖c7 66.♔g6 b4 67.♕e6
♗d4**
White resigned.

In one moment, Caruana had become, in many people's eyes, the main challenger for the World Championship! In the October rating list, he moved into second place (2844) with only Carlsen (2863) ahead of him. Caruana underlined his high quality with victory in the 2014-2015 FIDE Grand Prix series and for the first time obtained the right to play in the Candidates tournament.

From his 2015 games, we choose Caruana's victory over the American GM Wesley So. In recent years, So has become one of Caruana's closest rivals and a clear candidate for the World Championship.

Game 16 Nimzo-Indian Defence E43
Fabiano Caruana 2810
Wesley So 2788
Shamkir 2015 (7)

1.d4 ♞f6 2.c4 e6 3.♞c3 ♝b4 4.♞f3 b6 5.e3 ♞e4 6.♛c2 ♝b7 7.♝d3 f5 8.0-0 ♝xc3 9.bxc3 0-0

On the board we have a *tabiya* of the Nimzo-Indian Defence, for a long time considered safe for Black.
10.c5!?
This positional pawn sacrifice, seen in a number of variations, enriches this variation with dynamism and has made it interesting again. White strives to open diagonals for his bishops. One of the first examples on this theme was the following: Ehlvest-Vaisser (Volgodonsk 1983): 10.♞e1 ♛h4

11.f3 ♞g5 12.c5! bxc5 13.♖b1 ♝c6 14.♝a3 ♖f6 15.♛f2 ♛h5 16.dxc5! (trying to keep the knight on b8) 16...e5 17.♝c4+ ♚f8 18.♛g3 f4 19.exf4 exf4 20.♛g4 ♞xf3+ 21.gxf3 ♖g6 22.♞g2 ♖xg4 23.fxg4.

And Black resigned. The present author has been acquainted with this game from his schooldays and it made a great impression on me.
10...♖f6
In the game Vitiugov-Anand (Alekhine Memorial 2013) the black rook did not leave the 8th rank: 10... bxc5 11.♖b1 ♛c8 12.♝a3 ♖e8 13.dxc5 ♞a6 with mutual chances.
11.♞e1 bxc5 12.♖b1 ♛c8 13.f3 ♞g5 14.♝e2! cxd4 15.cxd4 ♞c6 16.♞d3 ♝a6 17.♝b2
The unopposed dark-squared bishop on the long diagonal is

sufficient compensation for the sacrificed pawn.

17...♘e7 18.d5 ♖h6 19.dxe6 ♘xe6

20.♘f4!

White consistently plays to enlarge the scope of the ♗b2.

20...♘xf4 21.exf4 ♗xe2 22.♕xe2 ♖e6 23.♕d3 ♘g6?!

This proves a significant loss of time.

There were good chances to maintain dynamic equality after 23...♖b8 24.♕d4 ♖f6.

24.g3!

Perhaps Black was counting on 24.♕xf5 ♕f8, exchanging queens and equalising.

24...♖b8

He has to return the pawn in a less favourable version, since after 24...♘e7 there is the unpleasant 25.♖fe1.

25.♕xf5 ♖eb6 26.♗d4 ♖xb1 27.♖xb1 ♖xb1+ 28.♕xb1

Despite the exchange of rooks and the presence of two connected

passed pawns in the centre, Black's position is quite unpleasant.

The white bishop is clearly stronger than the black knight and, together with the queen, it creates unpleasant threats against the king.

28...c5 29.♕b3+ c4

On 29...♔f8 there follows the nice double attack 30.♕c3!.

30.♕b5 ♘e7 31.♕g5 ♕f8 32.♗c5 ♔f7 33.♕e5 ♕e8 34.♔f2 ♘c6 35.♕h5+

The dominance of the white pieces leads to material gains.

35...g6 36.♕xh7+ ♔e6 37.♕g7 ♕f7 38.♕xf7+

The exchange of queens is the simplest way to realise the advantage. In the endgame with passed pawns, the superiority of bishop over knight is obvious.

38...♔xf7 39.♔e3 ♔e6 40.g4 d6 41.♗a3 d5 42.♗b2 ♘b4 43.a4 ♘c2+ 44.♔d2 ♘b4 45.h4 ♘d3 46.♗d4 a6 47.h5 gxh5 48.f5+ ♔d6 49.gxh5 ♘e5 50.♔e3 ♘f7 51.♗g7 1-0

In June 2015, Caruana quit the Italian federation and returned to the US rating list. This same period saw another change of trainer – Fabiano took on as his new assistant the ex-FIDE World Champion Rustam Kasimdzhanov.

Caruana's rating began gradually to drop and by the start of the Moscow Candidates tournament (March 2016) was below 2800.

Shared 2nd-3rd places in the Candidates with Anand, victory in the US Championship and Olympiad gold as a member of the US team – these were our hero's principal achievements in 2016.

The following game may justifiably be regarded as the golden one for the US Olympiad team. In the match against their main rivals Ukraine, peace was signed on board two, three and four. The fate of the match therefore depended on the battle of the two team leaders.

Game 17 Sicilian Defence B31
Fabiano Caruana   2818
Pavel Eljanov   2739

Baku ol 2016 (6)

1.e4 c5 2.♘f3 ♘c6 3.♗b5 g6 4.♗xc6 bxc6 5.0-0 ♗g7 6.♖e1 ♘h6 7.c3 0-0 8.h3

Black gets sufficient counterplay in the event of the immediate 8.d4 cxd4 9.cxd4 d5 10.e5 f6!.

The move h2-h3 aims to restrict the enemy pieces.

8...f5 9.e5

Now the strategical battle rages around the e5-square.

9...♘f7 10.d3

10...♖b8

Holding the ♗c1 on its original square. If 10...d6 there could follow 11.♗f4.

11.♘a3 ♗a6

And now Black prevents the knight appearing on c4.

12.♘c4 ♗xc4 13.dxc4 d6 14.e6 ♘e5 15.♘xe5 ♗xe5 16.♗h6 ♗g7 17.♗xg7 ♔xg7

Black has played the opening stage confidently, and has equalised. Although White has established a 'wedge' in the enemy position, in the future the pawn on e6 may become an object of attack.

18.♖b1 ♕a5 19.a4 ♖f6 20.♖e3 ♕a6 21.b3 ♕c8 22.♕e1 a5

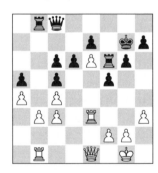

We have a position of dynamic equality. The e6-pawn has drawn to itself the attention of the white pieces, whilst Black's defences on both flanks are solid. Even so, Caruana continues to seek the smallest chance to continue the battle.

23.b4! axb4 24.cxb4 cxb4 25.罩xb4
So, White creates a passed pawn on
a4, but maybe it is vulnerable?!
**25...罩a8 26.營a1 f4 27.罩e4 f3 28.g4
查g8 29.營d1 罩xe6?!**
Black strives for simplifications, but
this decision proves far from best.
By continuing 29...c5 30.罩b5 營f8
followed by ...營h6, Black could
have confidently controlled the
situation thanks to his counterplay
against the white king.
30.營xf3 罩xe4 31.營xe4 營c7

32.c5!
An effective blow, breaking up the
opponent's pawn structure.
**32...dxc5 33.營c4+ 查g7 34.營c3+
查g8 35.營c4+ 查g7 36.營xc5**
Emphasising White's positional
advantage. He has two pawn islands
against the opponent's three, and
an outside passed pawn on a4. In
addition, the protection of the
black king is less solid than that of
White's.

**36...營d6 37.營c3+ 營f6 38.營e3 罩f8
39.罩e4 罩f7 40.罩e5**
The white pieces gradually take
over the whole board!
40...營d6 41.a5 營d1+ 42.查g2 營a1

43.營e2!
A small move with large
consequences. Now the advance of
the black pawn to e6 is unavoidable.
Black cannot protect the many
weaknesses in his position.
**43...e6 44.a6 營d4 45.罩xe6 c5
46.罩e7 營d5+ 47.f3 c4 48.罩xf7+
營xf7 49.營e5+ 查h6 50.營e3+ 查g7
51.營d4+ 查h6 52.a7 營b7 53.h4**
Black resigned.
A characteristic Caruana game,
in which the victory was created
practically out of nothing. An
important factor in such games
is undoubtedly Fabiano's absolute
determination to fight to the last
pawn. This quality was also typical
of Bobby Fischer in his day.

In the January 2017 rating list, Caruana again returned to second place,
with only Carlsen ahead...

At the start of 2017, Caruana played in a new series of events – an open
(!) tournament in Gibraltar, the US Championship and a tournament in
Baden-Baden. However, he did not achieve any great laurels. As a result,

he lost rating points and dropped (in the 1 May 2017 list) to fourth place. There is nothing surprising in these swings. Caruana plays much and often, and therefore, as the reader has already seen, his results fluctuate somewhat. His fans only need patiently to await new successes!

At the last of the above-mentioned tournaments in Baden-Baden, Caruana shared 2nd-3rd places with World Champion Magnus Carlsen, but both were 1.5 points behind Levon Aronian! Already in the first round, Caruana suffered a sensational defeat against the women's World Champion Hou Yifan, but demonstrating his immunity against misfortune, he won in the next two rounds.

Game 18 Vienna Game C28
Arkadij Naiditsch 2702
Fabiano Caruana 2817
Baden-Baden 2017 (2)

1.e4 e5 2.♗c4 ♘f6 3.d3 ♘c6 4.♘c3 ♘a5

One of the most solid lines against the Vienna. Black is prepared to sacrifice several tempi, to achieve the exchange of White's active light-squared bishop.

5.♘ge2 ♗c5 6.0-0 0-0 7.♘g3 h6 8.h3 d6

9.♗b3

More energetic is 9.♔h1 ♘xc4 10.dxc4 ♗e6 11.b3 c6 12.f4 with mutual chances.

9...c6 10.♘a4 ♘xb3 11.axb3 ♗b4 12.♗d2 ♗xd2 13.♕xd2 d5

As a result of his opponent's somewhat tame play, Black has managed to become active in the centre and obtain comfortable play.

14.♕b4?!

This turns out to be a blank shot and only leads to loss of time.

14...b6!

Since 15.♘xb6? is impossible due to 15...♖b8, Black can now activate his queenside pawn mass with tempo.

15.♘c3 c5 16.♕a3 d4 17.♘ce2 a5!

Now White has to spend a good deal more time to get his queen out of trouble. In addition, the fixed white queenside pawns may become an object of attack in the future.

18.f4 ♗e6 19.♖ae1 exf4 20.♘xf4 ♘d7 21.♕a1 ♕g5 22.♔h2 ♘e5 23.♕d1 ♖ae8

Having completely centralised and established control over the dark squares, Caruana has achieved a clear advantage.

24.♘ge2 ♘g6 25.♕c1 ♕e5 26.♔g1 ♘h4 27.g3 ♘g6 28.♔g2 ♕d6 29.♔h2

Short of time, White decides to adopt waiting tactics. Maybe he should have preferred simplification: 29.♘xg6 fxg6 30.♖xf8+ ♖xf8 31.♖f1 etc.

29...♘e5 30.♔g2

30...f5!?

In view of his opponent's time-trouble, Caruana goes over to active operations. The alternative was a gradual strengthening of the position by means of 30...♗d7.

31.♘xe6 ♖xe6 32.exf5 ♕d5+ 33.♔g1?

The mistake soon comes. It was essential to play 33.♔h2 ♖ef6 34.g4 ♘f3+ 35.♖xf3 ♕xf3 36.♕f4 ♕c6 37.♘g3, establishing a solid position for the sacrificed exchange.

33...♖ef6 34.♘f4

Now the variation 34.g4 ♘f3+ 35.♖xf3 ♕xf3 is bad for White, because of the undefended pawn on h3.

34...♘f3+ 35.♔f2

After 35.♔h1 ♕b7 36.♖e4 ♘g5 Black wins. White had placed his hopes on the text, but it meets a simple refutation.

35...♕xf5 36.♔xf3 ♕xh3!

After this quiet move, White is defenceless.

37.♖e4 g5 38.♔e2 ♕xg3 39.♖f3 ♕g4 40.♕h1 ♖xf4 0-1

The American grandmaster's climb to the top continued. The saying 'genius is 10% inspiration and 90% perspiration' is well-known.

'There is no particular secret. I have simply always taken chess seriously and I understand that chess is my job! One must never relax or permit oneself indulgences. Although nobody can completely explain why one person keeps on advancing, while another ceases to go beyond what they have already achieved. There is no magic recipe.'

(from Caruana's interview on Chess Pro).

That Caruana is a real chess worker is well-known. 'And what about the 10% in the formula?' the reader may ask. I think the answer to this question is provided by the splendid chess creations of our hero, which can be found in the second half of this book. For myself, I can only say that I obtained enormous pleasure from working on this book about the games of Caruana!

Two rapid wins

In August 2017 in St Louis, a sensational rapid tournament took place, in which ex-World Champion Garry Kasparov took part, after an absence of 12 years from tournament play. Although the event did not have major sporting significance, it attracted the interest of chess lovers the world over.

In the rapid tournament, Caruana shared 2nd-3rd places with Nakamura (Aronian was first). But probably the most memorable things for Fabiano were his wins against Karjakin and the 13th World Champion. These games were very instructive and add some splendid extra instructional material to this book.

The Pillsbury Attack

The famous Pillsbury attacking formation, involving the establishment of a knight outpost on e5, supported by white pawns on d4 and f4, was for a long time a source of terror to defenders of the Queen's Gambit. Pillsbury first used this strategy in his triumphant tournament victory at Hastings 1895.

And lo and behold, over 120 years later, the Pillsbury Attack was used to overcome one of the strongest modern grandmasters.

Game 19 Nimzo-Indian Defence E53
| **Fabiano Caruana** | 2807 |
| **Sergey Karjakin** | 2773 |

St Louis 2017 (3)

1.d4 ♘f6 2.c4 e6 3.♘c3 ♗b4 4.♘f3 b6 5.e3 ♗b7 6.♗d3 0-0 7.0-0 d5
Now Black turns the game into lines more reminiscent of the Queen's Gambit.
Alternative approaches were 7...c5 8.♘a4 cxd4 9.exd4 ♖e8 10.a3

♗f8 followed by ...d7-d6, going into a sort of Hedgehog structure, or 7...♗xc3 8.bxc3 ♗e4 9.♗e2 c5, constructing a blockading position along Nimzowitsch-type lines.
8.cxd5 exd5

9.♘e5
At the end of the 19th century, there was a joke going round: 'If Pillsbury gets a knight on e5, it is mate!' The other popular continuation is 9.a3 ♗d6 10.b4, aiming to develop an initiative on the queenside.
9...c5
A responsible decision, cutting off the ♗b4 from the kingside.

The flexible continuation
9...♗d6 10.f4 c5 enjoys greater
popularity, e.g. 11.♕f3 ♘c6 12.♕h3
g6 (necessary prophylaxis. An
instructive crush resulted after
12...♘e7? 13.♘d7!, Simagin-
Razuvaev, Moscow 1967) 13.♔h1 a6
14.♗d2 b5 15.♖ad1 cxd4 16.♘xc6
♗xc6 17.exd4 b4 18.♘e2 ♗b5 19.f5
♗xd3 20.♕xd3 ♘e4 21.♗f4 with
roughly equal chances, Sadler-
Kortchnoi, Tilburg 1998.

10.f4 ♘c6 11.♘e2
Directing the knight towards the
kingside and leaving the ♗b4 in no
man's land.

11...c4
Undoubtedly, taking the pressure
off d4 frees White's hands for
operations on the kingside, but
after 11...♘e4 12.a3 ♗a5 13.♖b1 the
position of the bishop on a5 causes
concern.

12.♗c2

12...♘e7?!
The manoeuvre begun with
this move leads Black into
serious difficulties. It was worth
considering the consolidation of
the position by means of 12...♖e8

13.♗d2 ♗f8 14.♘g3 ♖c8 15.♕f3 ♖c7
etc.

13.♘g3 ♘c8 14.♘h5 ♗e7
The move 14...♘d6 is now
impossible because of 15.♘xf6+
♕xf6 16.♘d7.
But now the ♘c8 is ready to
continue its journey to e4.

15.b3!
An outstanding example of play
on the whole board! The white
dark-squared bishop gains the
possibility of coming into the game
via a3, which completely upsets the
opponent's plans.

15...cxb3?!
More chances of a successful
defence were offered by 15...♘d6
16.♘xf6+ ♗xf6 17.♗a3 ♖c8.

**16.axb3 ♘d6 17.♘xf6+ ♗xf6 18.♗a3
♗c8?!**
This leads to an obvious loss of
time, but it is already hard to offer
Black any good advice. The problem
is that there is no way his knight
can reach e4, e.g. 18...♗e7 19.♗xh7+!
♔xh7 20.♕h5+ ♔g8 21.♖f3 or
18...♖e8 19.♗xd6 ♕xd6 20.♗xh7+!
with a decisive attack for White in
both cases.

19.♕f3 ♗b7 20.♗d3 a5 21.♖ac1 a4 22.♕h3 g6

23.♘d7
Leading to the win of the exchange, with an irresistible attack on the kingside.

23...♗e7 24.♘xf8 ♗xf8 25.f5! axb3 26.fxg6 hxg6

27.♗xg6!
A crushing blow, crowning White's purposeful play.

27...fxg6 28.♕e6+ ♔h7 29.♗xd6 ♕xd6 30.♖f7+ ♔h6
After 30...♔g8 the move 31.♖xf8+ decides.

31.♕h3+ ♔g5 32.g3
Black resigned.

Meeting a legend
In this game, Black confidently solved his opening problems, but no quick draw agreement followed. Caruana was in the mood for a long battle and was able to maintain minimal pressure. In his best years Kasparov would undoubtedly have confidently neutralised his opponent's pretensions, but his 12-year absence from the game told. The fate of the game was decided by Black's mistake at move 35.

Game 20 Sicilian Defence B52
Fabiano Caruana   2807
Garry Kasparov   2812
St Louis 2017 (9)

1.e4 c5 2.♘f3 d6 3.♗b5+
Fabiano has respect for his great opponent's exceptional Sicilian skills and takes play into more positional channels.
There is nothing surprising in this decision, because in the 20th century, Kasparov dominated in the Sicilian, both with the white and the black pieces!
3...♗d7 4.♗xd7+ ♕xd7 5.c4

Preparing to go into a Maroczy set-up.
5...♘c6 6.♘c3 g6 7.d4 ♗g7

A subtle move, introduced into practice by Kasparov himself back in the day.

In the event of the natural 7...cxd4 8.♘xd4 ♗g7 9.♘de2! the white bishop later occupies the active square g5.

Now, however, White has the choice between developing the bishop to e3 or advancing d4-d5.

8.♗e3

Caruana is ready to settle for the minimum. A more tense struggle, in the spirit of the Nimzo-Indian, results from 8.d5 ♗xc3+! 9.bxc3 ♘a5 10.0-0 f6 11.♘d2 b6, as was seen in the game Shirov-Kasparov, Yerevan 1996.

8...cxd4 9.♘xd4 ♘f6 10.f3 0-0 11.0-0 a6

Black's plans include preparing the freeing advances ...b7-b5 or ...d6-d5.

12.♘a4

In Kasparov's practice, the following continuation has been tested twice: 12.a4 e6 13.♖c1 ♘e5 14.b3 (or 14.♕e2 ♖fc8 15.b3 d5 16.cxd5 exd5 17.f4 ♖xc3!? 18.♖xc3 ♘xe4 with the initiative for the sacrificed exchange, Sadvakasov-Kasparov, Astana 2001) 14...d5

15.cxd5 exd5 16.♘xd5 ♘xd5 17.exd5 ♖fe8 18.♗f2 ♕xd5 with equality, Akopian-Kasparov, Bled 2003.

12...♖ab8 13.♘xc6

Formally this move is a novelty. White gets nothing at all from 13.♘b6 ♕d8 14.c5 ♘d7! 15.♘xc6 bxc6 16.♘xd7 ♕xd7 17.♗d4 dxc5 18.♗xg7 ♕xd1 19.♖axd1 ♔xg7 20.♖f2 with an equal rook endgame, Smeets-Yilmaz, Germany Bundesliga 2012/13.

13...♕xc6

The alternative is 13...bxc6 14.♕d2 (premature is 14.c5?! d5 15.e5 ♕e6 16.♗d4 ♘d7 17.f4 f6 etc.) 14...♕c7 with a solid position. With the text, Black retains the possibility of the break against the c4-pawn with ...b7-b5.

14.♘b6 ♘d7 15.♘xd7 ♕xd7

We have on the board a position of dynamic equality. White's space advantage is offset by the flexibility of the black position. The outpost on d5 does not exert a significant influence on the game, after the exchange of knights.

16.♖f2

But the battle continues! In putting his rooks on d2 and c1, Caruana is counting on breathing life into the position, by playing the break c4-c5.

16...b5

True to his active style of play, the 13th World Champion forces an immediate change of circumstances.

17.c5 ♕a7 18.♖c1 dxc5 19.♗xc5 ♕c7 20.f4

It is essential to establish control of the dark squares in the centre. If not, he must constantly reckon with ...♗e5 or ...♗h6.

20...♖fd8 21.♕e1 ♖d3 22.e5

Limiting the activity of the ♗g7, which, however, is compensated for by Black's control of the d-file.

22...♕d7 23.h3

23...♕e6

A rather direct attempt to prepare a break against the e5-pawn with ...f7-f6. He could have brought the ♗g7 into play, whilst retaining control of the d-file, with 23...♖bc8 24.b4 ♗f8 followed by ...e7-e6.

24.♖d2 ♖xd2 25.♕xd2 f6 26.exf6 ♗xf6 27.b4

The upshot is that White has a microscopic advantage, due to his superior pawn structure.

27...♖e8 28.♖f1 ♔f7 29.♖f3 h5 30.a3 ♕c4 31.♕d7 a5

Exchanging off pawns and getting rid of the potential weakness on a6. Commentators recommended as a more solid alternative 31...♕e6, but Kasparov never did like passive waiting.

32.f5!

The only way to maintain the flagging initiative.

32...g5 33.♕e6+ ♕xe6 34.fxe6+ ♔xe6 35.bxa5

It may appear that with his active king in the endgame, Black should have nothing to fear, but the passed pawn on a5 requires heightened attention.

35...♖a8?

This is effectively the only mistake in the game, but it proves decisive.

Equality could be maintained with 35...♖c8! 36.♗b6 ♖c4!, followed by the transfer of the rook to a4.
The text leads to a passive position for the black rook.
36.♗b6 ♔d5 37.♖f5+ ♔c4 38.♖c5+ ♔b3 39.♖xb5+ ♔xa3 40.♔f2 ♔a4 41.♖f5
The black king is cut off on the 5th rank and the game is decided by the triumphal march of the white monarch.
41...♔b3 42.♔e3 ♔c4 43.♔e4 g4
No better is 43...♖a6 44.♖c5+ ♔b4 45.♔d5, winning.
44.♖xh5 gxh3 45.gxh3 ♗c3 46.♖c5+ ♔b3 47.h4 ♗b4 48.♖g5 ♔c4 49.h5 ♗d6 50.h6
Black resigned.

The first half of 2018 was the most brilliant period of our hero's career. Although January's Wijk aan Zee tournament was a failure (5 out of 13; 10th-12th places), maybe this event was used by Caruana to 'accumulate' energy before the most important event, the Candidates tournament in Berlin, which began in March.

Candidates tournament, Berlin 2018 (March)

The Berlin tournament saw Fabiano realise his dream of obtaining the right to play a match for the world title against Magnus Carlsen!

The drama of the event reached its climax two rounds before the end, when Caruana, the leader at that point, was defeated by Karjakin! At this critical moment, Fabiano demonstrated his best personal qualities and, by winning his last two games, finished first (9 out of 14!), a full point ahead of his nearest chaser.

The 'Catalan bomb'

At the Candidates' tournament, Caruana's principal weapon as White in the closed games was the Catalan, with the white queen coming to b3. Already in the opening round, he scored an important victory in this system.

Game 21 Catalan Opening E00
Fabiano Caruana   2784
Wesley So   2799
Berlin 2018 (1)

1.d4 ♘f6 2.c4 e6 3.g3 ♗b4+

A popular manoeuvre. Only after luring the enemy bishop to d2 does the black bishop retreat to its intended e7-square.
In the game Caruana-Karjakin (round 5), Black chose 3...d5 4.♗g2

♗e7 5.♘f3 0-0, probably aiming for the variation 6.0-0 dxc4 7.♕c2 a6 etc. But here too, Caruana chose 6.♕b3, aiming to take play into the same closed line that he had prepared 'in the quiet of his study', since after 6...dxc4 7.♕xc4 a6, White is not required to castle, but can instead fight for the initiative with 8.♗f4!. Therefore Karjakin settled for the continuation 6...c6 7.0-0 dxc4!?, and after 8.♕xc4 b5 9.♕c2 ♗b7 10.♘bd2 c5 11.dxc5 ♘a6 12.♘b3 ♗e4 13.♕c3 ♖c8, successfully solved his opening problems.

4.♗d2 ♗e7 5.♗g2 d5 6.♘f3 0-0 7.0-0 c6 8.♕b3

The idea of bringing the queen to b3 is to prepare to develop the queen's knight to its natural and active square on c3. The text has been known for a long time, but until now was not regarded as a serious alternative to the main continuation 8.♕c2.

8...♘bd7

In the game Caruana-Ding Liren (round 9) Black chose the principled retort 8...b6 9.♘c3 ♗a6, forcing White to release the tension in the centre, since he cannot protect the c4-pawn with the move b2-b3. But even in the resulting symmetrical position, Caruana was able to pose problems for his opponent: 10.cxd5 cxd5 11.♘e5 ♗b7 12.♖fc1 ♘c6 13.♘xd5 ♘xd4 14.♘xe7+ ♕xe7 15.♕c4 ♗xg2 16.♕xd4 ♖fd8 17.♕f4 ♗b7 18.♗b4 ♕e8 19.♖c7 ♘d5 20.♕xf7+ ♕xf7 21.♖xf7 ♗a6 22.♗a3 ♗xe2 23.♖c1 ♗h5 24.♖b7 with the advantage to White in the endgame.

9.♗f4 a5

The advance of the a-pawn prevents the intended 10.♘c3, after which there follows 10...a4!. Even so, in a strategic sense, the advance of the a-pawn is very committal, since it practically forces Black to continue the queenside demonstration with a subsequent ...b7-b5.

10.♖d1 ♘h5 11.♗c1 ♘hf6

The position has almost repeated, but White has managed in the process to 'correct' the position of his queen's bishop.

12.♘bd2 b5 13.c5

The b5-pawn is invulnerable because of 13.cxb5 cxb5 14.♕xb5 ♗a6.

13...b4 14.♕c2 a4

15.♖e1!

The activity of the black queenside pawns should not cause anyone to panic: White only needs to play e2-e4, and his advantage will be obvious. It is to prepare this advance that White moves his rook from d1 to e1.

After the immediate 15.e4?! there could follow either 15...b3, exploiting the insufficiently-defended e4-square, or 15...♘xe4 16.♘xe4 dxe4 17.♕xe4 ♘xc5, and the hanging white rook on d1 is exposed.

15...e5

Black is practically forced to decide on this central advance, since otherwise he will have a prospectless position after White pushes e2-e4.

16.♘xe5 ♘xe5 17.dxe5 ♘d7 18.♘f3 ♗xc5

In the event of 18...♘xc5 19.♗e3 the black rook would be forced to occupy an awkward position on a5. On the other hand, the text move is quite risky, because it leads to a weakening of the black king's pawn cover.

19.♘g5! g6 20.♗f4 ♕b6

21.e4!

The thematic Catalan break is achieved! The opponent replies with a queenside counterattack.

21...b3! 22.axb3 axb3 23.♕e2

23...♗a6?!

By transferring the bishop to c4, Black succeeds in strengthening the all-important point d5, but this logical idea does not solve all his problems.

Immediately afterwards, commentators suggested 23...♖a2!?, aiming for counterplay with the bishop subsequently coming to a6. This recommendation looks extremely unstable in a practical game, although computer analysis shows that Black can repulse a direct attack:

24.e6 (or 24.exd5 ♗a6 25.♕f3 ♖xb2 with mutual chances) 24...fxe6 25.exd5 (25.♘xe6?! ♗a6 26.♕d2 ♗b4) 25...exd5 26.♕e6+ ♔g7 27.♗e3 h6 28.♖ac1 hxg5 29.♖xc5 ♕b4!! (he loses after 29...♘xc5? 30.♗d4+ ♔h6 31.♕e7 ♖g8 32.h4 and mate) 30.♖xc6 (30.♖cc1 ♖xb2) 30...♖f6, and White's offensive is beaten off. Even so, such head-spinning variations always require serious checking.

It is also worth examining the quiet move 24.♖ab1!?.

analysis diagram

The manoeuvre 24...♗a6 25.♕f3 ♗c4 again proves to be no panacea: White can decide things in his favour with the combinative blow 26.♘xf7! ♖xf7 27.e6 ♖e7 28.exd7 ♖xd7 29.exd5 ♗xd5 30.♖e8+ ♔f7 31.♕e2, and the black king is defenceless.

The computer recommends provoking the knight sacrifice on f7 in a form more favourable to Black, by means of 24...h6. Then there could follow 25.♘xf7! ♖xf7 (25...♔xf7 is bad because of 26.e6+! ♔xe6 27.exd5+ ♔f7 28.♗xh6)

analysis diagram

26.exd5! (or 26.e6 ♖xf4 27.gxf4 ♘f6), and although White's initiative

looks very promising, by means of 26...♘f8 27.e6 ♖e7 28.♗xh6 cxd5 29.♗xd5 ♗b7 Black manages to hold the position.

24.♕f3

The white queen creeps, catlike, closer to the enemy king's residence.

24...♗c4

25.♖xa8

Deflecting the black king's rook from its defensive duties.

25...♖xa8 26.e6!

As a result of the sharp battle on the queenside and in the centre, White has been left with a numerical superiority in his attack on the opposite flank. Such situations, ending in the demolition of the black king's defences, are typical of many Catalan battles.

26...dxe4

If 26...fxe6? White wins with either 27.♗c7 or the more striking 27.♗b8.

27.exf7+ ♗xf7 28.♘xe4

The combinational fire has died down and it is time to draw conclusions. The insecure position of the black king determines White's clear superiority.

28...♗d4

After 28...♖e8 29.♖d1 ♗d5 30.♕g4
♗e6 31.♕e2 ♗d5 32.♕d3 Black's
position is also difficult.
29.♘d6 ♗d5 30.♕e2 ♘f8

It may momentarily appear that
Black has miraculously managed
to cover the holes in his king's
protective wall, but White ends the
game with a few accurate moves.
31.♗xd5+ cxd5 32.♕f3! ♕a5 33.♖e7!
Black resigned. It is impossible to
prevent the decisive penetration of
the white queen to f7.

The decisive encounter
The game below was played in
the final round. By the moment
the first time-control was passed,
it had become obvious that a
draw was enough for Caruana to
win the tournament. However,
the American GM showed his
maximalist side and converted his
advantage to victory.

Game 22 Petroff Defence C43
Alexander Grischuk   2767
Fabiano Caruana   2784
Berlin 2018 (14)

1.e4 e5 2.♘f3 ♘f6

In the Candidates tournament, the
Petroff Defence proved a splendid
weapon for Fabiano against 1.e4,
yielding him 2.5 points out of 4
games!
3.d4
Vladimir Kramnik, Wesley So and
Sergey Karjakin all played 3.♘xe5
against Caruana in this top-level
event.
3...♘xe4 4.dxe5 d5 5.♘bd2

5...♘xd2
The alternative is 5...♘c5, but the
text leads to a sharper game.
Two weeks later, Caruana played the
interesting novelty 5...♕d7!? against
Nikita Vitiugov.

The idea of this original queen
move, as Fabiano himself explained,
is that Black for the moment
neither retreats the knight, nor

exchanges it off on d2, but intends simply to continue developing.
In doing so, the move 5...♗e7, for example, would be bad because of 6.♘xe4 dxe4 7.♕xd8+ ♔xd8 8.♘d4. This threat is prevented by the queen move to d7.
In the game Vitiugov-Caruana, Baden-Baden 2018, there followed 5...♕d7 6.♗d3 ♘c5 7.♗e2 g6 8.♘b3 ♘e6 9.♗e3 c5 10.♘g5 b6 11.♘xe6 fxe6 12.a4 ♗b7 13.0-0 ♘c6 14.f4 ♗h6 15.a5 ♘e7 16.♗g4 d4 17.♗c1 0-0 18.♕d3 ♗d5 19.♕h3 ♗g7 20.♘d2 ♘f5 21.c4 dxc3 22.bxc3 ♖ad8 23.axb6 axb6 with excellent play for Black.

6.♗xd2 ♗e7

7.♗d3

The continuation 7.♗e2 is interesting, neutralising the possible pin on the h5-d1 diagonal. In the game Nepomniachtchi-Mamedyarov, Moscow rapid 2018, there followed 7...0-0 8.0-0 c5 9.♗f4 ♘c6 10.♕d2 ♗e6 11.c3 ♕d7 12.h3 ♖ad8 13.♖fd1 h6 14.♗d3 ♗f5 15.♗g3 ♗xd3 16.♕xd3 ♕e6 17.a3 b6 18.b4 d4!, and Black successfully beat off the opponent's pressure.
7.c4 has also been seen.

7...c5 8.c3 ♘c6 9.0-0 ♗g4 10.♖e1 ♕d7 11.h3 ♗h5

In Vallejo Pons-R.Perez Garcia (Spain tt 2009) Black immediately sought the exchange of light-squared bishops by means of 11...♗f5. After 12.♕c2 ♗xd3 13.♕xd3 0-0 14.♖ad1 ♕e6 15.a3 a6?! (15...♖ad8) 16.♗e3 ♖ad8 17.b4! cxb4 18.axb4, White obtained the advantage thanks to the weakened d4-square.
The text looks more logical, since it retains the unpleasant pin on the knight at f3.

12.♗f4

White gets nothing from the continuation 12.♕c2 ♗xf3 13.♗f5 ♕c7 14.gxf3 ♘xe5 etc.

This was the turning point in the game. It is tempting to transfer the knight to the blockading square e6, but after 12...♘d8 13.g4 ♘e6 (13...♗g6? is refuted by 14.e6! ♘xe6 15.♘e5) 14.gxh5! (14.♗g3 ♗g6) 14...♘xf4 15.e6! ♘xe6 16.♘e5 ♕d6 17.♕a4+ ♔f8 18.♗f5, the pawn sacrifice gives White a strong initiative.
After the other natural move 12...0-0 there follows 13.♕c2 ♗g6 (13...♗xf3? 14.♗xh7+ ♔h8 15.♗f5

♗e4 16.♕xe4!) 14.♗xg6 hxg6
15.♖ad1 ♖ad8 16.♗g5, and White's
chances are superior.

12...♕e6!

A subtle move, significantly
limiting the opponent's
possibilities. It seems that Black is
not playing 'according to the rules'
(the queen is a poor blockader!),
but now 13.♕c2? ♗xf3 14.♗f5 is
impossible because of 14...♗e4!, and
the black queen is defended.

13.a3 0-0 14.b4

Again, after 14.♕c2 there follows
14...♗xf3 15.♗xh7+ ♔h8 16.♗f5 (16.
gxf3 g6) 16...♗e4!.

14...h6!

After the 'automatic' 14...b6 the
move 15.♕b1! is possible, because
in the variation 15...♗xf3? (15...♗g6
16.♗g5!, and White's chances are
somewhat preferable) 16.♗xh7+
♔h8 17.♗f5 ♗e4 18.♗xe6 ♗xb1
19.♗xd5, the undefended ♘c6 tells.

15.♗g3

After 15.bxc5 ♗xc5, the d4-square
comes under the control of the
black pieces.

15...b6 16.♘d4?!

The wish to escape the pin is
perfectly understandable, but

the transformation of the pawn
structure forced by the text move
proves unfavourable for White.
There was approximate equality
after both 16.♗e2 and 16.♕b1 ♗g6.

16...♗xd1 17.♘xe6 fxe6 18.♖axd1

If White was counting on obtaining
dividends from having the two
bishops in the ending, then he
was to be disappointed, as Black's
next move gives the game a closed
character.

18...c4!

Preventing the move c3-c4 forever.

19.♗c2 b5 20.a4 a6

The structure of the position has
been determined. Strategically,
the threat of the advance ...d5-d4
hangs over White, after which his
pawn structure will be completely
undermined.

21.f3

The attempt to change the
unfavourable course of the game by
violent means with 21.f4 ♖ac8 (21...
d4? 22.♗e4) 22.f5 fails because of
22...d4! 23.cxd4 ♘xb4 etc.

**21...♗g5 22.♗f2 ♗f4 23.♗c5 ♖fd8
24.♗d6**

The appearance of the bishop on d6
does not bring White great benefits,

and Black just strengthens his
position methodically.

**24...♗g3 25.♖e2 g5 26.♔f1 ♔f7
27.♗c7 ♖e8 28.♗d6 ♖ac8 29.♖a1**

If White continues to keep his rook
on d1, then Black can proceed to
the preparation of an attack on the
kingside, involving the advance of
the g- and h-pawns.

29...♖ed8 30.♗b1 ♖d7 31.♖a3

The queenside demonstration
31.axb5 axb5 32.♖a6 could be
countered by 32...h5 (32...d4?!
33.♗e4 d3 34.♗xc6) 33.♖b6 d4
34.♗e4 ♖a7!, and it is already Black
who has the a-file along which to
penetrate.

31...d4!

The thoroughly-prepared
breakthrough finally comes!

32.axb5 axb5 33.cxd4 ♘xd4 34.♖ea2

If 34.♖e4 White's defences crumble
after 34...♘f5, whilst after 34.♖ee3
there follows 34...♗f4 35.♖e4 ♘f5.

**34...♘c6 35.♗e4 ♗xe5 36.♗xc6
♖xd6 37.♗xb5**

Going into an opposite-coloured
bishops endgame only increases
Black's winning chances, since with
rooks on, the insecure position of
the white king comes into play.

37...♖d1+ 38.♔e2 ♖g1 39.♔e3

39...♖b1

White can't defend the b4-pawn,
as he still has to fight against the
passed c-pawn. Even so, it was
even more accurate to play 39...
c3!, depriving the opponent of
the possibility of 40.♖a8! (which
could have followed after the text)
40...♖xa8 41.♖xa8 ♖xb4 42.♗a4
to exchange a pair of rooks and
improve his drawing chances.

**40.♖a7+ ♔f6 41.♗d7 ♗f4+ 42.♔e2
♖d8 43.♖c2 ♖xb4**

So, Black wins a pawn, whilst
retaining all the advantages of his
position.

44.♗c6 c3 45.♖d7 ♖c8 46.♗e4

46...h5!

By advancing the pawn to h4, Black
fixes the weakness of the g2-pawn
and ensures his king a path via

e5-f4-g3-h2 to enter the enemy camp.

From a practical point of view, White's position is already pretty much indefensible, because he is under pressure on both flanks.

47.♔d3 ♖b2

Black is ready to exchange the rooks on b2, which would sharply increase the strength of his passed pawn.

48.♔e2 h4 49.♖d1 ♔e5 50.♖a1 ♖d8 51.♖d1 ♖db8 52.♖a1 ♗d2 53.♖a6 ♖d8 54.♖c6 ♖b1 55.♔f2 ♖a1 56.♖c4 ♖d4 57.♖c8 ♖b4 58.♔e2 ♔f4 59.♔f2 ♖bb1 60.♖f8+ ♔e5 61.♗d3 ♖b2 62.♔e2 ♖e1+ 63.♔f2

63...♖c1!

Forcing the exchange on the square b2, which finally breaks the opponent's defences.

64.♖xb2 cxb2 65.♖b8 ♗c3 66.♗e4 ♗d4+ 67.♔e2 ♔f4 68.♖b4 e5 69.♖b7 ♔g3 0-1

Baden-Baden 2018 (April)

Just days after the end of the Candidates tournament, Caruana started the tournament in Baden-Baden. Having fortunately escaped defeat in the opening round in a principled battle against Magnus Carlsen, Fabiano then hit 'cruising speed' and finished first (6.5 out of 9), a point ahead of the World Champion! It was hard to believe that, after such an exhausting event as the Candidates, it was possible still to have so much energy!

The g7-pawn advances!

At the Candidates tournament, a great deal of attention was paid to the game Aronian-Kramnik, in which the ex-World Champion threw his g-pawn forward as early as move 9: 1.e4 e5 2.♘f3 ♘c6 3.♗b5 ♘f6 4.d3 ♗c5 5.♗xc6 dxc6 6.0-0 ♕e7 7.h3 ♖g8! 8.♔h1 ♘h5 9.c3 g5!, developing a powerful attack on the king.

Caruana uses an analogous idea in a somewhat different variation of the Spanish, and also with great success.

Game 23 Ruy Lopez C69
Georg Meier   2648
Fabiano Caruana   2784
Baden-Baden 2018 (3)

1.e4 e5 2.♘f3 ♘c6 3.♗b5 a6 4.♗xc6 dxc6 5.0-0 ♕f6

This old move has become popular in recent years. By comparison with the line 5...♛d6, the queen's position on f6 has certain plusses.

6.d4 exd4 7.♗g5 ♛d6

It may look as though Black has lost a tempo, but, as we will see, the white bishop on g5 is not especially well-placed.

8.♘xd4

Going into the endgame with 8.♛xd4 ♛xd4 9.♘xd4 ♗d7 10.♘c3 f6 11.♗e3 0-0-0 doesn't pose Black any problems.

8...♗e7

Black's king's bishop comes quickly into play.

9.♗e3

Retaining the tension. Simpler play results from 9.♗xe7 ♘xe7 10.♘c3 ♗d7 11.♘b3 ♛xd1 12.♖axd1 b6 13.♘c1 0-0-0 14.b4 ♗e6 15.f3 ♖d6, and Black's position is very solid,

Naiditsch-Grandelius, Stockholm 2010.

9...♘h6

In his game against Naiditsch (Baden-Baden, 2013), Caruana brought his knight to f6, but after 9...♘f6 10.f3 0-0 11.♘d2 c5 12.♘c4! ♛d8 13.♘e2 ♛e8 (in the endgame after 13...♗e6?! 14.♛xd8 ♖fxd8 15.♘a5! ♖ab8 16.♘f4 the advantage is on White's side) 14.♗f4 b5 15.♘e3 c4 16.♔h1! ♛c6 17.♘d4 ♛b6 18.♘df5 ♗c5 19.♛e1! faced serious problems: White's growing attack on the kingside is extremely dangerous.

10.♛d2

10...g5!?

An interesting novelty! Black prevents the enemy bishop coming to f4 and prepares the knight raid to g4.

Previously here, Black had tried 10...♛g6 11.f3 ♗d7 12.♘c3 0-0-0 13.♛f2, and White's position is somewhat preferable, Naiditsch-Maiorov, Bastia 2013.

11.♘f3

On 11.♗xg5 Black had prepared 11...♗xg5 12.♛xg5 ♖g8! 13.♛h4 ♛xd4 14.♛xh6 ♛xb2 15.♘d2 ♛c3, and Black takes over the initiative.

11...♖g8 12.h4?!

Played in principled fashion, but as the further course of events shows, he should have preferred the quiet 12.♕xd6 cxd6 13.h4 f6 14.♘bd2 with equal chances in the endgame.

12...♕g6!
By sacrificing a pawn, Black develops a strong attack!
13.hxg5 ♘g4 14.♘c3 h6! 15.♗f4 ♗e6
As the commentators pointed out, a more energetic line is the immediate 15...hxg5 16.♗xc7 ♖h8 17.♘e2 ♕h7 18.♘g3 ♗e6, although it is only when armed with the computer that one can appreciate the difference between these two lines.
16.♗xc7 ♖c8 17.♗b6 hxg5 18.♘e2

Urgently transferring the cavalry to defend the danger zone on the h-file.

18...c5!
'Cutting off the infantry from the tanks'! Now the ♗b6 will be out of play.
19.♘g3 ♖h8 20.♖fd1 ♕h6 21.b4?!
White's desire to bring his bishop back into the game is understandable, but this move proves to be a serious mistake. The calm defence 21.a4! ♘h2 22.♖a3! allows the queen's rook to take part in events on the queenside. After 22...♘xf3+ 23.♖xf3 ♕h2+ 24.♔f1 ♗c4+ 25.♖d3 White obtains sufficient compensation for the exchange, because of the weakness of the light squares in the enemy position.
21...cxb4 22.♗d4 f6 23.c3 bxc3 24.♗xc3

24...♔f7?!
Playing for a logical strengthening of his position, Caruana misses an effective possibility: 24...♘h2! 25.♘d4 ♘f1!! 26.♔xf1 ♗c4+ 27.♘de2 ♕h1+ 28.♘xh1 ♖xh1#!. If 25.♘xg5 then again 25...♘f1!! decides.
The only defence is 25.♘e1!, but after 25...♗g4 26.f3 ♕h4! the black attack should be crowned with success.

25.♖ac1 ♖c4

Now on 25...♘h2, a possibility
is 26.♘xg5+ fxg5 27.♗xh8 ♖xh8
28.♖c7 with serious counterplay.

26.♗d4 b5 27.♕a5 ♘h2

If 27...♗d6 White defends by means
of 28.e5 ♗xe5 29.♗xe5 ♘xe5
30.♘xe5+ fxe5 31.♔f1 etc.

28.♕xa6?

The decisive mistake. It was
essential to play 28.♘e1!, e.g.
28...♖xc1 29.♖xc1 ♗g4 30.♖c7 ♘f1
31.♖xe7+ ♔xe7 32.♕c7+ ♔e8 33.f3
♘xg3 34.♕xg3, and the battle flares
up with renewed strength.

28...♘xf3+ 29.gxf3 g4?

In mutual time-trouble, the players
exchange mistakes.

There was an immediate win with
29...♕h2+ 30.♔f1 ♖hc8!, and on

31.♖b1 Black decides things with
31...♖xd4! 32.♖xd4 ♖c2.

30.f4 ♕xf4

Now too, he could win with
30...♕h2+ 31.♔f1 ♖hc8!.

31.♖xc4 bxc4 32.♗e3?

The manoeuvre 32.♕a5! ♖h3
33.♕d2! ♕f3 34.♖e1 allows White to
strengthen his defences.

32...♕f3 33.♖d6

33...♖h3!

An effective finish: there is no
defence against a crushing sacrifice
on g3!

34.♖xe6

If 34.♗c5 then the push 34...c3 is
decisive.

**34...♖xg3+ 35.fxg3 ♕xe3+ 36.♔h2
♕f2+ 37.♔h1 ♕f1+**

White resigned.

USA Championship, St Louis 2018 (April)

Ten days after the end of the Baden-Baden tournament, Fabiano was
already starting the battle for the title of US Champion! He showed a good
result (8 out of 11), but this was 'only' enough for the silver medal. The US
Champion was Sam Shankland, who scored half a point more.

Breakthrough

This game is something of a
lightweight encounter, certainly.
But undoubtedly the effective

breakthrough against the French
Defence brought the spectators a lot
of pleasure!

Game 24 French Defence C11
Fabiano Caruana 2804
Varuzhan Akobian 2647
St Louis 2018 (7)

**1.e4 e6 2.d4 d5 3.♘c3 ♘f6 4.e5
♘fd7 5.f4 c5 6.♘f3 ♗e7 7.♗e3 ♘c6
8.♕d2 b6**

Black chooses a relatively rare line
of the Steinitz Variation.
9.♗b5!?
In the game Quesada-Akobian, St
Louis 2017, there occurred 9.♗e2
0-0 10.♘d1 cxd4 11.♘xd4 ♘xd4
12.♗xd4 ♘b8 13.0-0 ♗a6 14.♗xa6
♘xa6 15.♘e3 ♘c5 16.♕e2 f5, and
Black satisfactorily solved his
opening problems.
Caruana chooses a more dynamic
continuation. White is prepared to
'sacrifice' his light-squared bishop
for the knight on c6, which will
reduce the opponent's pressure
against the pawns on d4 and e5.
9...♕c7
The game Anand-Pelletier, Zurich
2017, developed in instructive
fashion: 9...♘db8 10.♕f2! c4 11.♘e2
a6 12.♗xc6+ ♘xc6 13.c3 b5 14.g4
h5 15.gxh5 ♖xh5 16.h4 ♖h8 17.♕g2
♗f8 18.f5! exf5 19.♗g5 ♕c7 20.h5,

and White developed a dangerous
initiative.
10.0-0-0
Caruana plays consistently
to sharpen the position. The
alternative was kingside castling.
10...a6?!
There is little point in provoking
White into the exchange on c6. It
was worth considering 10...cxd4!?
11.♘xd4 ♘xd4 12.♗xd4 0-0, aiming
for normal development.
11.♗xc6 ♕xc6 12.f5! c4

Beginning a race between opposing
attacks!
13.f6!
His lead in development tells White
he should open the position.
13...gxf6 14.exf6 ♗xf6 15.♖hf1 b5?!
Black goes for a desperate
counterattack, but with his
queenside pieces undeveloped, it
is doomed to failure. He should
have considered completing his
mobilisation with 15...♗b7.
16.♕f2 b4 17.♘e2
Here it was possible to play va
banque: 17.♘e4! dxe4 18.♘e5 with a
very strong attack. But the move in
the game is also good enough.
17...b3

18.♘e5!

The black pawn has advanced a long way, but in the process has limited the scope of its own forces. But in White's attack, all his pieces take part!

18...♗xe5 19.♕xf7+ ♚d8 20.dxe5

The square d4 is freed for the decisive appearance of the white knight.

20...bxa2 21.♚d2 ♖f8 22.♕xh7 ♖xf1 23.♖xf1 d4

24.♕g8+

Cutting out Black's counterplay. After the immediate 24.♘xd4 there

is 24...c3+! 25.bxc3 ♕xg2+ 26.♖f2 ♕d5 with complications.

24...♚c7 25.♘xd4 ♕d5 26.♕xe6 ♕a5+

In the event of the exchange of queens, the pawn on a2 does not present any threat at all, and White's material advantage decides the outcome of the game.

27.c3

27...♘xe5

The 'triumph' of the passed pawn by 27...a1♕ is 'crowned' by a beautiful mate of the black king: 28.♖xa1 ♕xa1 29.♕d6+ ♚b7 30.♕d5+ ♚b8 (30...♚c7 31.♘e6+) 31.♘c6+ ♚c7 (or 31...♚b7 32.♘a5+ ♚c7 33.♕d6+ ♚d8 34.♘c6+ ♚e8 35.♕e7#) 32.♕d6+ ♚b7 33.♘d8# !

28.♖f7+! ♘xf7

Or 28...♗d7 29.♖xd7+ ♘xd7 30.♗f4+ ♚c8 31.♕c6+ ♚d8 32.♕xa8+ ♚e7 33.♘c6+, winning.

29.♗f4+ ♚b7 30.♕xf7+

Black resigned.

Stavanger 2018 (May)

It is already a remarkable thing: having taken part in four very strong international tournaments in the space of four months, Caruana has taken first place in three of them! Admittedly, at the start of the event in Stavanger, the American again experienced problems in his principled match-up against Carlsen, this time losing. But his finishing burst, including wins in the last two rounds (5.5 out of 9), allowed Fabiano to finish half a point ahead of his three closest pursuers, among whom was the World Champion!

Make way for the bishops!

One of Tarrasch's aphorisms was 'He who has the bishops has the future'. The following game is a splendid demonstration of the 'Praeceptor Germaniae's' advice.

Game 25 English Opening A28
Fabiano Caruana   2822
Sergey Karjakin   2782
Stavanger 2018 (5)

1.c4 ♘f6 2.♘c3 e5 3.♘f3 ♘c6 4.e3 ♗b4 5.♕c2

5...♗xc3!?

This 'unforced' exchange of bishop for knight no longer surprises anyone these days. But why the hurry? The answer is to some extent shown by the rapid game Karjakin-Vidit, Rhiyad 2017: 5...d6 6.♘e2!? a5 7.a3 ♗c5 8.b3 0-0 9.♘g3 ♖e8 10.♗b2 ♗a7 11.♗e2 h6 12.0-0 ♗e6 13.♗c3 ♘e7 14.d4 exd4 15.♘xd4, and White obtained the advantage. A more prosaic illustration is the variation

5...0-0 6.♘d5, considered the main line of this set-up.

6.♕xc3 ♕e7 7.b3

In the game Giri-Aronian, Geneva 2017, there followed 7.♗e2 d5 8.d4 (Black had good play after 8.cxd5 ♘xd5 9.♕b3 ♘b6 10.d3 0-0 11.0-0 ♖d8 12.♗d2 ♗f5 13.♖fd1 ♖d7 14.♗e1 ♖ad8 in Allander-Vachier-Lagrave, Rhodes 2013) 8...exd4 9.♘xd4 ♘xd4 10.♕xd4 c5 11.♕h4 dxc4 12.♗xc4 ♗e6 13.♗e2 ♘d5 14.♗b5+ ♔f8 15.♕e4 ♗d7 16.♕c4 ♗e6 17.♕e4, and the players repeated the position.

7...0-0

Black usually plays 7...d5 here, e.g. 8.cxd5 ♘xd5 9.♕b2 0-0 10.d3 ♗g4 11.♗e2 ♖ad8 12.a3 ♘f6 13.♕c2 e4 14.dxe4 ♘xe4 15.0-0 ♗f5 16.♕b2 a5 (Trapl-Lilienthal, Decin 1977) or 8.♗b2 d4 9.♕c1 ♗g4 10.♗e2 0-0-0 11.0-0 dxe3!? 12.fxe3 h5 (Rezan-Kir. Georgiev, Croatia tt 2015) with good play for Black in both cases.

Perhaps after 7...d5 Caruana was intending to continue 8.d4 ♞e4 (if 8...exd4 9.♞xd4 ♞xd4 10.♛xd4 c5 11.♛f4 White, compared with the game Giri-Aronian, has made the useful move b2-b3) 9.♛b2 ♛b4+ 10.♝d2 ♞xd2 11.♛xd2 ♛xd2+ 12.♚xd2 with chances of taking over the initiative in the endgame.

8.♝b2 ♜e8 9.a3 a5

If 9...d5 10.cxd5 ♞xd5 11.♛c2 e4 12.♞d4 ♞xd4 13.♝xd4 White's chances are somewhat preferable.

10.h3!?

A subtle move. The advance h2-h3 could prove useful later, whilst the ♝f1 retains a wide choice of possibilities, in the event that Black plays 10...d5.

In the game Van Wely-Piket, Wijk aan Zee 1996, White played more directly: 10.d3 d5 11.cxd5 ♞xd5 12.♛c2 ♝g4 13.♝e2 ♜ad8 14.0-0 ♜d6!? with a good game for Black.

10...b6 11.♝e2 ♝b7 12.0-0

12...d5

Black decides on the advance ...d7-d5 after all, which can only please the ♝e2! More in keeping with the spirit of the position was 12...♞e4 13.♛c2 ♞c5 14.d3 d6, striving to limit the possibilities of the white bishops.

13.cxd5 ♞xd5 14.♛c2 e4?!

Continuing the same 'active' strategy. Now great prospects also open up for the ♝b2.

Black should have preferred 14...♜ad8, intending in reply to 15.♝b5 to strengthen the position by means of 15...♜d6.

15.♞h2!

The knight retreats to a flexible position, underlining the far-sightedness of the move h2-h3.

15...♛g5 16.f4! exf3?!

This exchange too, further opening the position, should have been avoided.

17.♞xf3 ♛g3

It may appear that the black pieces have developed enormous activity, as he threatens both 18...♞f4 and 18...♜xe3.

18.♜f2!

After this modest move, Black's initiative ends and the issue of the two bishops in an open position takes centre stage. White's threats on the diagonals a2-g8 and a1-h8, and also on the f-file, develop of their own accord.

18...♖ad8 19.♗c4 ♘f6

A desperate attempt to eliminate the two bishops, at the cost of a weakening of the black king's pawn cover.

20.♗xf6 gxf6 21.♖af1 ♖d6

The leap 21...♘e5 would be refuted by means of 22.♘xe5 ♖xe5 23.♗xf7+! ♔xf7 24.♕xc7+, and White wins.

22.b4!

Pressing the opponent over the whole board.

22...axb4 23.axb4 ♖e7

The pawn on b4 is immune because of the nice variation 23...♘xb4 24.♗xf7+! ♔xf7 25.♕xc7+ ♖e7 26.♘g5+! ♕xg5 27.♕xd6 ♘d5 28.♖f5, winning.

24.b5 ♘e5 25.♘d4 ♗c8 26.♔h1 ♔g7 27.♗e2 ♔h8 28.♕c3 ♔g7

Black can only wait, while White methodically strengthens his position.

29.♗d1! ♔g8 30.♗c2 ♕h4 31.♖f4 ♕g3 32.♗f5 ♗b7 33.♗e4 ♗c8

By refraining from the exchange of bishops, Black exploits his only chance of stopping a white knight appearing on f5.

34.♕a3!

Black's position has too many vulnerable points. The queen cannot be prevented from marching into a8.

34...♔g7 35.♕a8

After 35...♗d7 36.♗f5 the black bishop can no longer avoid the exchange and the outcome of the game will be decided by the white knight's appearance on f5. In an impossible situation, Black decides on a desperation sacrifice.

35...♗xh3 36.gxh3 ♕xh3+ 37.♔g1 ♖xd4

38.♗g2!

Destroying the opponent's last illusions. White has more trouble after 38.exd4 ♕g3+ 39.♗g2 ♘g4 40.♖xg4+ ♕xg4 41.♕d8 ♖e6.

38...♕g3 39.♖xd4 ♘g4 40.♖f3 ♕e1+ 41.♗f1 1-0

PART II

Learn from Fabiano's best games

The second part of this book presents Caruana's best games, with detailed commentaries. In choosing (albeit subjectively) this selection of games, the author has intended that they should combine beauty and crystal-clear strategic clarity.

To give the material a greater didactic quality, the games are grouped by theme, and within each group are arranged chronologically. This allows the material to be used as a textbook on the middlegame.

The games are arranged in the following thematic order:
Chapter 5: Attacking the enemy king
   A) Attack on the king in the centre (26-31)
   B) Same-side castling (32-36)
   C) Opposite-side castling (37-41)
Chapter 6: Centralisation as a weapon (42-49)
Chapter 7: Attacking on the queenside (50-52)
Chapter 8: Playing on two flanks (53, 54)
Chapter 9: Defence and counterattack (55, 56)
Chapter 10: The Berlin endgame (57, 58)
Chapter 11: The Dortmund pearls (59, 60)
Chapter 12: Queen sacrifices (61, 62)

I should warn the reader at once that this classification is to some extent arbitrary. In any chess battle, many different ideas occur and the master's sharp eye covers the whole board and embraces many different themes.

For example, Game 50, which is included in the chapter on attacking the queenside, ends in mate on the kingside! Therefore, in looking at games by theme, the author has paid especial attention to what he sees as the 'dominating' factor in each separate case.

Biel 2011

CHAPTER 5

Attacking the enemy king

The above words are such as warm the heart of every chess player. The possibility of a masterpiece of sacrificial play brings enormous aesthetic pleasure to such games.

A) Attacking the king in the centre

In five (!) games (26, 27, 28, 30 and 31) Black suffers a catastrophe in the region of the squares e6, f7 and g6. In total, these three squares attract sacrifices of two rooks, two bishops and a knight! The aim of these sacrifices is to destroy the enemy king's pawn cover. From this fact, one can draw a useful conclusion – if the enemy king remains in the centre, then these squares are always a permanent focus of potential sacrifices!

Game 29 demonstrates another characteristic problem of not having castled, namely that the king's rook cannot get into the game.

Game 26 Caro-Kann Defence B17

Fabiano Caruana 2528
Peter Prohaszka 2443

Budapest 2007 (8)

1.e4 c6 2.d4 d5 3.♘d2 dxe4 4.♘xe4 ♘d7 5.♘g5 ♘gf6 6.♘1f3 e6 7.♗d3 ♗d6 8.♕e2 h6 9.♘e4 ♘xe4 10.♕xe4

10...♕c7

An ambitious continuation. Black keeps his knight on the flexible

square d7 (from where it supports the advance ...c6-c5 and controls the square e5) and in return is prepared to allow the unpleasant queen move to g4.

A quieter game with a small advantage to White results from 10...♘f6 11.♕e2 b6 12.♗d2 ♗b7 13.0-0-0 ♕c7, planning queenside castling.

11.♕g4 ♔f8

The king loses the right to castle, but the white queen's position on g4 is also not ideal. Black intends ...b7-b6, ...♗b7 and ...c6-c5, with counterplay.

12.0-0 b6 13.♖e1

White has also tried developing the bishop on the long diagonal a1-h8, with the aim of making the advance ...c6-c5 more difficult. In the game Karjakin-Bologan (Tomsk 2006), which was important for the theory of this variation, there occurred 13.b3 ♗b7 14.♗b2 ♘f6 15.♕h4 c5 16.dxc5 ♕xc5 17.♗xf6 gxf6 18.♕xf6 ♕h5! 19.♗e2! ♗xf3 20.h3 ♕e5 21.♕xe5 ♗xe5 22.♗xf3 ♗xa1 23.♗xa8 ♗c3 24.♗e4 ♔e7 25.f4 f5 26.♗d3 ♔f6, and the extra pawn, with opposite-coloured bishops, did not bring White any particular dividends.

13...c5 14.c3 ♗b7 15.♕h3

Putting the queen on a safer and more convenient square.

15...c4

In this way, Black ensures his pieces use of the d5-square, but, on the other hand, frees his opponent's hands for operations on the kingside. It was more promising to maintain the tension in the centre, e.g. 15...♖d8 16.♗e4 ♗xe4 17.♖xe4 ♘f6 18.♖e1 g6! 19.b3 ♔g7 20.dxc5 ♗xc5 21.♗b2 ♖d5 22.c4 ♖h5! 23.♕g3 ♗d6 24.♘e5 ♖d8 with good play for Black, Leko-Bareev (Elista 2007).

16.♗e4 ♗xe4 17.♖xe4 ♕c6

Better was 17...♘f6 – the knight heads to d5, whilst the ♗d6 keeps control of the square e5.

18.♖h4!

Thanks to his strong centre, White's rook can head to the kingside, making it harder for the black king to find safety.

18...♖g8 19.♗f4!

After the exchange of dark-squared bishops, White's plan will involve putting his rook on the e-file and the knight on e5.

19...♔e7 20.♖d1 ♗xf4 21.♖xf4 ♕d6 22.♕g3 ♕d5

Parrying the threat of 23.♖xf7+.

23.♖e1 g5 24.♖fe4 ♘f6 25.♖e5 ♕d7 26.♖f5!

An interesting manoeuvre, allowing him to approach the enemy defences.

26...♕b7 27.♕e5 ♘d7

28.♖xf7+!

The rook sacrifice completely destroys the black king's pawn protection. Events now develop forcibly.

28...♔xf7 29.♕xe6+ ♔g7 30.♕e7+ ♔h8

The black king has finally managed to flee to the kingside, but with his forces dominating the centre, White manages to organise a decisive attack there as well.

**31.♖e6! ♖g7 32.♖xh6+ ♔g8
33.♕e6+ ♖f7 34.♖g6+ ♔f8 35.♘xg5
♘f6 36.♘xf7 ♖e8 37.♕d6+ ♕e7
38.♖xf6 ♔g7 39.♕e5 ♕xf6 40.♕xe8
♕g6 41.h3**
Black resigned.

Game 27 French Defence C14
Fabiano Caruana   2528
Martin Neubauer   2474

Szeged 2007 (2)

**1.e4 e6 2.d4 d5 3.♘c3 ♘f6 4.♗g5
♗e7 5.e5 ♘fd7 6.h4**

The famous Alekhine-Chatard
Attack is one of the sharpest
continuations in the classical
system of the French Defence.
6...♘c6
The main lines are considered to
be either the acceptance of the

sacrifice with 6...♗xg5 7.hxg5
♕xg5, where, as well as Alekhine's
8.♘h3, the move 8.♕d3 has become
popular, and the immediate central
counterattack 6...c5.
The text involves the preliminary
mobilisation of the queenside
(...♘b6, ...♗d7), and became popular
thanks to the efforts of the Moscow
GM Alexander Morozevich.
7.♘f3
In the game Nataf-Morozevich
(Istanbul 2001) the continuation
was 7.♗xe7 ♕xe7 8.a3 ♘b6 9.f4 ♗d7
10.♕d2 0-0-0 11.♘f3 ♔b8 12.h5 h6
13.♘d1 f6 14.♘f2 fxe5 15.fxe5 ♖hf8
16.0-0-0 ♗e8, and Black obtained a
comfortable position.
7...♘b6

8.♗d3
The usual continuation here
is 8.♕d2, preparing queenside
castling.
Caruana carries out a different idea,
for the moment leaving his king in
the centre.
8...♗d7 9.a3 a6
On 9...♘a5 there could follow
10.b3, and the mobility of the black
knights is limited.
10.♖h3!

The rook comes into play along the third rank, whilst the white king, in case of necessity, can sidestep to f1.

10...h6

11.♗e3!

An excellent positional decision. Of course, in the French Defence, White usually dreams of exchanging his opponent's dark-squared bishop, but in this case, it is more important to emphasise the cramped nature of the black position.

11...♘a7

Trying to untangle the position by an exchange on b5.

12.♖g3 ♗f8

13.♘e2!

By heading the knight towards h5, White seems to allow the opponent to exchange light-squared bishops (and this is usually Black's dream in the French!). However, the young player had reinforced his positional play with accurate calculation.

13...♗b5 14.♘f4 ♘d7

It turns out that after 14...♗xd3 15.♕xd3 ♕d7 16.♘h5, the pawn on g7 is lost.

With the text, Black strengthens the vulnerable square f6, hoping that now nothing can stop him exchanging off the active enemy bishop on d3.

15.♘h5 g6

Again he cannot play 15...♗xd3 because of 16.♕xd3 g6 17.♖xg6! fxg6 18.♕xg6+ ♔e7 19.♘g5!, and White wins. But now surely Black's dream will be realised...

16.♖xg6!

This brilliant rook sacrifice crowns White's subtle play!

16...f7xg6 17.♗xg6+ ♔e7 18.♘g5!

This effective knight jump allows White to include in the attack his strongest piece. The threat is 19.♕f3 or 19.♕g4.

18...♗g7 19.♘xe6 ♕g8

Or 19...♔xe6 20.♘xg7+ ♔e7 21.♘f5+ ♔f8 22.♕h5, winning.

20.♘exg7 ♖f8 21.f4 ♔d8 22.f5

It is obvious that the white pawns will sweep away all in their path.
22...♔c8 23.♕g4 c5 24.0-0-0 cxd4 25.♗f4 ♘c6 26.f6 1-0

Game 28 Caro-Kann Defence B12
Fabiano Caruana   2767
Petar Genov   2463
Italy tt 2012 (5)

1.e4 c6 2.d4 d5 3.e5
For a long time, it was considered that the move 3.e5 gave White nothing, because it allows freedom to the ♗c8, and after 3...♗f5 4.♗d3 ♗xd3 5.♕xd3 e6 we reach a favourable French Defence for Black. However, in contemporary practice, White strives not to exchange the ♗f5, but to attack it!
3...♗f5 4.♘f3 e6 5.♗e2 ♘e7 6.c3 ♘d7

7.0-0

White develops calmly, whilst Black still has to solve the problem of mobilising his kingside.
7...♘c8
The ♗f5 occupies the convenient post of the king's knight and so the latter seeks pastures new. Even so, the text is too passive. The principled line was 7...c5 8.dxc5 ♘xc5 9.♘d4 ♗g6. However, if Black wishes to avoid a premature opening of the position, then it is more useful to play 9...h6, reserving the square h7 for the bishop.
8.♘bd2 ♗e7 9.♘e1
An elastic retreat. The white pawns are ready to attack the kingside (f2-f4 and g2-g4), whilst the ♘e1 is ready to come via c2-e3 or f4.
9...♗g6
This prophylactic move aims to reduce the effectiveness of the advance of the white infantry, but now the ♘e1 gets a concrete target!
10.♘d3 c5 11.♘f4 cxd4 12.♘xg6 hxg6 13.cxd4 ♕b6 14.♘f3 a6

Preparing to transfer the ♘c8 to c6. Black's position may look perfectly solid, because with the centre closed, it is not so easy for White to develop activity, but...

15.g3!

The start of a typical plan, which allows White to expose the weakness in the enemy position. White intends to strengthen his position by means of h2-h4, ♔g2 and ♖h1, ensuring his minor pieces a post on g5, and in the event of kingside castling by Black, threatening to open the h-file (h4-h5). In the coming kingside attack, an important role will be played by the light-squared bishop, which has no opponent.

15...♘a7 16.h4 ♖c8 17.♖b1 ♘c6 18.♔g2 ♘b4 19.a3 ♘c6 20.♗e3 ♘a5

It is hard for Black to obtain counterplay and he tries to create a small hook to bite on (the squares b3 and c4). Black has to leave his king in the centre, hoping to shelter it behind the pawn chain.

21.♘d2!

Caruana has a remarkable ability to breathe life into his pieces! The knight retreat limits as far as possible the opponent's possibilities and prepares to strengthen the position by means of ♗d3 and ♕g4.

21...♕c7

The immediate 21...♘c4 is impossible because of 22.♘xc4 dxc4 23.d5.

22.♗d3 ♘c4 23.♕g4

Consistently strengthening the position and drawing the opponent's attention to the ♘c4. The exchange on e3 only gives the white rooks the open f-file.

23...b5 24.♘f3 ♘db6

Black's demonstration on the queenside is effectively just a defensive measure.

The ♘d7 can retreat to f8 to strengthen the squares e6 and g6, but in this case, Black will have problems with his opponent's activity on the c-file.

25.♗g5 a5

Black hurries to safeguard his queenside by means of ...a5-a4, but allows a knockout blow from the other side. It was essential to play 25...♕d7, which allows him to hold the defence.

On the other hand, 25...♔d7 leads to a collapse after 26.b3! ♘xa3 27.♗xe7 ♔xe7 28.♖bc1 ♕d7 29.♕g5+ ♔e8 30.♕d2! ♕e7 31.♖xc8+ ♘xc8 32.♕a5 etc.

26.♗xg6!

The bishop sacrifice leads to the destruction of the enemy pawn structure and an attack on the king.
26...fxg6 27.♕xe6 a4 28.b3
Including the queen's rook in the attack.
28...axb3 29.♖xb3 ♕d7 30.♕xg6+ ♔f8 31.♖e1

31...♗xg5
Losing at once. But even after 31...♕e8 32.♕f5+ ♔g8 33.♕e6+ ♔f8 34.♖xb5 ♗xg5 35.♘xg5 ♕xe6 36.♘xe6+ ♔f7 37.♘f4 ♖hd8 38.a4 ♖a8 39.♖eb1 ♘xa4 (or 39...♖xa4 40.♖xb6 ♘xb6 41.♖xb6 ♖xd4? 42.♘e6) 40.♖b7+ ♔g8 41.♘e6, Black's position is hopeless.
32.♘xg5 ♖h6 33.♘h7+
In view of the variation 33...♔g8 34.♘f6+ ♔h8 35.♕xh6+ gxh6 36.♘xd7 ♘xd7 37.♖xb5, Black resigned.

Game 29 French Defence C10
Fabiano Caruana   2757
Georg Meier   2640
Baden-Baden 2013 (1)

1.e4 e6 2.d4 d5 3.♘c3 dxe4 4.♘xe4 ♘d7

Georg Meier is one of the main experts on the Rubinstein French and demonstrates with enviable regularity its defensive qualities.
5.♘f3 ♘gf6 6.♘xf6+ ♘xf6

7.♗e3
This move has become highly popular in recent times. White holds up the freeing break ...c7-c5 and draws the black knight to d5.
7...♘d5
This jump involves the idea of the quickest possible advance ...c7-c5. The alternative is gradual development by 7...♗d6 (or 7...♗e7) 8.♗d3 0-0 9.♕e2 b6 10.0-0-0 ♗b7 11.♗g5 with a complicated battle, in which White's chances are somewhat preferable.
8.♗d2 c5 9.♗b5+ ♗d7 10.♗xd7+ ♕xd7 11.c4 ♘b6
The necessity to prevent the white queen raid on the e8 diagonal (11...♘f6? 12.♘e5) forces the knight to retreat to this rather awkward position.
12.♖c1 f6
The main line is 12...♗e7 13.dxc5 ♗xc5 14.b4 ♗e7 15.c5 ♘d5 16.♘e5 ♕c7 17.♕a4+ ♔f8, where Black hopes to compensate for the loss

of castling and the active white queenside pawn majority by the occupation of d5 by his knight and his extra pawn in the centre.

We would point out that the following line is unsatisfactory for Black: 12...cxd4 13.c5 ♘d5 14.♘e5 ♕b5 15.♕f3 ♘f6 16.a4 ♕a6 17.b4 etc.

The text looks somewhat strange from the point of view of opening principles, but continues the idea of taking control of the square c5.

13.0-0

This move was introduced into practice by Dutch GM Friso Nijboer. Fighting for a lead in development, White sacrifices the d4-pawn.

In the game Bacrot-Meier (France tt 2010) there followed 13.dxc5 ♗xc5 14.b4 ♗e7 15.♕b3 0-0 16.0-0 ♖ac8 17.♖fd1 ♖fd8 18.♗e1 ♕a4, and Black successfully solved his opening problems.

13...cxd4

A principled decision. In the stem game there followed 13...♖c8 14.dxc5 (14.♖e1!?) 14...♗xc5 15.b4 ♗e7 16.♕b3 ♔f7 17.♖fe1, and White's chances were preferable in Nijboer-Mellema, Hoogeveen 2012.

14.♖e1 ♖c8

Among other possibilities, we would mention 14...e5? 15.♘xe5! fxe5 16.♖xe5+ ♔f7 17.c5 ♘d5 18.♕f3+ ♘f6 19.♕b3+, winning, and 14...♗e7 15.c5 ♘d5 16.♘xd4 e5 17.c6! bxc6 18.♘xc6 0-0 19.♕b3 ♔h8 20.♖ed1, with initiative to White.

15.♕b3!

An important move, strengthening the pressure against the square e6 and preparing the advance c4-c5. Less accurate is 15.♕e2, since after 15...e5 the knight sacrifice loses in strength: 16.♘xe5? fxe5 17.♕h5+ (or 17.♕xe5+ ♔f7) 17...g6 18.♕xe5+ ♔f7 19.♕xh8 ♗g7 20.♕xh7 ♖h8 etc.

15...♗e7

The advance 15...e5? is now refuted by 16.♘xe5! fxe5 17.♖xe5+ ♔d8 18.c5, winning.

The computer suggests strengthening the square d4 with the paradoxical 15...♔f7 16.♕d3 ♔g8 (!?), but after 17.b4 e5 18.♘h4, with the idea of f2-f4, Black's position is unenviable.

16.c5 ♖xc5

Unsatisfactory is 16...♘d5? 17.♘xd4 e5 18.♘b5 ♗xc5 (or 18...0-0 19.♘d6) 19.♖ed1, and Black loses material.

17.♖xc5 ♗xc5 18.♖xe6+ ♔d8
19.♖e1

In Caruana's words, only at this point did his opening preparation end. Black has managed to hold onto the d4-pawn, but his centralised king makes White's chances preferable.

19...♕d5 20.♕d3 ♘d7?!

As Caruana pointed out in New In Chess 2013/2, Black should not hang onto his material advantage, but should instead evacuate his king from the centre as quickly as possible – after 20...♔c8! 21.♗f4 ♗d6 22.♗xd6 ♕xd6 23.♘xd4 ♔b8 White has only a small advantage.

21.b4 ♗b6 22.a4 a6?

The same mistake. Black should offer the exchange of rooks with 22...♖e8, and if 23.♖c1 ♖e4! (Caruana) he retains good chances of defending.

23.a5 ♗a7?

After 23...♗c7 24.♘xd4 ♔c8 25.♖c1 ♔b8 26.♗e3 ♘e5 27.♕e2, the black king, hiding behind the pawn, manages to escape to the queenside. But here too, thanks to the advance b4-b5, he comes under attack. Even so, this was the lesser evil.

24.♗f4!

Domination! One of White's threats is to break into the enemy camp by means of 25.♕e2.

24...♘b8

It is already hard for Black to find any sort of adequate answer. For example, 24...g5 25.♗g3 g4 26.♕e2! gxf3 27.♕e7+ ♔c8 28.♕e8+! ♖xe8 29.♖xe8# (Meier); 24...♘f8 25.♕c2! ♘e6 (or 25...♔c6 26.♕b3 followed by ♖c1) 26.♖xe6! ♕xe6 27.♕c7+ ♔e8 28.♕xb7, winning (Caruana); 24...♖e8 25.♗c7+! etc.

25.♗xb8 ♗xb8 26.♘xd4

Material equality is re-established, but the bad position of his king leaves Black no chance of saving the game. There followed:

26...♕d6 27.♘e6+ ♔e7 28.♘c5+
♔f7 29.♕c4+ ♔g6 30.g3 h5

31.♕e4+ ♔h6 32.♕xb7 ♕d2
33.♖e7 ♕d1+ 34.♔g2 h4 35.♕d7
♗d6 36.♘e4
Black resigned.

Game 30 Sicilian Defence B48
Fabiano Caruana 2791
Peter Svidler 2758
Stavanger 2014 (2)

1.e4 c5 2.♘f3 e6 3.d4 cxd4 4.♘xd4
♘c6 5.♘c3 ♕c7 6.♗e3 a6 7.♕d2
♘f6 8.0-0-0 ♗e7
Black meets the modern English
Attack with the Paulsen set-up,
keeping his pawn on d7. One of
the main ideas of the line is the
aggressive 8...♗b4 9.f3 ♘e5 10.♘b3
b5 with a sharp battle. The text has
the plus that Black's bishop does
not obstruct the path of his b-pawn.
9.f3 b5

Typical Sicilian strategy – Black
does not hurry to castle, striving to
win time for creating counterplay
on the queenside.
10.♔b1
A poisonous prophylactic move. In
improving the position of his king,
White also to some extent waits to
see what his opponent will do.

In a game between the same
players, played a year earlier, there
followed the immediate 10.g4
♘xd4 11.♗xd4 ♗b7 12.♔b1 0-0
13.♕f2 ♖ac8 14.♖g1 ♗c6 15.♗d3 b4
16.♘e2 d5 with good play for Black
(Caruana-Svidler, Rhodes 2013).
10...♘e5
After 10...♘xd4 11.♗xd4 ♗b7
White, as well as 12.g4, has another
possibility: 12.♕g5!? b4 (12...0-0?
13.e5 ♘d5 14.♘xd5+–) 13.♘a4 0-0
14.♘b6 ♖ae8 15.♕g3 d6 16.♘c4 e5
17.♗b6 ♕c6 18.♗e3 ♖c8 19.♗d3,
and White's chances are preferable
(Ivanchuk-Wang Yue, Beijing 2013).
And after the immediate 10...♗b7
an interesting line is 11.♗f4!? e5
12.♘f5 exf4 13.♘d5 with an attack
for the sacrificed piece (Anand-
Movsesian, Dubai 2014).
11.g4 b4
The hasty 11...d6?! allows White to
obtain an attacking position in the
centre after 12.g5 ♘fd7 13.f4 ♘c4
14.♗xc4 ♕xc4 15.♖he1 (Svidler-
Maksimenko, Tivat 1995).
12.♘a4

12...h6
Black strives at least temporarily to
hold up the advance g4-g5, so as to
establish counterplay in the centre.

13.♖g1 d5

The modern way of handling the Sicilian – refraining from castling, Black opens the centre! The justification for this seemingly risky strategy is the offside knight on a4.

14.♗f4!

By sacrificing the central pawn, White pins the ♘e5 and organises pressure against it.

14...dxe4

After 14...♗d6 15.exd5 ♘xd5 16.♘f5! 0-0 17.♘xd6 ♘xf3 (17...♕xd6? 18.g5 with a strong attack) 18.♕f2 ♘xg1 19.♖xd5 exd5 20.♕xg1 play turns out in White's favour.

Completely unsatisfactory for Black is 15...♘d5? 16.♗xe5 ♕xe5 17.fxe4 ♕xe4 18.♗g2 etc.

15.g5

15.♗xe5?! ♕xe5 16.♘c6 would be a blank shot because of 16...♕d5.

15...hxg5 16.♖xg5 ♘fd7

Trying to break up the coordination of the enemy attacking forces by 16...e3? does not succeed: 17.♕g2! (17.♕xe3 ♘d5) 17...♘fd7 18.♖xe5! ♘xe5 19.♕xg7 ♖h5 20.♘b5! axb5 21.♗xb5+ ♗d7 22.♗xe5 ♗f8 23.♕f6 ♗e7 24.♖xd7! ♗xf6 25.♖xc7+ ♔f8

26.♗xf6 ♖xb5 27.♘c5! e2 28.♘d3 ♖d5 29.♗e7+ ♔g8 30.♗xb4, and White wins.

17.♖xg7 exf3

It was worth considering 17...♕a5!?. In this case, White can develop the initiative by means of 18.b3 exf3 19.♘b2, trying to include his queen's knight in the attack via c4.

18.♘xe6!

A typical Sicilian sacrifice. Its difficulty consists in the fact that the attack is continued with 'quiet' moves.

18...fxe6 19.♗d3

It is not easy immediately to point to concrete white threats, but Black's main problem is that the coordination of his pieces is disrupted.

19...♗f6?!

Tempting moves based on unpinning the ♘e5 lead Black to immediate disaster, e.g. 19...♕c6? 20.♗xe5 ♘xe5 21.♕f4 with the unstoppable threat of 22.♗g6+; or 19...♕a5? 20.♗g5! ♗f8 21.♖xd7! ♗xd7 22.♗g6+! with mate.

Later, analysts with the help of the computer suggested the cold-blooded 19...♖b8!.

Now there is a forcing route to a draw: 20.♗g6+ ♔d8 21.♗g5 ♘xg6 22.♗xe7+ ♘xe7 23.♕g5 ♖e8 24.♖xe7 ♖xe7 25.♕g8+ with perpetual check.

But White can also continue the battle without any special risk, hoping to exploit the exposed position of the enemy king. For example: 20.♕e3 ♖b5! 21.c4!? bxc3 (21...♖a5? 22.♗g6+ ♔d8 23.c5) 22.♘xc3 ♖a5 (or 22...♖xb2+!? 23.♔xb2 ♔f8! 24.♖xe7! ♔xe7 25.♔c2 ♕a5 with unclear chances, since now both kings are insecure) 23.♗g6+ ♔d8 24.♖xe7 ♔xe7 25.♗g5+ ♔f8 (25...♘f6? 26.♕f4 ♖f8 27.♘e4+−) 26.♗h6+ ♔e7 27.♕f4!? ♖xh6 28.♕g5+ ♘f6 29.♕xh6 ♖d5! 30.♘xd5+ ♘xd5, and Black can probably hold the balance.

With the text, which involves giving up the queen, Svidler tries to give the position a more stable character, but he does not manage to solve his problems completely.

20.♗g6+ ♘xg6

The only move. The king retreats 20...♔d8? 21.♗xe5 or 20...♔f8? 21.♖f7+! ♔g8 22.♖g1 ♕a7 23.♗e3!

♘xf7 24.♗xa7 ♖xa7 25.♕e3 lead to a win for White.

21.♗xc7 ♗xg7

Black has managed to obtain sufficient compensation for the queen and significantly simplify the position. Even so, the poor coordination of his pieces makes his position difficult.

22.♕d3!

The most precise – White wants to eliminate the aggressive pawn on f3.

After 22.♕xb4 ♖a7 23.♕g4 0-0! Black manages to consolidate.

22...♘ge5 23.♗xe5 ♗xe5

If 23...♖xe5 24.♕d8+ ♔f7 25.♕c7+ ♗d7 (25...♔f6 26.♘b6 leads to the loss of the ♖a8) 26.♖xd7+ ♘xd7 27.♕xd7+ ♔f6 28.♘c5 ♖ae8 29.♕c6 White wins the f3-pawn and keeps a material advantage.

24.♕e4!?

The immediate capture on f3 was also possible, but Caruana finds a more precise form in which to carry out his idea.

24...♖a7

He loses after 24...♖b8? 25.♘c5!.

25.♘c5 ♔e7 26.♖f1! ♖f8 27.♘xd7 ♖xd7 28.♕xe5 ♖d5 29.♕e3 ♖df5

White now has the material advantage, but the passed pawn on f3 allows Black to continue his resistance.

30.♕f2

The start of a precise plan to realise the advantage. The queen temporarily blockades the pawn on f3, and then, after strengthening the king's position, the queen and white rook will seek a way to break through to the enemy king.

30...a5 31.b3 ♗d7 32.♖g1 ♗c6 33.♔b2 ♖8f7 34.♖g8 ♖f8 35.♖g4 ♖8f7 36.a3! bxa3+ 37.♔xa3 ♔d6 38.♖c4 ♗d5 39.♖c8

Black resigned. The correctness of this decision is illustrated by the following variation: 39...♗e4 40.♕d4+ ♗d5 (or 40...♖d5 41.♕xe4 f2 42.♖c6+!) 41.c4 f2 42.cxd5 f1♕ 43.♖c6+ ♔e7 44.♖e6+ ♔f8 45.♕h8#!.

Game 31 Sicilian Defence B46
Fabiano Caruana 2801
Veselin Topalov 2772
St Louis 2014 (6)

1.e4 c5 2.♘f3 e6 3.d4 cxd4 4.♘xd4 ♘c6 5.♘c3 a6

In this move order (as opposed to 5...♕c7) it makes no sense to go for the English Attack, since after 6.♗e3 ♘f6 7.♕d2 ♗b4 8.f3 d5! Black has saved time on the queen move and seizes the initiative. However, now White has another tempting possibility.

6.♘xc6 bxc6 7.♗d3 d5 8.0-0 ♘f6

Having strengthened the enemy's position in the centre with his 6th move, White has obtained an advantage in development. Black, in his turn, hopes to be able to sit behind his strong pawn centre and later exploit his trumps – the pawn centre and the open b-file.

9.♖e1

A solid alternative is 9.♕e2 ♗e7 10.b3 0-0 11.♗b2, followed by ♘a4 and c2-c4.

9...♗e7 10.e5 ♘d7 11.♕g4

11...♔f8

In view of the strength of his central position, Black is prepared to abandon castling, not allowing the creation of weaknesses in his kingside structure.

The move 11...g6 is regarded as similarly good. Thus, in the game Caruana-Svidler, Dubai 2014, there followed: 12.♗h6 ♖b8 13.♘d1! ♖b4 14.c4 dxc4 15.♗xc4 ♕a5 16.♘e3 ♘xe5 17.♕d4 f6 18.♕c3 ♕c5 19.♖ac1 with the initiative for the sacrificed pawn.

12.♘a4 ♕a5

A novelty at that moment. Black usually plays 12...c5 here, e.g. 13.c4 ♕a5 (less accurate is 13...d4 on account of 14.b4!) 14.♕d1 d4 15.♗d2 ♕c7 16.♕e2 ♖b8 17.b3 ♗b7 18.♖ad1 h5 19.♘b2 g6 followed by ...♔g7, and a solid position for Black (Andreev-N.Popov, Taganrog 2013). With the text, Topalov aims to solve his opening problems tactically, in all likelihood having banked on the continuation 13.♗g5 ♗xg5 14.♕xg5 ♗b7 (14...♕xa4?? 15.♕d8#) with roughly equal chances.

13.♖e2!

Caruana replied almost at once, demonstrating his theoretical erudition. In the opinion of GM Chuchelov, this strong reaction, overlooked by Topalov's camp, completely threw the Bulgarian grandmaster.

White prepares the move ♗d2, which underlines the poor position of the enemy queen on a5.

13...h5

Going into the endgame with 13...♕b4 14.♕xb4 ♗xb4 15.c4 gives White a clear initiative on the queenside.

In an attempt to justify his 12th move, Topalov goes for a sharp pawn advance on the kingside.

14.♕f4 g5 15.♗d2

This tactical nuance is the point of White's 13th move.

15...♕c7

In the endgame that would arise after 15...gxf4 16.♗xa5, Black was doubtless worried about the f4-pawn, which is cut off from its own forces.

16.♕g3 h4 17.♕g4

The critical moment of the game.

The Bulgarian GM's choice proves to be a mistake:

17...♖g8?!

Black had to seek a concrete continuation, so as to escape a strategically dangerous position. The attempt to exploit the cramped position of the ♗d3 is beautifully refuted: 17...c5? 18.♗xg5 ♗xg5 19.♕xg5 c4 20.♗f5! exf5 21.♖ae1!! (less accurate is 21.e6?! fxe6 22.♖xe6 ♘e5), and there is no satisfactory defence against the breakthrough e5-e6. For example: 21...♘c5 22.♘xc5 ♕xc5 23.♕d8+ ♔g7 24.♕f6+ ♔g8 25.e6! ♗xe6 26.♖xe6 fxe6 27.♕g6+ ♔f8 28.♖xe6 with mate.

However, perfectly possible was 17...h3!? 18.♗xg5 (18.g3? is bad because of 18...♘xe5 19.♖xe5 ♕xe5 20.♗c3 d4 21.♗xd4 ♕d5!) 18...♗xg5 19.♕xg5 hxg2 with hopes of consolidating with ...♗b7 and ...♕d8. In the variation 20.c4 ♗b7 21.cxd5 cxd5 22.♖c1 ♕d8 23.♕xd8+ ♖xd8 24.♖c7 ♖h3 25.♖xb7 ♖xd3 26.♔xg2 ♖d4 27.b3 ♔g7 Black retains compensation for his minimal material deficit, thanks to the opponent's broken kingside pawns.

But the most interesting thing is that the capture on e5 is also possible: 17...♘xe5!?. After 18.♖xe5 ♕xe5 19.♗c3 ♕f4 20.♕xf4 gxf4 21.♗xh8 f6, Black manages to isolate the extra bishop on h8 and later win it back. For example: 22.♘b6 ♖b8 23.♗xa6! ♖xb6 24.♗xc8 ♔f7 25.♖e1 e5 26.♗d7 ♔g8 27.♗xf6 ♗xf6, and again Black has compensation for the pawn in the endgame, this time thanks to his strong centre.

18.♖ae1

Now White strengthens the pawn on e5 and obtains a clear advantage, thanks to the weakness of the enemy kingside.

18...c5 19.c4 dxc4

Black hopes somehow to enliven his pieces. After 19...d4 20.♕h5 White's advantage is also not in doubt.

20.♗xc4 ♗b7 21.h3 ♖d8 22.♗c3

22...♘b8

Showing the idea behind Black's 19th move – the knight heads for d4.

23.♖e3

Unhurriedly strengthening the position and awaiting the

opponent's continuing with his idea...

23...♘c6?

Consistent, but this is refuted beautifully. However, it is hard to know what to recommend for Black. For example, in the variation 23...♗d5 24.♗xd5 ♖xd5 (24...exd5? 25.e6!) 25.b3 ♘c6 26.♘b2 followed by ♘c4 White's advantage is obvious.

24.♗xe6!

The bishop sacrifice totally destroys the black king's protection.

24...fxe6 25.♖f3+ ♔e8

After 25...♔g7 White wins with the subtle move 26.♕h5! (weaker is 26.♕xe6 ♖df8) 26...♖df8 27.♖f6! ♖xf6 (or 27...♗xf6 28.exf6+ ♖xf6 29.♖xe6+–) 28.exf6+ ♗xf6 29.♕xg5+ etc.

26.♕xe6 ♖g7 27.♕h6 ♘d4

28.e6!

An effective finish!

28...♘xf3+ 29.gxf3 ♗f8

Or 29...♖g8 30.♕h5+ ♔f8 31.♕f7#.

30.♕h5+ ♔e7 31.♗xg7

Black resigned. The variation 31...♗xg7 32.♕f7+ ♔d6 33.e7 is hopeless for him.

B) The attack with same-side castling

A classic example of an attack with same-side castling is Game 33. The attack, the main motif of which is the centralised knight on e5, ends with logical sacrifices on the squares f7 and e6, drawing the black king out of his fortress.

In Game 34 White's piece attack is helped by a powerful pawn wedge on e6, arising as a result of a knight sacrifice on that square.

Games 32 and 35 are examples of a piece and pawn attack on the castled position.

An original picture can be seen in Game 36. By sacrificing a piece for two pawns, Black completely destroys the pawn protection of the enemy king. However, the resulting open lines are exploited by... the white pieces, which go over to a decisive counterattack against Black's monarch!

Game 32 Queen's Indian Defence E11

Zlatko Ilincic   2451

Fabiano Caruana   2412

Budapest 2007 (6)

1.d4 ♘f6 2.c4 e6 3.♘f3 ♗b4+ 4.♗d2 ♕e7

One of the solid variations of the Bogo-Indian Defence. Black's main idea is, after the exchange of dark-squared bishops, to put his pawns on d6 and e5.

5.g3 ♘c6 6.♗g2

A popular alternative is 6.♘c3 ♗xc3 7.♗xc3 ♘e4 8.♖c1 d6 etc.

6...♗xd2+

7.♘bxd2

Now we see Black's idea – White has to capture with the knight, putting it on a less active square than c3, since after 7.♕xd2?! ♘e4 8.♕c2 ♕b4+ the white king must lose castling rights, in order to avoid loss of a pawn, or the destruction of his pawn structure after 9.♘c3 ♘xc3 10.♕xc3 ♕xc3+ 11.bxc3.

7...d6 8.0-0 a5

More often seen is 8...0-0 9.e4 e5 10.d5 ♘b8, and now one of White's main plans is 11.♘e1 a5 12.♘d3 ♘a6 13.f4, trying to seize space on the queenside.

9.e4 e5 10.d5 ♘b8 11.♘e1

Black's delay in castling gives White another possibility – 11.c5!? 0-0 (Black faces unpleasant pressure after 11...dxc5 12.♘c4 ♘bd7 13.d6!) 12.cxd6 cxd6 13.♘e1, opening lines in his favour on the queenside.

11...h5!?

This march of the h-pawn to h4 is the idea of Black's move order. It is not so much an attack on the king as a prophylactic measure against the advance f2-f4.

12.♘c2

It is interesting that the players have played a whole series of games against each other, in which this position has arisen. Just a month after this game, the Serbian GM tried the move 12.♘ef3. There followed 12...♘bd7 13.b3 ♘c5 14.♕c2 h4! 15.a3 (if 15.♘xh4 ♖xh4! 16.gxh4 ♘h5 the exchange sacrifice promises Black excellent play on the dark squares) 15...hxg3 16.fxg3 ♘g4 17.♕c3 ♗d7 18.b4 ♘a4 19.♕b3 b5 20.h3 ♘f6 21.cxb5 axb4 22.axb4 ♗xb5 23.♘h4 g6 24.♖fc1 0-0 with mutual chances, Ilincic-Caruana, Budapest 2007.

12...h4 13.♘e3

13...hxg3

In principle, there was no need to hurry with the exchange on g3. But what continuation should Black then choose? He does not want to castle yet, because his rook is doing good work on the h-file.

It would be useful to play 13...♘a6, but after 14.♕a4+ the a5-pawn is lost. On the other hand, the black knight would be less well-placed on d7. Playing 13...b6 means reducing the flexibility of his queenside pawn chain, whilst after 13...♗d7 there is the possible reply 14.♕b3. In this context, one can understand why in Meduna-Rashkovsky, Lviv 1981, Black chose 13...g6 14.b3 ♘a6 15.a3 ♔f8 16.b4 ♔g7 17.♘b3 b6 18.♘c1 ♗d7 19.♘d3 ♖h7 20.♖a2 ♖ah8, and he had achieved all he could dream of. White has to play more dynamically, for example with the interesting pawn sacrifice 14.c5 dxc5 15.♘dc4, after which Black should first of all consolidate by means of 15...0-0.

14.hxg3 ♘h5?!

The idea of this move is obvious – to deprive the opponent of any chance of the advance f2-f4. But

the coordination of the black pieces is somewhat disrupted – the rook on h8 has to fulfil obligations defending the ♘h5, which, in its turn, leaves the centre.

15.♖e1?!

Too academic. The minuses of the opponent's previous move could be demonstrated with 15.c5!, and in the event of the sacrifice being accepted, Black gets into serious difficulties, e.g. 15...dxc5 16.♘dc4 ♖a6 17.♘f5 ♗xf5 18.exf5 ♘d7 19.d6! etc.

15...♗d7 16.b3 g6 17.♕c2

17...♔f8

Black has successfully overcome a wobbly moment and gradually restores the harmony of his pieces. His king heads to g7, which allows the rooks to coordinate and keep in mind the open h-file.

18.a3 ♔g7 19.b4 ♘a6 20.♕c3 ♖ae8

Necessary prophylaxis. In the event of the direct 20...♖h7?! 21.c5! dxc5 22.bxa5 Black has problems.

21.♖ac1

White over-prepares his queenside advance. The immediate 21.c5! was possible, offering a positional pawn sacrifice of a type we are already familiar with. However, in this case, the game does not move beyond the boundaries of dynamic equality, e.g. 21...axb4 22.axb4 dxc5 23.bxc5 ♕xc5 (or 23...♘xc5 24.♖ec1 b6 (24...♘a6 25.♘dc4) 25.♖a7 ♖c8 26.♘dc4 ♖he8 27.d6 with the initiative) 24.♕xc5 ♘xc5 25.♖ec1 b6 26.♖a7 ♖c8 27.♘dc4 ♖he8 28.d6 b5 29.dxc7 bxc4 30.♘xc4 ♘b3 31.♖b1 ♘d4 32.♘d6 ♘c6 33.♘xe8+ ♗xe8 34.♖ab7 ♗d7 35.♗f1 ♘a5 36.♖a7 ♘c6, and the battle ends in a repetition of moves.

21...b6!

An important defensive device, allowing him to keep control of the square c5. After 22.bxa5 ♘c5 23.axb6 cxb6 Black manages to strengthen his dark squares at the cost of a pawn.

22.♗f1 ♗c8

Meeting the threat of 23.c5.

23.♘f3 ♘f6

The situation on the queenside has more or less stabilised, and Black begins manoeuvres aimed at creating pressure on the kingside. His main resource is the open h-file.

24.♗d3 ♘g4 25.♔g2 ♘xe3+ 26.♖xe3 ♗h3+ 27.♔g1

27...♘b8!

Characteristic for Caruana – he brings his only badly-placed piece into play!

The knight is headed on the route to g4.

28.bxa5

After 28.c5 axb4 29.cxd6 cxd6 30.axb4 ♖h7 Black also retains a solid position on the queenside and can prepare operations on the other flank.

28...♘d7! 29.axb6 cxb6 30.♗f1

White tries to exchange off his relatively inactive bishop, but now the position of his king acquires some weaknesses.

30...♘f6 31.♗xh3 ♖xh3 32.♔g2 ♖eh8 33.♖3e1

33...♕d7

Exploiting the opponent's dubious manoeuvres, Black begins a direct attack on the king.

34.♘g1 ♖h1 35.♕f3 ♘g4 36.♖e2 ♖8h2+ 37.♔f1 ♖h5 38.♕b3 ♘h2+ 39.♔g2 ♕g4

An effective strengthening of the position – the threat is 39...♘f3. Another decision was also possible: 39...♖xg1+! 40.♔xg1 ♕g4! (the direct 40...♕h3 41.f4 ♘g4 42.♕f3 exf4 43.♕g2 does not bring the desired result) 41.♖e3 ♕h3 42.♖e2 g5! (42...♘f1 43.♕f3), and White has no satisfactory defence against ...g5-g4 and ...♘f3+.

40.♖e3

On 40.♔xh1 Black settles things with 40...♘f3+ 41.♔g2 ♖h2+ (41...♘xg1 42.♖xg1 ♕xe2 43.♕e3) 42.♔f1 ♖h1 43.♔g2 ♘xg1 44.♖xg1 (44.♔xh1 ♘xe2) 44...♕h3+ 45.♔f3 ♖xg1 46.♕xb6? ♕h1+ 47.♔e3 ♖b1 48.♕xd6 ♖b3+ 49.♔d2 ♕a1!, winning.

40...♘f1!

A nice final blow!

41.♔xf1 ♖xg1+! 42.♔xg1 ♕h3

White resigned.

Game 33 French Defence C10
Fabiano Caruana 2640
Emanuel Berg 2628
Dresden ol 2008 (7)

1.e4 e6 2.d4 d5 3.♘c3 dxe4 4.♘xe4 ♘d7 5.♘f3 ♘gf6 6.♘xf6+ ♘xf6 7.♗d3 c5 8.dxc5 ♗xc5 9.♕e2 0-0

At one time, this *tabiya* was the basic one in the Rubinstein French. For a long time it was considered that White obtains the advantage by castling queenside. But everything changed, and after 10.♗g5 Black found the resource 10...h6! 11.♗d2 (or 11.h4 ♕a5+ 12.♗d2 ♕b6 13.0-0-0 e5!, Pelletier-Morozevich, Biel 2004) 11...e5! (Fedorov-Supatashvili, Yekaterinburg 1997), and the sacrifice of the central pawn promises Black excellent counterplay!

Therefore, Caruana settles for the quieter plan of kingside castling.

10.0-0 b6 11.♗g5 ♗b7 12.♖ad1 ♕c7 13.♘e5

Because practice has demonstrated the solidity of the black position in the variation 13.♗xf6 gxf6 14.♗e4 ♖fd8, White tries another plan. He occupies e5 with the knight, hoping to use it to create threats on the kingside.

13...♖fd8

The king's rook is the one that belongs on d8, the point being that in variations such as ♗xf6, gxf6 and ♕h5, the black king has a flight square on f8.

14.♔h1!?

An interesting idea. The modest king move aims to include the f2-pawn in the battle. Other ideas do not bring White any special dividends:

A) 14.♖fe1 ♖d5 15.♗f4 (the active 15.c4? fails to 15...♖xe5! 16.♕xe5 ♗xf2+! 17.♔f1 ♕c6 with advantage to Black, Nurkevich-Vysochin, Warsaw 2009) 15...♖d4 16.♗g3 ♘e4 17.c3 ♘xg3 18.hxg3 ♖dd8 19.♗e4 ♗xe4 20.♕xe4 ♖ac8 21.g4 h6 with equality, Kveinys-Speelman, Plovdiv 2003;

B) Or 14.c3 ♖d5 15.♖de1!? ♖ad8 16.♗b1 ♗a6!? 17.♕xa6 ♖xe5 18.♗f4 ♗xf2+! 19.♔xf2 ♕c5+ 20.♔f3 ♕d5+ 21.♔f2 ♕c5+ 22.♔f3 ♕d5+ with perpetual check, Miroshnichenko-Meier, Bad Zwesten 2005.

14...♗e7

Having mobilised his queenside, Black returns the bishop to e7. The

drawback of this is the reduced surveillance of f7.

The alternative is 14...♖d5 15.♖de1 or 14...♗d4 15.♖de1, which requires practical tests. In the last case, the following direct variation is possible: 15...♗xb2 16.♗xf6 gxf6 17.♕g4+ ♔h8 18.♕h4 f5 19.♕f6+ ♔g8 20.♕g5+ ♔h8 21.♕f6+ with perpetual check.

15.♖fe1!

A subtle set-up of the white rooks. It is clearly directed at developing activity on the e- and f-files, whilst at the same time avoiding possible exchanges on the d-file. An analogous idea was mentioned in the note to move 13, but here the white pawn remains on c2, which makes the ♗d3's position more secure.

15...h6 16.♗h4

The thematic knight sacrifice 16.♘xf7 is currently not dangerous for Black because of 16...♕c6! (16...♔xf7? 17.♕xe6+ ♔f8 18.♗xf6 ♗xf6 19.♗c4+−) 17.♘xh6+ gxh6 18.♕xe6+ ♕xe6 19.♖xe6 hxg5 20.♖xe7 ♖d7, and in the endgame, the only issue is whether White can equalise.

16...♘d5

Black aims to reduce the kingside pressure by exchanges, which his opponent naturally avoids.

17.♗g3 ♗d6 18.♕e4 ♘f6 19.♕h4 ♘d7?

The Swedish GM consistently plays against the opponent's active pieces. However, now the black king is the only defender of f7, which allows White to carry out an effective combination.

Black could retain a solid position with 19...♖ac8. Counterplay in the centre allows Black not to fear the kingside attack.

20.♘xf7! ♚xf7 21.♖xe6!

With a series of blows, White destroys the protection of the enemy king, which finds itself unsupported by its own army.

21...♘c5

Black does not manage to organise a defence after either 21...♚xe6 22.♗c4+ ♗d5 23.♕e4+ ♚f6 24.♗xd5+− or 21...♘f6 22.♗c4 ♘d5 23.♕h5+ ♚xe6 (23...♚g8 24.♗xd5 ♗xd5 25.♕xd5 ♗xg3 26.♖e8+ ♚h7 27.♕e4+ g6 28.♖e7+) 24.♕g6+ ♚d7 25.♕f5+ ♚e8 26.♖e1+ ♘e7 27.♕f7+ ♚d7 28.♖xe7++−.

The most tenacious defence was 21...♘e5, although after 22.♖xe5 ♗xe5 23.♕h5+ ♚g8 (23...♚e6? 24.♖e1+−) 24.♗xe5 ♕e7 25.f4 White's advantage is obvious.

22.♖xd6! ♖xd6 23.♕f4+ ♚e7 24.♖e1+ ♚d7

After 24...♘e6, among various choices there is 25.♕g4 ♖g8 26.♗h7+−.

25.♗b5+ ♗c6 26.♕f5+ ♘e6 27.♗xd6 ♕xd6 28.♖xe6

Black resigned.

Game 34 Sicilian Defence B42

Fabiano Caruana	2640
Aloyzas Kveinys	2533

Dresden ol 2008 (10)

1.e4 c5 2.♘f3 e6 3.d4 cxd4 4.♘xd4 a6 5.♗d3

It is worth noting that the development of the bishop to d3 was Fischer's favourite way of responding to the Paulsen.

5...♘f6

In the famous 7th match game Fischer-Petrosian (Buenos Aires 1971) there followed 5...♘c6 6.♘xc6 bxc6 7.0-0 d5 8.c4! ♘f6 9.cxd5 cxd5 10.exd5 exd5 11.♘c3 ♗e7 12.♕a4+

♕d7 13.♖e1! ♕xa4 14.♘xa4 ♗e6
15.♗e3 0-0 16.♗c5 with a clear
positional advantage to White.
In the present game, Black goes for
a Hedgehog set-up.

**6.0-0 ♕c7 7.♕e2 d6 8.f4 ♗e7 9.c4
♘bd7 10.♘c3 b6 11.♔h1 ♗b7
12.♗d2**

12...g6

More common is 12...0-0 13.f5
(if 13.♖ae1 ♖fd8 Black indirectly
prevents the advance e4-e5) 13...
e5 14.♘c2 (or 14.♘b3), and White's
position is somewhat preferable.
Now, however, after 13.f5 there
follows 13...gxf5 14.exf5 e5, and
Black has counterplay in the centre
and on the kingside.

13.♖ac1

In the game Wegener-Mainka,
Dortmund 2000, there followed
13.♖ae1 0-0 14.f5 gxf5 15.exf5 e5
16.♘f3 ♘c5 17.♗b1 b5!? 18.cxb5 axb5
19.b4 ♘a4 20.♘xb5 ♕d7 and Black
had the initiative for the sacrificed
pawn.

13...0-0 14.f5

The game Dominguez-Vasques, Las
Tunas 2001, developed in a spirit of
unhurried manoeuvring: 14.b4 ♖fe8
15.♘f3 ♗f8 16.a3 ♗g7 17.♘g5 ♖e7

18.♖ce1 ♖d8 19.♕f2 ♘f8 20.♖c1 h6
21.♘f3 etc.
The young grandmaster prefers
more active measures against the
Hedgehog.

14...gxf5 15.exf5 e5 16.♘d5 ♕d8

17.♘e6!?

This positional knight sacrifice
gives White chances of a direct
attack on the enemy king.
The alternative was the quiet 17.♘c2
♔h8 (not 17...♘xd5 18.cxd5 ♗xd5?
(the lesser evil was 18...♘f6 19.♘b4,
when Black is just worse because
of the weakness of c6) 19.♘e3 ♗b7
20.f6! ♘xf6 21.♘f5 with decisive
threats) 18.♘ce3 ♖g8 – the white
pieces are beautifully placed, but
Black's defences are sufficiently
solid.

17...fxe6 18.fxe6 ♘c5 19.♗f5

The direct 19.♖xf6 ♖xf6 (or
19...♗xf6 20.e7 ♗xe7 21.♗xh7+
♔xh7 22.♕h5+ ♔g8 23.♕g6+
♔h8 24.♕h6+=) 20.♗xh7+ ♔xh7
21.♘xf6+ ♗xf6 22.♕h5+ ♔g7
23.♕f7+ ♔h8 24.♕h5+ leads to an
immediate draw.
Caruana takes a brave decision, to
continue the fight a piece down,
placing his hopes on the pawn at

e6, which splits the enemy position into two halves.

19...♔h8!

The immediate attempt to get rid of the powerful knight on d5 leads to catastrophe: 19...♘xd5? (hoping after 20.cxd5 ♖xf5 21.♖xf5 ♗xd5 22.♗h6 ♔h8 to beat off the attack) 20.♗xh7+! ♔xh7 21.♕h5+ ♔g8 22.♖f7! ♖xf7 23.exf7+ ♔g7 24.♗h6+ ♔f6 25.cxd5 ♗xd5 26.♖f1+ ♗f3 27.♖xf3+ ♔e6 28.f8♕, winning.

20.♖c3 ♘xd5

The alternative is 20...♗xd5 21.cxd5 ♘xd5 22.♖h3 ♖xf5 23.♖xf5 ♘f6, and White has nothing better than to force a draw with 24.♖xf6! ♗xf6 25.♖xh7+! ♔xh7 26.♕h5+ ♔g8 27.♕f7+ ♔h8 28.♕h5+ and perpetual check.

But the Lithuanian GM is also a lover of the battle and so the game continues!

21.cxd5 ♗xd5 22.♖h3 ♗h4

Avoiding the latest hidden reef: 22...♖xf5? 23.♖xf5 ♕g8 24.♖f7 ♗xe6 25.♖fxh7+ ♕xh7 26.♖xh7+ ♔xh7 27.♕h5+ ♔g8 28.♗h6 ♗f8 29.♕g6+ ♔h8 30.b4, and White wins.

23.♗e1

An unpleasant shot.

After the direct 23.♕h5, the white attack runs out of steam: 23...♖xf5 24.♖xf5 ♗xe6 25.♗g5 ♕d7 26.♕f3! ♕c8! 27.♖xe5 dxe5 28.♗xh4 ♗f5 29.♗f6+ ♔g8 30.♕d5+ ♘e6 31.♖c3 ♕f8 32.♖g3+ ♔f7 etc.

23...♖g8?

Practically the only, and the decisive mistake of the game! Maybe White's last move had been underestimated by Black and this threw him out of kilter.

Bad was 23...♗g5? 24.♖xh7+ ♔g8 25.♕h5 ♕f6 26.h4, and White wins. After 23...♘xe6 24.♗xh4 ♕d7 25.♕d1! (equality results from the exchange of blows 25.♗xh7 ♘f4 26.♖xf4 ♕xh3 27.♗e4 ♗xe4 28.♕xe4 ♕e6 29.♗f6+ ♖xf6 30.♖xf6 ♕xf6 31.♕xa8+ ♔g7) 25...♕b7 (25...♕c6? 26.♗f6+! ♖xf6 27.♖xh7+ ♔g8 28.♕g4+ ♔f8 29.♕h4 ♗xg2+ 30.♔g1, winning) 26.♖g3 the activity of the white bishops prevents the black king from feeling safe.

The most accurate defence is 23...♗xe6! 24.♗xh4 (or 24.♗xe6 ♖xf1+ 25.♕xf1 ♗xe1 26.♗d5 ♖c8 (26...♖a7? 27.♖f3 ♔g7 28.♕xe1 with irresistible threats) 27.♕xe1 ♕e7

with approximate equality) 24...♕d7
25.♗xe6 ♕xe6 26.♖hf3 ♘d7, and
the resulting position is one of
dynamic equality, in which Black's
extra pawn is offset by the exposed
position of his king.
**24.♗xh4! ♖xg2 25.♕xg2 ♗xg2+
26.♔xg2 ♕f8**

The presence of queens on the
board does not bring Black any
happiness, as four white pieces
surround the black king!
27.♗g6 ♘xe6
Mate follows 27...♖c8 28.♗f6+ ♔g8
29.♗xh7+ ♔f8 30.♗g5+ etc.
**28.♗f6+ ♔g8 29.♗xh7+ ♔f7
30.♗xe5+**
Black resigned. After 30...♔e7
31.♖xf8 ♖xf8 32.♗g3 White has an
extra piece.

Game 35 Sicilian Defence B85
Fabiano Caruana   2646
Krishnan Sasikiran   2711
Wijk aan Zee 2009 (11)

**1.e4 c5 2.♘f3 d6 3.d4 cxd4 4.♘xd4
♘f6 5.♘c3 a6 6.♗e2 e6 7.0-0 ♕c7
8.f4 ♗e7 9.♗e3 ♘c6 10.♔h1 0-0
11.♕e1**

This position is one of the *tabiyas*
of the Scheveningen Sicilian. The
plan of bringing the queen to g3,
introduced by Chigorin, allows
White to create piece pressure
against the enemy king.
A fashionable alternative is 11.a4
♖e8 12.♗f3 ♖b8 13.♕d2 ♗d7 14.♘b3
b6 15.g4, and White advances his
pawns against the enemy king.
**11...♘xd4 12.♗xd4 b5 13.a3 ♗b7
14.♕g3**

14...♖ad8
Twenty years ago the main line
was considered to be 14...♗c6
15.♖ae1 ♕b7 16.♗d3 b4! 17.axb4
♕xb4 18.♘e2 ♕b7 19.♘c3 ♕b4,
and Black maintains dynamic
equality. Then popularity switched
to the continuation 17.♘d1!? bxa3
18.bxa3 with the idea of ♘g4, which
brought good practical results –

at the cost of a weakening of his queenside pawns, White improves his kingside attacking chances. Since then, a lot of water has flowed under the bridge. Black has developed some interesting prophylactic methods, allowing him to limit the development of the enemy initiative. Thus, by placing his rook on d8, Black eyes up the bishop on d4, thereby reducing the effectiveness of the advance e4-e5. The black queen remains on c7 for the time being, forcing White continually to reckon with the typical central counter ...e6-e5!. However, as we will see, Black's defensive set-up has certain tactical drawbacks.

15.♖ae1

If Black now plays some sort of useful 'neutral' move, such as 15...♗c6, then 16.♗d3 is possible, not fearing the standard reaction 16...e5 17.fxe5 ♘h5 because of 18.♕f2 dxe5 19.♗b6, winning an exchange.

15...♖d7

This move, getting the rook off the compromised square, also contains an active idea: by means of ...♖e8 and ...♗d8 to prepare the counterblow ...e6-e5!.

16.♗d3

It turns out that White can still put the bishop in this active position, because now after 16...e5 17.fxe5 ♘h5 there follows 18.♕h3 dxe5 19.♗xe5! ♕xe5 20.♕xd7. Admittedly, Black keeps some compensation for his material loss:

20...♗d6 21.♕h3 (21.g3? ♘xg3+! 22.hxg3 ♕xg3 23.♖e2 ♕h4+ 24.♔g1 ♕g5+! 25.♖g2 ♕c5+! 26.♖ff2 ♗c8, and Black wins) 21...♗c8 22.♕h4 ♗e7 23.♕f2 ♗d6 24.g3 ♗h3 25.♖g1 ♗c5 26.♕f3 ♗xg1 27.♖xg1 ♗e6 or 24.♕g1 (instead of 24.g3) 24...♗c5 25.♖f5 ♗xf5 26.exf5 ♕c7 27.♕f1 ♘f6 28.♘e4, but in both cases, Black faces a battle for a draw.

16...♖e8

17.♖f3!?

Caruana on ChessBase: 'This rare move was recommended to me by Chernin. Maybe it is insufficient to yield an advantage, but Black faces a concrete problem, which is not so easy to solve at the board. I felt that this was an unpleasant surprise for my opponent.'

The main line here is considered to be 17.e5. Thus, in Ni Hua-Jakovenko, Nyzhnij Novgorod 2007, after 17...dxe5 18.♗xe5 ♕d8 19.♘e4 ♘h5 20.♕e3 ♘f6?! 21.♗xf6 ♗xf6 22.♘c5 White obtained some advantage. Later the move 20...♕c8 was found to be more reliable for Black.

It should be noted that the attempt to prepare e4-e5 with 17.♕h3 fails to the counterblow 17...e5.

One of the ideas of the text is the 'secret' doubling of the white rooks on the f-file, which could occur if the opponent achieves his 'dream' and plays ...e6-e5.

17...♕d8?!

Black prepares to retreat the bishop to f8, but for a moment removes control of e5.

The principled continuation was 17...♗d8 18.♖ef1 e5 19.fxe5 dxe5 20.♗e3 ♔h8, inviting the opponent to demonstrate the effectiveness of the doubling of rooks on the f-file. Caruana, in his notes, illustrates the possibilities of the position with the following imaginative variation: 18.f5 e5 19.♗e3 d5 20.♗h6 ♘h5 21.♕g4

analysis diagram

21...♖d6! 22.f6 g6 23.♕xh5 gxh5 24.♖g3+ ♔h8 25.♗g7+ with perpetual check.

We would add that in the game Ni Hua-Hou Yifan (China tt 2010) there followed 18.♘d1 e5 19.♗c3 ♕c8 20.♘f2 ♘h5 21.♕g4 ♘f6 22.♕g3 ♘h5 23.♕g4 ♘f6 24.♕f5 ♖de7 25.♕xc8 ♗xc8 26.♗b4 exf4 27.♗xd6 ♖e6 28.♗xf4 ♗b7 29.♔g1 ♘xe4 with mass exchanges and a draw.

18.♕h3

Now the counterblow ...e6-e5 is not possible, and the white queen, by attacking h7, forces a weakening of the black kingside.

18...g6 19.♖ef1

The threat is f4-f5, which follows after, for example, 19...♗c6 20.f5 exf5 21.exf5 ♗xf3 22.fxg6 hxg6 (22...hxg6 23.♕xf3+−) 23.♕e6+ ♔g7 24.♖xf3+− or 19...♗f8 20.f5 exf5 21.exf5 g5 (21...♗xf3 22.fxg6 hxg6 23.♗xf6 ♕xf6 24.♕xd7+−) 22.♖g3 h6 23.♘d1! ♗g7 24.♗xf6 ♕xf6 25.♘e3 with the hard-to-meet threat of 26.♘g4 (variations by Caruana).

19...d5?

Failing to notice the opponent's knockout blow. The best defensive resource, in Caruana's opinion, was 19...♘h5!? 20.f5 exf5 21.exf5 ♗xf3 22.♕xf3 ♗g5 (22...♗f8 23.♘d5+−) 23.♘d5 ♖e5! with the possibility of a stubborn defence.

20.f5!

A beautiful breakthrough, including all the pieces in the attack.

20...dxe4 21.fxg6 fxg6

Bad was 21...exf3? 22.♕xh7+ ♘xh7 23.gxh7+ ♔f8 24.h8♕# or 21...hxg6? 22.♖xf6 ♖xd4 23.♖xf7+−.

22.♖xf6

The tempting check 22.♕xe6+?
♔h8 leads the attack to a dead end.
22...♖xd4

Or 22...♗xf6 23.♗xf6 ♕a8 24.♗e2+–.
23.♖f7 ♗h4 24.♗e2

It turns out that both black bishops
are under attack – the threats are
25.♖xb7 and 25.g3.
24...♗c6 25.g3 e3+ 26.♔g1 a5

It is already impossible to maintain
material equality – 26...♕g5
27.♖7f4 ♖d2 28.♖g4! (28.♖xh4?
♖xe2 29.♘xe2 ♕d5–+; 28.♕xh4
♕xh4 29.gxh4 ♖xc2 30.♗f3±)
28...♕e5 29.gxh4+– (pointed out by
Caruana).
**27.gxh4 b4 28.axb4 axb4 29.♘d1
♕d5**

30.♘xe3 ♕c5

Or 30...♕h1+ 31.♔f2 ♕e4 32.♗d3
♕e5 33.♔g1, winning.
31.♗d3

Black has no compensation at all for
his lost piece. There followed:
**31...b3 32.♕g3 bxc2 33.♗xc2 ♖d2
34.♖7f2 ♖ed8 35.♖xd2 ♖xd2 36.♖f2
♖d4 37.♗xg6! hxg6 38.♕xg6+
♔h8 39.♕h6+ ♔g8 40.♕xe6+
♔h8 41.♕h6+ ♔g8 42.♕e6+ ♔h8
43.♕c8+ ♔g7 44.♖g2+ 1-0**

Game 36 Ruy Lopez C88
Fabiano Caruana   2778
Levon Aronian   2816
Sao Paulo/Bilbao 2012 (9)

**1.e4 e5 2.♘f3 ♘c6 3.♗b5 a6 4.♗a4
♘f6 5.0-0 ♗e7 6.♖e1 b5 7.♗b3 0-0
8.d3**

A solid continuation, allowing
White to avoid the sharp variations
of the Marshall Gambit.
**8...d6 9.a4 ♗d7 10.c3 ♘a5 11.♗c2
c5 12.♘bd2 ♖e8**

This position had already been seen
in Caruana's practice. In the game
Caruana-Jakovenko, Poikovsky
2011, there followed 13.♘f1 h6
14.♘e3 ♗f8 15.h3 ♘c6 16.♘h2 b4
(less committal is 16...♗e6 17.♘hg4
♘xg4 18.hxg4 ♕d7 19.♗b3 ♖ab8
with a solid position for Black,
Kryvoruchko-Erdös, Germany
Bundesliga 2012/13) 17.♘hg4 ♘xg4
18.hxg4 ♗e7 19.♗b3 ♗e6 20.♗d5
♖c8 21.♘f5 ♗g5 22.♗c4 ♗xc4
23.dxc4 with some advantage to
White.

13.d4

This time Caruana refrains from
the preparatory manoeuvres
typical of the variation with 8.d3,

and forces an immediate central confrontation.

From a theoretical point of view, advancing the pawn to d4 in two moves should not bring White any benefits at all.

13...exd4

Black has quite a wide choice of continuations, from a closed set-up typical of the Chigorin (13...♕c7 14.d5 c4! with decent play) to more open constructions such as after 13...cxd4 14.cxd4 ♘c6, underlining the vulnerability of the b4-square.

14.cxd4

14...♗g4!?

Here too 14...♘c6 was possible, bringing the knight off the edge of the board.

The text aims to sharpen the game, but the ♗g4 risks being pushed offside and getting 'under arrest' on g6. One cannot help remembering the classic game Capablanca-Bogoljubow, London 1922, in which a similar pawn structure arose.

15.h3 ♗h5 16.d5

Sharply reducing the scope of the ♘a5 and recalling another, more recent classic, Fischer-Kortchnoi, Stockholm 1962.

After the immediate 16.g4 ♗g6 17.d5 ♗f8 the ♘d2 is tied to the defence of the e4-pawn.

16...♕c8!?

An original treatment of the position. Black intends to meet the advance g2-g4 with a piece sacrifice, and at the same time prepares the manoeuvre ...♗e7-d8-b6.

Even so, it looks more natural to play the standard 'Indian' regrouping 16...♘d7 17.g4 ♗g6 18.♘f1 h6 19.♘g3 ♗f6, establishing control over the key square e5.

17.♘f1

After 17.g4?! ♘xg4! 18.hxg4 ♕xg4+ 19.♔f1 ♗f6 Black has good positional compensation for the sacrificed knight, since the opponent simply cannot untangle his cluster of pieces.

17...♗d8

18.g4

Consistently playing to exclude the enemy bishop from the game.

A more restrained alternative was pointed out by Caruana in New In Chess 2012/8: 18.♘g3 ♗xf3 (or 18...♗g6 19.♗f4 followed by ♘f5) 19.♕xf3 g6 (on 19...♘xd5 there follows 20.e5! ♘b4 21.e6! ♖xe6 22.♖xe6 fxe6 23.♕h5 with a strong attack) 20.♗h6, and the possibility of the raid ♘f5 shows that White has the initiative.

18...♗g6

Now 18...♘xg4? fails to 19.hxg4 ♕xg4+ 20.♘g3!, and White wins.

19.♘g3 b4

The conflict assumes clear outlines. Black has activated on the queenside, trying to push his pawns through to the third rank, whilst White, in his turn, develops his kingside initiative.

20.♘h4

Leading to unnecessary tactical complications.

Again, Caruana avoids the quieter alternative 20.♗f4! b3 (on 20...♕d7 there follows 21.b3! c4 22.bxc4 ♘xc4 23.a5!) 21.♗b1 ♕d7 22.♗d2 with the transfer of the bishop to c3, which gives White the advantage.

20...b3

Preparing the conditions for the following piece sacrifice.

As Caruana pointed out, he spent a lot of time looking at the variation 20...c4 21.♘hf5 b3 22.♗b1 ♗b6 23.♕f3 ♕c5, which opens up many possibilities. Here is one of the variations found by him: 24.♗f4 c3 25.♗xd6 cxb2 26.♗xc5 bxa1♕ 27.♗xb6 ♕xa4 28.♗d4, and White's powerful attacking position compensates for his material deficit.

21.♗b1 ♘xg4!? 22.♘xg6 ♘xf2

23.♘e7+!!

A brilliant zwischenzug. After 23.♔xf2 fxg6! 24.♔g2 ♗f6 Black achieves a compact pawn structure on the kingside and can develop without hindrance an attack on the other wing.

23...♖xe7?

Another original decision by the Armenian GM in this game, which, however, proves to be bad.

The objective assessment of the two sides' opposing ideas depends on the key position arising after 23...♗xe7 24.♔xf2 ♗f6 25.♘f5 c4. Black has managed to bury the

♗b1 and ♖a1 on the queenside, but White, with the support of the ♘f5, has chances to develop an attack on the enemy king along the g-file. The following analysis, carried by Caruana in his 'home laboratory', shows the richness of the possibilities in this position: 26.♖g1 ♔h8 27.♗e3!? ♗xb2 28.♘xd6 (after 28.♖xg7 ♗xg7 29.♘xg7 ♕xh3! the battle suddenly ends in perpetual check, whilst after 28.♗d4 ♗xd4+ 29.♕xd4 ♕c5 30.♕xc5 dxc5 31.♖xg7 we reach a sharp endgame which is not easy to assess) 28...♕c7 29.♘xe8 (things remain unclear after 29.♗d4 ♗xa1 30.♗xa1 c3 31.♕d4 f6 32.♗xc3 ♕xd6 33.♗xa5) 29...♖xe8 30.d6 ♕b8! 31.e5! (the subtlety of the move 30...♕b8! is shown by the variation 31.♗d4 ♗xa1 32.♗xa1 b2, whilst after 32.♖xg7 ♗xd4+ 33.♕xd4 ♘c6 34.♕f6 ♕a7+ 35.♔f1 ♖e6 Black fights off the mating threats) 31...♖xe5 (31...♗xa1? is bad because of 32.♖xg7! ♔xg7 33.♕g4+ ♔h8 34.♕f5 with mate)

analysis diagram

32.♕f3!! (the prelude to a surprising combination, which brings White victory!) 32...♗xa1 33.♖xg7! ♔xg7

34.♗h6+! ♔xh6 35.♕f6+ ♔h5 36.♕xf7+ ♔g5 37.♕g7+ ♔h5 38.♕xh7+ ♔g5 39.♕g6+ ♔f4 40.♕g3#!.

Caruana concludes his analysis with the following words: 'This fantastic variation would be impossible to see at the board, of course, with limited time. In a practical game, any result is possible here.'

24.♔xf2 ♖e5

Aronian's idea is revealed – after ♗f4 and the reply ...♗f6, he is ready to sacrifice a whole rook (!) for a blockade on the dark squares! The problem, however, is that White is not obliged to accept the Trojan Horse.

25.♔g2 c4 26.♘f5 ♗f6

At first, Aronian was prepared to play 26...♖xf5 27.exf5 ♗f6, but after closer examination, he refrained from this possibility. After 28.♖e2 Black does not have sufficient compensation for the sacrificed rook.

27.♕f3 c3

As pointed out by Caruana, after 27...♖xf5 28.♕xf5 ♕xf5 29.exf5 c3 White wins without any special difficulty: 30.♖e2 c2 31.♗xc2 bxc2

32.♖a3 ♘c4 33.♖b3 ♖c8 34.♔h1 ♘e5
35.♖xc2, etc.

28.♘h6+ ♔h8

Much the same consequences as
in the game result from 28...♔f8
29.♗d3.

29.♗d3 ♖e7

30.e5!

Opening lines for the decisive
attack on the king!

30...♗xe5 31.♕e4 g6 32.♕h4 f6

**33.♖xe5 dxe5 34.♕xf6+ ♖g7
35.♕xe5**

The outcome of the game is
decided. There followed:

**35...♕e8 36.♕xc3 ♖c8 37.♕xa5
♖e7 38.♗g5 ♖e2+ 39.♔g1 1-0**

C) The attack with opposite-side castling

The most important criterion of success in positions with opposite-side
castling is opening lines for the attack!

In Game 37 the activity of the black rook on the g-file was supported
by the ♗c6. To establish this coordination Black had to clear the pawn
barriers in the centre, by achieving the break ...d6-d5.

Games 38-40 are characterised by mutual pawn storms on opposite
flanks. Here we would draw attention to the combining of the attack with
subtle prophylactic measures.

Game 41 is interesting for the fact that matters do not come down to
the traditional pawn storms on opposite wings – with an open centre, this
strategy looks less promising. For the reader, the manoeuvres of the white
pieces are highly instructive, as they find a path into the enemy king's
position via the central lines!

Game 37 Sicilian Defence B43

Tibor Fogarasi	2425
Fabiano Caruana	2549

Budapest 2007 (1)

**1.e4 c5 2.♘f3 e6 3.d4 cxd4 4.♘xd4
a6 5.♘c3 ♕c7 6.♗d3 ♘f6 7.0-0 ♗c5**

The elasticity in developing Black's
king's bishop is a characteristic of
the Paulsen System.

8.♘b3 ♗a7 9.♔h1 ♘c6 10.♗g5 h5!?
An interesting novelty. Black
usually plays 10...d6 11.♗xf6 gxf6
12.♕h5, and the white queen has

managed to occupy an excellent blockading position.

The text prevents this idea and creates the threat of 11...♘g4.

11.♗xf6

Caruana in his comments on ChessBase considers this exchange too direct and recommends 11.♕d2! with the idea of meeting the move 11...♘g4 with 12.♗f4.

I suspect the Hungarian GM did not like the variation 11...♗b8 12.f4 ♘h7 13.♗h4 g5.

Admittedly, after 14.♗e1 gxf4 15.♗h4 Black's position looks dangerous, because it is not easy for him to meet the typical Sicilian jump ♘d5. But Black is not obliged to take on f4. It is worth considering 14...♘f8 15.e5! gxf4 16.♗h4 (16.♕xf4 f5) 16...♘xe5 17.♗f6 ♖h6 (17...♖g8 18.♘d5!) 18.♘d5! ♕c6 19.♕xf4 ♘g4 20.♕b4! ♗d6 (or 20...♕d6 21.♕xd6 ♗xd6 22.♗g7 exd5 23.♗xh6 ♘e6 (23...♘xh6 24.♖f6) 24.♗d2 ♗xh2 25.♖f5 etc.) 21.♕a5! b6 22.♕xb6 ♗b7 23.♘a5 ♕xd5 24.♘xb7 ♗xh2 25.♗g7 ♖g6 26.♗xg6 ♘xg6 etc.

The reader will of course feel that we are sinking into the debris of computer analysis. Very well, it is not too late to halt this pernicious practice. From a human point of view, the truth about these complications should be in White's favour...

11...gxf6 12.f4

It was worth considering 12.♕d2, aiming for the fastest possible concentration of major pieces on the d-file and making it harder for the opponent to regroup with ...d7-d6, ...♗d7 and ...0-0-0. Then, for example, there could follow 12...h4 13.h3 b5 14.♖ae1 ♗b7 15.a4 b4 16.♘d5! exd5 17.exd5+ ♘e7 18.♕xb4 d6 19.c4!? and White has excellent compensation for the sacrificed piece.

But Black can also insist on the plan with ...d7-d6: 12.♕d2 h4 13.h3 d6 14.♖ad1 ♗d7 15.♗e2 0-0-0! (15...♔e7!?) 16.♕xd6 ♕xd6 17.♖xd6 ♔c7, and the two bishops in the endgame provide compensation for the lost pawn.

12...d6 13.♗e2 ♗d7 14.♕d2

The move 14.♗xh5 need not even be considered – after 14...♖h7!?, followed by ...0-0-0 and ...♖h8, Black gets open lines for the attack.

14...0-0-0 15.♖ad1 ♗e8

The upshot is that Black has a comfortable version of a Richter-Rauzer structure. The key difference is that the white king is not castled on the queenside, but on the king's wing, where he can come under attack, whilst the black bishop is actively placed on the a7-g1 diagonal, rather than its usual modest square e7.

16.♖f3

The white rook is excellently placed on the third rank – it can take part in the attack on the d6-pawn or support the tactical ideas ♘d5 or (after a2-a4) ♘b5.

It is worth adding that in the Richter-Rauzer itself, this rook manoeuvre was introduced in the classic game Keres-Botvinnik, Moscow 1956.

16...h4!

Excellently played! Black believes in the flexibility of his position and, without losing time, utilises his attacking trumps on the kingside. Superfluous prophylactic manoeuvres, such as 16...♔b8 17.♖d3, could lead to unnecessary problems defending the d6-pawn, because the bishop lacks the square b8.

17.h3

On 17.♖d3 Black can react quietly with 17...♖g8!, having in mind the variation 18.♖xd6? ♕xd6 19.♕xd6 ♖xd6 20.♖xd6 ♗b8 21.♖d1 ♗xf4∓. Meanwhile the jump 17.♘d5? is impossible for the moment, in view of 17...exd5 18.exd5 h3!.

17...♖g8 18.♕e1?

This was not the time to turn attention to the h4-pawn, and Black is able to seize the initiative. Another blank shot was 18.♘d5 exd5 19.exd5 ♔b8 (19...♘e7 20.♖c3 ♗c5 21.♘xc5 dxc5 22.d6) 20.♖c3 ♗c5!! ('This move, which I spent a long time finding, gives Black a clear advantage' – Caruana; equality results from 20...♕b6 21.dxc6 ♗xc6 22.♗f3) 21.♘xc5 (21.dxc6 ♗b4! 22.cxb7 ♗xc3 23.bxc3 ♗c6 24.♗f1 ♗xb7??? 21.♗f3 ♘a7) 21...dxc5 22.♖xc5 ♕b6 (22...♖g3!? – Caruana) 23.♕e3 ♘a7, and White does not have sufficient compensation for the piece.

Caruana considers White's best continuation to be the consolidating 18.♖d3! (freeing the f3-square for the bishop),

analysis diagram

intending to meet 18...♘b4 with the counterblow 19.♘d5! exd5 20.♕xb4 dxe4 21.♕xe4 ♗c6 22.♕f5+ ♚b8 23.♗f3 with equality.

18...♘e7!

A splendid manoeuvre! Black's defensive pawn set-up in the centre is ready to start moving, and the advance f4-f5 will open rich attacking prospects for the ♗e8!

19.f5

Blockading the f6-pawn. In reply to the calm 19.♕xh4 Caruana gives the following variation: 19...f5 20.♗d3 fxe4 21.♘xe4 ♗c6 22.♘a5! ♕xa5 23.♕xe7 ♕h5, with good attacking possibilities. For example, an immediate disaster occurs after 24.♘f6? ♕xf3! 25.gxf3 ♗xf3+ 26.♚h2 ♖g2+ 27.♚h1 ♖e2#.

19...♗c6 20.♘d4

Immediately fighting against the powerful ♗c6.

There is no time for grabbing material, as Caruana illustrates with the following variation: 20.fxe6 fxe6 21.♖xf6 ♘f5! 22.♗g4 ♘g3+ 23.♚h2 ♖xg4! 24.hxg4 ♕g7 25.♖xe6 ♕xg4 26.♖f6 ♕g5! with the decisive transfer of the queen to e5.

20...♗xd4

The ♗a7 has already done its job and now the light-squared bishop takes over as 'first violin' in the attack.

21.♖xd4 d5! 22.exd5 ♘xd5 23.♖c4?

The decisive mistake, perfectly understandable given the complexity of the defensive task facing Fogarasi. White adopts tough measures against the ♗c6, but still does not manage to 'cut off its legs'! Essential was 23.fxc6 (23.♗f1? ♘e7!) 23...fxe6 (the attempt to crush the opponent immediately does not work: 23...♖xg2!? 24.♚xg2 ♘e3+ 25.♚f2 ♖xd4 26.exf7!, and the strong pawn on f7 forces Black to take a draw – 26...♕h2+ 27.♚xe3 ♕e5+ 28.♚f2 ♕h2+ with perpetual) 24.♗f1, succeeding in consolidating the position.

Caruana now gives the surprising variation 24...♚b8! 25.♕xe6? ♕e5!! 26.♕xe5+ fxe5 27.♖d2 ♘xc3! 28.♖xd8+ ♖xd8 29.♖xc3 ♖d1 30.♚g1 ♗b5 31.♖f3 e4, and Black wins. Better is 25.♖fd3 ♘f4 26.♖xd8+ ♖xd8 27.♖xd8+ ♕xd8 and Black's pressure is unpleasant, but plenty of fighting lies ahead.

23...♖xg2!

A nice blow! White resigned. He cannot neutralise the ♗c6 – after 24.♔xg2 ♘e3+ 25.♔f2 ♘xc4 or 24.♖xc6 ♖h2+ 25.♔g1 ♖g8+ 26.♔f1 ♕xc6 Black wins.

Game 38 Slav Defence D11
Vladimir Potkin   2606
Fabiano Caruana   2680
Russia tt 2010 (5)

1.d4 ♘f6 2.♘f3 d5 3.c4 c6 4.e3

Who would have believed that this modest move, which used to be regarded as a way for older players to avoid many sharp variations, would today become one of the main lines against the Slav!
The reason for this is a change in the philosophy of the opening. Youngsters now want to play chess and not just test the accuracy of each others' computer analysis in sharp variations.
4...♗g4
If the bishop develops to f5, it can also be chased: 4...♗f5 5.♘c3 e6 6.♘h4.
5.h3 ♗xf3 6.♕xf3 e6 7.♘c3 ♘bd7 8.♗d2 ♗d6

Each side can be satisfied – Black has solved the problem of developing his light-squared bishop and obtained a solid central position, whilst White, in his turn, has the two bishops, although they are hard to exploit in this relatively closed position.
9.cxd5
A relatively rare continuation. White immediately determines the pawn structure in the centre, so as then to form a concrete middlegame plan independent of it.
9...exd5
A solid alternative is 9...cxd5 10.♗d3 0-0 11.0-0, and White's chances are only slightly better.
The text leads to an asymmetrical pawn structure and a sharper game.
10.g4
It is interesting that this position was reached by Caruana with colours reversed! In the game Caruana-l'Ami, Wijk aan Zee 2009, there followed 10.♗d3 ♘f8?! (10...0-0) 11.g4 ♘e6 12.h4 ♕e7 13.♕e2 0-0-0 14.0-0-0 ♔b8 15.♔b1 ♘d7 16.f4 with an initiative for White.
10...0-0 11.g5 ♘e8

Opening the game with 11...♘e4 12.♘xe4 dxe4 13.♕xe4 ♕xg5 14.♗d3 favours the side with the two bishops.

12.h4

White's plan is clear – to castle queenside and conduct a pawn storm against the black king's fortifications.

12...♗b4

Freeing the d6-square for the knight and including it in the battle for the e4-square.

13.0-0-0 ♘d6 14.♗d3

14...a5

The logical continuation, supporting the ♗b4 and making it easier to organise counterplay with the advance ...b7-b5. However, in Caruana's opinion (on ChessBase), this move is too slow and allows White to create a strong attack. 'The best decision was 14...f5!. I thought about this move, but rejected it because of 15.g6 (if 15.gxf6 ♘xf6 16.♕g2 ♗xc3 (16...♕e7!?) 17.♗xc3 ♘fe4 18.♗e1 ♕f6 19.♖f1 ♘f5 20.♗b4 ♖fe8. Black's position looks satisfactory, whilst 21.f3 will be met by the variation 21...♘eg3 22.♖g1 ♖xe3 23.♗e1 ♖xe1

24.♖dxe1 ♕xd4 25.♗xf5 ♘xf5) 15...h6 16.♘xd5 ♗xd2+ 17.♖xd2, but here I overlooked the possibility of 17...♘e4!, which gives Black a good position' – Caruana.

I think that this assessment of the promising move 14...f5 is too categorical.

analysis diagram

Let us consider this interesting possibility, for instance: 15.♘xd5!? ♗xd2+ 16.♖xd2 ♘e4 (if the knight is accepted by 16...cxd5 17.♕xd5+ ♘f7 18.♕xf5 g6 19.♕g4 ♘b6 20.♔b1, White's chances are better because of his attacking prospects and the lack of mobility of the black knights) 17.♘f4 (equality results from the variations involving 17.♘f6+) 17...♘xd2 18.♕d1!! (18.♗xd2 ♕a5+) 18...♕a5 (after 18...♘e4 a well-known combinational motif follows: 19.♗c4+ ♔h8 20.♘g6+! hxg6 21.h5 ♕xg5 22.hxg6+ ♕h6 23.♕g1!, and Black is in a bad way) 19.a3 ♘b6 20.♕xd2 ♕xd2+ 21.♔xd2, and in the endgame, White has a pawn for the exchange, the better pawn structure and excellent outposts for his pieces. In my opinion, his chances are superior.

It should be added that both before and after this game, Black has always played 14...♕e7, which looks more solid, e.g. 15.♖dg1 (15.♔b1 – with the threat of 16.♘xd5 – 15...a5 transposes to a position from the game) 15...f5 16.gxf6 ♘xf6 17.♕g2 ♖f7 18.♖h3 ♗xc3 19.♗xc3 ♘fe4 20.♗e1 ♘f5 with mutual chances, S.Ernst-Stellwagen, Hilversum 2008.

15.♔b1?!

This move out of general considerations Caruana also regards as not sufficiently concrete, and he recommends the immediate 15.♖dg1 ♕e7 16.h5 f5 17.gxf6 ♘xf6 18.♕g2.

analysis diagram

We will quote some of his variations, which nicely illustrate the spirit of positions with opposite-side castling:

A) 18...♗xc3 19.♗xc3 ♘fe4 20.♗e1, and the black knights will be driven out of the centre by f2-f3;

B) 18...b5? 19.h6 g6 20.♗xg6 with a crush;

C) 18...♖f7 19.♗g6! ♖ff8 20.h6! hxg6 21.♕xg6 ♖f7 22.hxg7 ♖xg7 23.♕h6 ♔f8 24.e4! ♗xc3 25.bxc3 ♘dxe4 26.♕h8+ ♖g8 27.♖xg8+

♘xg8 28.♖h7 ♕e6 29.♕g7+ ♔e8 30.♗h6 ♘e7 31.♕f8+ ♔d7 32.♕xa8, and White's attack has achieved its aim;

D) 18...♘fe4 19.h6! g6 20.f3! ♘xc3 (after 20...♗xc3 21.bxc3 ♘xd2 White's main idea works: 22.♗xg6! ♔h8 23.♗xh7! ♖f7 24.♕g7+ ♖xg7 25.hxg7+ ♕xg7 26.♗d3+ ♔g8 27.♖xg7+ ♔xg7 28.♔xd2, and the ending is bad for Black) 21.bxc3 ♗a3+ 22.♔c2 – Black's position looks dangerous, but because the white king is potentially vulnerable, the likely outcome of the game remains undetermined.

15...♕e7 16.♖dg1

16...b5!?

Black plays to sharpen the situation.

Simpler play results from 16...f5 17.gxf6 ♘xf6 18.♕g2 ♘fe4 19.♗xe4 ♘xe4 20.♘xe4 dxe4 21.♗xb4 axb4 22.♖h3 ♖f7 with roughly equal chances.

17.♕d1

With the intention by ♕c2 to force a weakening of the black king's residence. However, the opponent finds a way to create serious counterplay.

The alternative was a more 'traditional' development of events: 17.h5 f5! 18.gxf6 ♘xf6 19.♕g2 ♘fe4 etc.

17...♗xc3!

Parting with the bishop without regret, as it was getting under the feet of its own pawns.

18.♗xc3 b4 19.♗e1 c5

Black's counterplay develops quickly, not leaving White time to exploit his trumps, i.e. the two bishops and his kingside space advantage.

20.dxc5

On 20.♕c2?! there would follow 20...♖fc8! 21.♗xh7+ ♔h8 22.♗d3 c4 23.♗e2 c3!, and Black's attack is faster!

20...♘xc5

21.♖g4?!

It made sense to keep the bishop with 21.♗c2 ♕e5 with mutual chances. Now White needs to show definite accuracy to hold the balance.

21...♘xd3 22.♕xd3 ♖ac8 23.♖d4

The opening of central lines after 23.♕xd5?? ♖fd8 is fatal for White.

23...♘e4 24.f3

As a first priority, White must establish some coordination between his pieces. The d5-pawn was again poisoned: 24.♖xd5? ♘c5 25.♕d4 ♖fd8 etc.

24...♘c5 25.♕d2

As Caruana pointed out, the most precise consolidating line was 25.♕d1! ♕xe3 (on 25...♖fd8 26.♗g3 ♕e6 there follows 27.e4!) 26.♖xd5 ♘e6 27.♗g3 ♖fd8 28.♖e1 with equality.

25...♕e6

The queen heads for the weakened diagonal b1.

Caruana also considers other ways of developing the initiative:

A) 25...♖fd8 26.♗g3 ♕e6 27.♗f4 (with the queen on d2, 27.e4?! fails to 27...♖e8! 28.♖xd5? ♘xe4!) 27...b3 (after 27...♕g6+ 28.e4 ♘e6?? 29.h5 the black queen turns out to be trapped) 28.a3, and White's position is fully defensible;

B) 25...b3!? 26.♖xd5 (26.a3? is bad because of 26...♕e6 27.♖xd5 ♘a4! with irresistible threats) 26...bxa2+ 27.♔xa2, and by sacrificing a pawn, Black opens the position of the white king, although this is not easy to exploit with limited attacking potential.

26.♔a1?

In mutual time trouble, White commits a serious mistake. He should have braved the critics and played 26.♖xd5!. Caruana gives these variations: 26...♕g6+ (26...b3 27.♕d4 bxa2+ 28.♔xa2) 27.♔a1 (also possible is 27.♕c2 ♘b3 28.♗c3!) 27...♘e4 28.♕d1 ♕c6, and after 29.♔b1 Black has to force a draw – 29...♕g6 30.♕d3 ♕c6 31.♕d1 etc.

26...b3

'A simpler path to the advantage was 26...♕f5 27.♖f4 ♕e5 28.♗g3 ♘e6 29.♖g4 ♕f5, and the white rook is driven to an unfortunate position' – Caruana.

27.♕d1!

Trying to strengthen the position by transferring the bishop to c3.

27...bxa2

28.♗xa5!

Cold-blooded defence! The automatic 28.♗c3 a4! leads to bad consequences: 29.♔xa2 a3! 30.bxa3 ♘e4 31.♗e1 (31.fxe4 ♖xc3 32.exd5 ♕xe3) 31...♘c3+ 32.♗xc3 ♖xc3 or 29.♖xd5 ♘b3+ (29...a3 30.bxa3 ♕xe3 31.♗b4!) 30.♔xa2 ♘c1+! 31.♔b1 ♘e2! with a decisive attack for Black in both cases (variations pointed out by Caruana).

28...♕xe3 29.♗c3 ♖a8 30.♖e1??

An oversight in serious time-trouble. After 30.♖b4 ♖fd8 31.♕d4! ♕xd4 32.♗xd4 ♘e6 White retains chances of a draw in the endgame a pawn down, thanks to the strong bishop on d4.

30...♕c1+!

A simple, but nice blow – 31.♕xc1 ♘b3#!.

White resigned.

Game 39 Ruy Lopez C65
Fabiano Caruana   2794
Hikaru Nakamura   2790
Moscow ct 2016 (8)

1.e4 e5 2.♘f3 ♘c6 3.♗b5 ♘f6 4.d3

Yet another revived opening fashion. This old move of Steinitz is now the main anti-Berlin variation for contemporary GMs.

4...♗c5 5.♗xc6 dxc6 6.♘bd2 0-0 7.♕e2 ♖e8 8.♘c4 ♘d7 9.♗d2 ♗d6

10.0-0-0

At the Wijk aan Zee 2016 tournament the continuation 10.h4!? was tested twice.

Thus, in Wei Yi-Navara there followed 10.h4 c5 11.h5 h6?! 12.0-0-0 ♘b8 13.♖dg1 ♘c6 14.g4 f6 15.g5!! fxg5 16.♘xg5 ♘d4 17.♕d1 hxg5 18.♗xg5 ♗e7 19.♗e3, and by sacrificing a piece, White developed a crushing attack.

Black played better in Caruana-Karjakin: 10.h4!? ♘f8 11.h5 ♘e6! 12.0-0-0 c5 13.♕f1 f6 14.♘h4 ♘d4 15.c3 ♘c6 with approximate equality.

The resulting position with opposite-side castling presages a sharp battle.

Lovers of chess classics should note that the first player to castle queenside in the Spanish was Wilhelm Steinitz!

10...b5

Immediately sending the queenside pawns into the attack.

11.♘e3 a5 12.♘f5 a4

13.♗g5!

A subtle move. Before advancing his kingside pawns, White provokes a weakening of the enemy kingside.

13...f6

Clearly Black did not wish to self-pin after 13...♘f6, but now the g2-pawn has an excellent target to bite on.

14.♗e3 ♘c5 15.g4 ♗e6 16.♔b1 b4

It was worth considering the manoeuvre 16...♕d7 17.♖hg1 ♕f7, also trying to force a weakness in the opposing king's pawn cover.

17.g5

The tension of the opposing pawn storms reaches its apex...

17...b3?

It is remarkable, but this natural move, apparently so in accordance with the usual principles of attack in opposite-side castling positions, proves to be a serious mistake. Numerous commentators have suggested here the variation 17...a3 18.b3 ♗xf5 19.exf5 e4, trying to get the knight to c3. The subtility of this idea consists in the immediate involvement of the black rook in the attack via the fifth rank: 20.dxe4 ♘xe4 21.♕c4+ ♔h8 22.♗d4 ♖a5! 23.gxf6 gxf6 with mutual chances.

18.♖hg1!
A surprisingly calm reply! Unexpectedly, it becomes apparent that it is hard for Black to make more progress on the queenside, whereas the white attack is just beginning to get up steam!
18...bxa2+ 19.♔a1 ♗xf5
Defending along the g-file with 19...g6 does not succeed: 20.gxf6 ♕xf6 21.d4! ♘xe4 22.♘h6+ ♔h8 23.dxe5 ♕g7 24.♗d4! (the sharpness of the battle is shown by the variation 24.exd6? a3 25.♗d4? axb2+ 26.♗xb2 ♕xb2+!! 27.♔xb2 a1♕+ 28.♖xa1 ♖eb8+ 29.♔c1 ♖xa1#!) 24...♗e7 25.♕xe4 ♕xh6 26.♕xc6, with a decisive advantage to White.
20.exf5 a3

On 20...♔h8 there follows 21.♘h4 followed by ♕h5.
21.b3 ♘a6

22.c3!?
The computer prefers the variation 22.d4 e4 (or 22...exd4 23.gxf6 ♕xf6 24.♕c4+ ♕f7 25.♖xg7+! ♔xg7 26.♖g1+ ♔f8 27.♗h6+ ♔e7 28.♖e1+, winning) 23.♕c4+ ♔h8 24.gxf6 ♕xf6 25.♘g5 ♖f8 26.♘e6 with a powerful attack for White.
The line chosen by Caruana is much more human – first White restricts his opponent's counterplay as much as possible.
22...♗f8
In reply to 22...♘c5 White had prepared 23.♗xc5 ♗xc5 24.d4! exd4 25.♕c4+ ♕d5 26.gxf6 with a winning position.
23.♘d2 fxg5 24.♖xg5 ♘c5

25.♖g3!

An excellent move, finally rendering the opponent helpless. Caruana's play in this game shows a subtle combination of attacking and prophylactic moves.

25...e4

No explanation is needed of the variations 25...♘xd3 26.♘e4 or 25...♕xd3 26.♕xd3 ♘xd3 27.♘e4 ♘b2 (27...♘f4 28.♘f6+) 28.♖dg1 ♔h8 29.f6 g6 30.♖h3, winning for White.

26.♗xc5 ♗xc5

26...exd3 fails to 27.♕g4.

27.♘xe4 ♗d6 28.♖h3 ♗e5 29.d4 ♗f6 30.♖g1

All of White's forces are included in the attack. There followed:

30...♖b8 31.♔xa2 ♗h4 32.♖g4 ♕d5 33.c4 1-0

Game 40 Sicilian Defence B31
Fabiano Caruana 2804
Teimour Radjabov 2726
Shamkir 2016 (5)

1.e4 c5 2.♘f3 ♘c6 3.♗b5

The Rossolimo Variation, a positional reply to the Sicilian Defence which leads, as a rule, to a manoeuvring battle.

3...g6

4.♗xc6

This 'unforced' exchange on c6 was worked out in his day by the late Moldavian trainer Viacheslav Chebanenko and clearly reveals White's strategic idea – the spoiled black pawn structure will inhibit the action of the second player's bishops. Therefore, it is important for White to give the game a closed character.

4...dxc6 5.d3 ♗g7 6.h3 ♘f6 7.♘c3 0-0 8.♗f4!?

Rather more common is 8.♗e3 b6 9.♕d2 e5 10.♗h6 ♕d6 with a complicated battle.

With the text, White refrains from gaining a tempo by attacking the c5-pawn; he aims instead to take control of the key square e5.

8...b6?!

An illogical continuation – he should fight for the centre! Possible, for example, is 8...♘h5 9.♗e3 ♕d6 10.♕d2 e5 11.g4 ♕f6 12.0-0-0 ♕xf3 13.gxh5 ♕xh5 14.♗xc5 ♖e8 15.♗e3 b5 with mutual chances, Artemiev-Khalifman, Kaliningrad 2015.

9.♕d2 ♖e8 10.0-0-0 a5

11.♘e5!

In positions with opposite-side castling, a great role is played not just by the speed of the pawn storms, but also by the control of key central squares!

11...b5 12.♕e3!

With his last two moves, Caruana has fought a subtle strategic battle, restricting Black's possibilities to the maximum extent.

The greedy 12.♘xc6 ♕b6 13.♘e5 a4 only hands the initiative to Black. Nor does the immediate 12.♗h6 work because of 12...♘xe4.

12...♕b6

The opposition of the queens results in a pin on the c5-pawn, which, as we will see, later proves significant.

13.♗h6 ♗h8 14.f4 a4 15.♖hf1

White has everything ready for the advance f4-f5.

15...e6

Trying to prevent the f4-pawn advancing, but weakening the square f6 and limiting the activity of the ♗c8.

Grandmaster Konstantin Landa recommended slowing up the white attack by 15...♘d7 16.♘xd7 ♗xd7 17.e5 f5! with a complicated battle. However, to my mind, the final position of this variation looks bad for Black. The ♗h8 is shut out of the game and without it, the queenside counterplay will be impossible to create. Meanwhile, White will gradually prepare an attack on the black king. Such a direct development of events is possible, for example: 18.h4 ♗e6 19.h5!? b4 20.hxg6 hxg6 (or 20...bxc3 21.gxh7+ ♔f7 22.bxc3) 21.♕g3 ♔f7 22.♘e4!! fxe4 23.f5 gxf5 24.dxe4 with a crush.

16.g4 a3

Equally, after 16...b4 17.♘b1! ♗a6 18.♘d2 ♗b5 19.♘dc4 Black's counterplay grinds to a halt before it has even started.

17.b4!

A beautiful resource! Now White takes complete control of the position.

17...♘d7 18.♘xd7 ♗xd7 19.e5

Burying the ♗h8.

19...f5 20.♘e2!

Caruana never has under-employed pieces! The knight heads to the kingside.

20...♗g7 21.♗xg7 ♔xg7

22.h4! fxg4 23.h5!

The black king is completely defenceless. White's breakthrough is simple and effective.

23...gxh5 24.♘g3 ♔h8 25.♘xh5 ♖e7 26.♘f6 ♗e8 27.f5! exf5 28.♖xf5 ♕c7 29.♖g5 ♖g7 30.♖h1 ♗g6 31.♖xg4 ♕f7 32.♔b1 cxb4 33.♕d4!

X-raying the black king.

33...♗f5

34.e6!

An elegant concluding combination!

34...♖xg4

Or 34...♗xe6 35.♖xh7+ ♖xh7 36.♘xh7+ ♔xh7 37.♕e4+ ♔h8 (37...♗f5 38.♕h1+) 38.♕e5+ ♔h7 39.♕h2+ with mate.

35.exf7 ♖xd4 36.♘e8!

Black resigned.

Game 41 French Defence C10

Fabiano Caruana 2817
Georg Meier 2621

Baden-Baden 2017 (3)

1.e4 e6 2.d4 d5 3.♘c3 dxe4 4.♘xe4 ♘d7 5.♘f3 ♘gf6 6.♘xf6+ ♘xf6 7.♗e3

This position had already been seen in the game between the same two players at Baden-Baden 2013 (Game 29). Then Black chose the forcing continuation 7...♘d5 8.♗d2 c5 9.♗b5+ ♗d7 10.♗xd7+ ♕xd7 11.c4 ♘b6, but did not completely solve his opening problems.

This time the German GM prefers gradual development.

7...♗d6 8.♗d3 0-0 9.♕e2 b6 10.0-0-0

The plan with queenside castling is the most principled response to the system of defence chosen by Black.

10...♗b7 11.♔b1

A subtle move. The direct continuations 11.c4 c5 12.dxc5 bxc5 13.♘g5 h6 14.♘h7 ♘xh7 15.♗xh7+ ♔xh7 16.♕d3+ ♔g8 17.♕xd6 ♕a5 (Anand-Meier, Baden-Baden 2013) or 11.♗g5 h6 12.♗h4 ♗e7 13.♔b1 ♘d5 14.♗g3 ♘b4 15.♗c4 ♗d5 (Ivanchuk-Pelletier, Cap d'Agde 2014) do not bring White any special benefits.

11...c5

In the game Ivanchuk-Drozdovski, Odessa 2006, Black played 11...♘d5 12.♗g5 ♗e7 13.h4 h6 14.♗c1! ♕d6 15.♘e5 ♘b4 16.♗c4 ♗d5 17.♗xd5 ♘xd5 18.g4, with advantage to White.

12.♗g5

Black has managed to solve the problem of the bad French bishop and has achieved the freeing advance ...c7-c5. But it is still too early to speak of complete equality, because the opponent's pieces occupy more aggressive squares.

12...h6 13.♗h4 ♖c8 14.c3 ♗e7

Escaping the unpleasant pin on the h4-d8 diagonal. Now after 15.dxc5 Black can go for a positional queen sacrifice: 15...♘d5 16.♗g3 ♖xc5 17.c4

♘b4 18.♗h7+ ♔xh7 19.♖xd8 ♖xd8 with sufficient compensation.

15.♗g3

This quiet bishop retreat reduces the effectiveness of the jump ♘d5 and takes convenient squares from the black queen. It is precisely concern about the future of his strongest piece that explains Black's next pawn exchange.

15...cxd4 16.♘xd4 ♖c5 17.♖he1 ♕c8 18.♗e5

Freeing the path of the g2-pawn.

18...♘d7 19.♗f4 ♘f6 20.h4 ♖d8

In positions with opposite-side castling, the usual plan is to launch a pawn storm against the enemy king as quickly as possible. However, with an open centre, this is not so simple. For example, the impatient 21.g4 fails to the unpleasant rejoinder 21...♘d5.

21.♗e5!

Caruana consistently carries out his favourite plan of centralisation. Only after he has established secure control of the middle of the board does he go over to a direct pawn storm against the black king. Now 21...♘d5 is refuted by 22.♘b3 ♖c6 23.♗b5, winning the exchange.

21...h5

Black could have driven the bishop from its dominating position by 21...♘d7, retaining approximate equality.

Evidently the German GM was afraid of the sacrifice 22.♗xg7!?. In the quiet of one's study one can establish that after 22...♔xg7 23.♕g4+ ♔f8! (23...♔h8? 24.♕f4 ♔g7 25.♖xe6!) 24.♘xe6+ (24.♖xe6? ♘f6; 24.♕f4 ♗f6) 24...fxe6 25.♕xe6 ♘e5! 26.♕xh6+ ♔f7 White has nothing more than perpetual check.

The text slows down the advance g2-g4, but weakens the position of Black's own king.

22.f3 ♗d6?!

Black starts to panic. Here too the retreat 22...♘d7 made sense. In this case, White can maintain the initiative by means of 23.♗f4 ♘f6 24.♗g5.

23.♗xf6 gxf6 24.♕e3 ♔g7 25.f4 ♖g8

26.♗c2!

The transfer of the bishop to b3 allows White to attack the Achilles'

Heel of the black position, the pawn on e6. It is interesting that in this game, White does not even start the traditional pawn storm, conducting his attack on the black king entirely with pieces!

26...♗b8 27.♗b3 f5?

The decisive mistake. All was still not lost after 27...e5! 28.fxe5 ♖xe5.

28.♘xe6+!

A blow in the very heart of the black position.

28...fxe6 29.♕d4+ ♔h7 30.♖xe6

Dominance of the centre allows White to follow up his piece sacrifice with quiet moves.

30...♗e4+ 31.♔a1 ♖g7

After 31...♖c7 possible is 32.♖xe4! (32.♕d6 ♕f8) 32...fxe4 33.♕xe4+ ♖g6 34.♖d6 ♖cg7 35.♖xg6 ♖xg6 36.♗f7 ♕g4 37.♗xg6+ ♕xg6 38.♕b7+, and White wins.

32.♕f6 ♗xf4 33.♖d8

The breakthrough by the major pieces to the 8th rank spells the end for the black king.

33...♕a6 34.♖ee8 ♕f1+ 35.♗d1

Black resigned.

USA $12.99 EUROPE €11.99   UK £8.99   2014#7   WWW.NEWINCHESS.COM

NEW IN CHESS

Italian writes history in St. Louis

Fabiano Caruana's Fabulous Streak

Carlsen-Anand
Sergey Shipov's preview

SOCAR sweeps European Club Cup

Hou Yifan wins Women's Grand Prix

And much more

ISBN 978-90-5691-504-9

CHAPTER 6

Centralisation as a weapon

The theme of centralisation is one of the main weapons in Caruana's armoury. It is reflected in our hero's opening preferences, which involve mainly classical schemes.

In Game 42 a sharp battle to centralise all the pieces is turned into a direct attack on the king.

In Game 43 both players appear to devote the same attention to centralisation. But when play opens up in the centre, it suddenly transpires that Caruana's pieces are more harmoniously placed.

Games 44 and 45 give us examples of effective piece operations against the enemy centre.

The popular topic of a knight outpost in the centre is shown in Games 46 and 47.

Game 48 demonstrates the strength of a mobile pawn centre, for which White sacrifices a gambit pawn on c4.

Even one piece established in the centre can exert a decisive effect on the course of the game. In Game 49 the white queen secures the post e4 and, without leaving the square, directs operations over the whole board!

Game 42 Ruy Lopez C99

Fabiano Caruana 2646
Mikhail Klenburg 2426

Budva tt 2009 (1)

1.e4 e5 2.♘f3 ♘c6 3.♗b5 a6 4.♗a4 ♘f6 5.0-0 ♗e7 6.♖e1 b5 7.♗b3 d6 8.c3 0-0 9.h3 ♘a5 10.♗c2 c5 11.d4 ♕c7

This system of development, suggested by Chigorin, retains popularity to this day.

12.♘bd2 cxd4

In the middle of the 20th century, Black often played Rubinstein's manoeuvre 12...♘c6 13.d5 ♘d8 followed by ...♘e8, ...g7-g6, ...♘g7, ...f7-f6 and ...♘f7, setting up a solid defensive line on the kingside. Nowadays, preference is given to the pawn exchange in the centre, which leads to more lively play.

13.cxd4 ♘c6 14.♘b3

Now 14.d5 is premature, because after 14...♘b4 15.♗b1 a5 16.♘f1 ♘a6 Black transfers the knight to c5 and achieves a comfortable position.

129

14...a5 15.♗e3 a4 16.♘bd2 ♗d7 17.♖c1 ♖ac8

Preparing the retreat of the queen to b8, from where she can control the squares b5 and e5.

More often seen is 17...♕b7, immediately opening the ♗e7's path to b6 and not yet determining the position of the rook.

18.a3

A typical Caruana choice. Most players would play the standard Spanish manoeuvre ♘d2-f1-g3 here, concentrating forces on the kingside. Fabiano, however, prefers to play in the centre – ♗d3 and ♕e2, striving to create pressure over the whole board.

18...♕b8 19.♕e2 ♖c7

It was worth considering 19...♘a5 20.♗d3 ♖fe8, strengthening b5 and e5.

20.♗d3 ♖fc8

21.♕f1!

This modest queen retreat defends the ♖c1 and creates a threat against the b5-pawn (the immediate 21.♗xb5? fails to 21...♘xd4!).

It is difficult for Black to maintain the tension any longer and he clears the centre.

21...exd4

He could have forced the exchange of all the rooks by 21...♘xd4 22.♘xd4 (22.♖xc7? ♘xf3+!) 22...♖xc1 23.♖xc1 ♖xc1 24.♕xc1 exd4 25.♗xd4 ♕b7, but even in this case, White's chances are preferable, thanks to his more aggressively placed pieces.

22.♘xd4 ♘xd4 23.♖xc7 ♖xc7?!

The positioning of the major pieces on the b8-h2 diagonal proves vulnerable. Better was 23...♕xc7 24.♗xd4 ♕b7, aiming for a more harmonious piece set-up.

24.♗xd4 ♗c6

25.e5!

The ideal moment to open the centre!

25...♘d7 26.e6!?

The continuation 26.exd6 ♗xd6 27.♕e2 ensures White the initiative in a symmetrical position, thanks to his more aggressively-placed pieces. With the text, Caruana aims for more.

26...fxe6 27.♖xe6 ♘c5!

Forcing the exchange of one of the white bishops, and getting rid of the weakness on d6.

28.♗xc5 dxc5 29.♕e2

Again Caruana prefers centralisation! The alternative is 29.♕b1 h6, forcing a weakening of the black king position.

29...♕d8 30.♘f3

In this open position, despite the opponent's two bishops, White has the advantage, because the defences of the black king are seriously weakened by the absence of the f7-pawn.

30...c4

31.♗c2

As Mihail Marin pointed out, rather more dangerous for Black was the move 31.♗f5!, when the white bishop is ready to develop activity, not only on the diagonal b1-h7, but also via the square e6. By way of an illustration of the possibilities, the Romanian GM gives the following variations:

A) 31...♗d7?? 32.♖xe7 ♗xf5 33.♖e8+;

B) 31...♗d5 32.♘g5! h6 33.♖e5 ♔h8 34.♘e6 ♗xe6 35.♖xe6 with a strong attack, which is strengthened further by the presence of opposite-coloured bishops;

C) 31...♗f8 32.♘e5 ♗b7? 33.♕h5 g6 34.♖xg6+! hxg6 35.♗e6+! with mate;

D) 31...♗f6 32.♘e5 ♕d5 33.♕g4 ♗xe5 34.♖e8+ ♗xe8 35.♗e6+, achieving a material advantage.

31...♗f8

After 31...♗f6 White develops the initiative by means of 32.♘e5 ♗xe5 (32...♗d5 33.♗xh7+) 33.♕xe5 with advantage.

32.♘e5 ♗d5?

The decisive mistake.

Also unsatisfactory was 32...♕d5 in view of 33.♘xc6 ♖xc6 34.♖e5. As Marin pointed out, it was possible to defend with 32...♗b7!, and it is not obvious how White can carry his attack to a victorious conclusion. Thus, after 33.♕h5 g6 the sacrifice of the white rook or any of his minor pieces on g6 leads only to perpetual check – 34.♖xg6+ hxg6 35.♕xg6+ ♖g7 36.♕e6+ ♔h8 37.♕h6+ etc.

33.♗xh7+!

The decisive combinational blow!

33...♔xh7 34.♕h5+ ♔g8 35.♖e8

With the bishop on b7 instead of d5, Black would have the move 35...♕d5!. Now, however, he suffers decisive material losses.

35...♕e7

After 35...♕f6 (or 35...♕d6) White decides things with 36.♘g6!.

36.♖xe7 ♖xe7 37.♘g6 ♖e1+ 38.♔h2 ♗d6+ 39.f4 ♗e4 40.♕h8+ ♔f7 41.♘e5+ ♗xe5 42.fxe5 ♗d5 43.e6+ ♗xe6 44.♕h5+ ♔f8 45.♕c5+ ♔g8 46.♕xb5 1-0

Game 43 Ruy Lopez C88

| **Fabiano Caruana** | 2773 |
| **Vladimir Georgiev** | 2586 |

Istanbul ol 2012 (7)

1.e4 e5 2.♘f3 ♘c6 3.♗b5 a6 4.♗a4 ♘f6 5.0-0 b5 6.♗b3 ♗b7

The introduction to the sharp Arkhangelsk Variation, the main lines of which are 7.♖e1 ♗c5 8.c3 d6 9.d4 ♗b6 or 7.c3 ♘xe4 8.d4 ♘a5 9.♗c2 exd4 etc.

7.d3

A quiet continuation, the main idea of which is to limit the activity of the ♗b7.

7...♗e7

Developing the bishop on the more aggressive Arkhangel square with 7...♗c5 has the drawback that Black may later feel its absence from the d8-h4 diagonal.

A typical illustration was the miniature Carlsen-Beliavsky (Wijk aan Zee 2006): 8.♘c3 d6 9.a4 ♘a5 10.♗a2 b4 11.♘e2 ♗c8 12.c3 bxc3 13.bxc3 ♗b6 14.♘g3 ♗e6 (14...h6!?) 15.d4 ♗xa2 16.♖xa2 0-0 17.♗g5 exd4 (the attempt to escape the pin with 17...h6 18.♗h4 g5? leads to catastrophe after 19.♘xg5!) 18.♘h5 dxc3 19.♘h4 ♔h8 20.♘f5, and Black resigned.

8.a4 0-0 9.♖e1 d6

Play has transposed into one of the lines of the Anti-Marshall, usually arising from the move order 5...♗e7 (instead of 5...b5) 6.♖e1 b5 7.♗b3 0-0 8.a4 ♗b7 9.d3.

10.♘bd2

There was a time when 10.♘c3 was regarded as the main line, aiming to provoke the move ...b5-b4, weakening the square c4. But practice showed that here Black retains full-fledged play: 10...♘a5 11.♗a2 b4 12.♘e2 c5 13.♘g3 ♗c8!, and the transfer of the bishop to e6 consolidates the position.

The continuation 10.♘bd2 came into fashion after the Kasparov-Short World Championship match in 1993. The white knight heads for its usual Spanish route via f1 to e3 – closer to c4! But in this case, of course, Black is not obliged to hurry with the advance ...b5-b4.

10...♘a5

In Game 7 of the Kasparov-Short match, Black played 10...♘d7 11.c3 ♘c5 12.axb5 axb5 13.♖xa8 ♗xa8 14.♗c2 ♗f6 15.b4 ♘e6 16.♘f1, and White's chances were somewhat preferable.

11.♗a2 c5 12.♘f1

12...b4

Black plays ...b5-b4 anyway, striving, as we will see, to shut out the Spanish bishop with ...b4-b3. In the game Kasparov-Leko, Linares 2001, Black played the advance ...c5-c4 with a similar idea: 12...♖e8 13.♘e3 h6 14.♗d2 c4. However, with the lovely manoeuvre 15.♗c3! ♕b6 16.♘d2! the 13th World Champion managed to dig the ♗a2 out of the mothballs.

The latest fashion in this variation is 12...bxa4, a favourite of GM Tomashevsky. In the game Caruana-Tomashevsky, Baku 2014, there followed: 13.♘e3 ♗c6 14.♘h4 ♗d7 15.♘hf5 ♖b8 16.♕f3 ♔h8 17.♕g3 ♘h5 18.♕g4 g6 19.♕f3 ♘c6 20.c3 ♘f4 21.♘xe7 ♕xe7 22.♘d5 ♘xd5 23.♗xd5 f6, and Black successfully solved his opening problems.

13.♘e3

White's strategy is crystal-clear – occupation of the light squares in the centre.

13...b3?!

This standard pawn sacrifice with the knight on e3 (but not g3) proves inadequate for equality here.

More solid was 13...♗c8 14.♘d2 ♖b8 15.♗c4 ♘xc4 16.dxc4 ♗e6 17.b3 ♖b7 18.♖f1 ♘d7 19.♕e2 ♘b8 20.♘d5 ♘c6 21.♗b2 ♗g5 22.♖ad1, and the white position is only slightly better, Svidler-Adams, Moscow 2001.

14.♗xb3!

Surprisingly, before this game White had only played 14.cxb3, keeping the ♗a2 from exchange. But after 14.cxb3 ♘c6 15.b4 ♘xb4 16.♗c4 ♗c8 Black does not have serious problems.

Caruana does not hang onto the two bishops – in a closed position, his knight acquires the great square c4!

14...♘xb3 15.cxb3 ♗c8 16.♘c4 ♖b8 17.♗d2 ♗e6 18.h3 ♕c8?!

More solid was 18...♕d7 19.♖c1 ♖fc8 (a recommendation of GM Sergei Erenburg), getting the king's rook into play as quickly as possible.

19.♖c1 ♕b7

Undoubtedly, the Bulgarian GM had counted on the closed nature of the position to reduce White's doubled and blockaded extra pawn to little significance. However...

20.b4!

This flank break takes the shackles off the centre! Suddenly the position opens up and it turns out that the white pieces are rather more actively placed than their opposite numbers.

20...cxb4?!

As Erenburg pointed out, more tenacious was 20...♘d7 21.♘a5 ♕a8 22.bxc5 ♘xc5 23.♗e3 ♖fc8, trying to keep the centre closed and retaining the possibility of counterplay along the b-file.

21.♘a5 ♕d7 22.d4!

Black's central barricades collapse like a house of cards and material losses are already unavoidable!

22...exd4 23.♘c6 ♖bc8 24.♘fxd4 d5?

Accelerating the inevitable end.

25.♗g5!

Tying the enemy pieces in the centre in knots!

25...h6

Black faces large material losses in any event – 25...dxe4 26.♘f5! ♗xf5 27.♕xd7 or 25...♗d8 26.e5.

26.exd5 ♘xd5 27.♗xe7

And Black resigned, since after 27...♘xe7 White wins with 28.♘xe6.

Game 44 Ruy Lopez C78
Victor Bologan 2692
Fabiano Caruana 2652
Reggio Emilia 2009 (1)

1.e4 e5 2.♘f3 ♘c6 3.♗b5 a6 4.♗a4 ♘f6 5.0-0 b5 6.♗b3 ♗c5

This old move is based nowadays on a strategic conception worked out by GM Leonid Yurtaev and is known as the 'New Arkhangel'. Its subtlety lies in the fact that after 7.c3 d6 8.d4 Black is not obliged to give up the centre, thanks to the variation 8...♗b6 9.dxe5 ♘xe5 10.♘xe5 dxe5 11.♕xd8+ ♔xd8 12.♗xf7 ♖f8 13.♗d5 ♘xd5 14.exd5 ♗b7, solving all his problems. Another important point is that after 7.♘xe5 ♘xe5 8.d4 ♗xd4 9.♕xd4 d6 Black obtains good dynamic compensation for his opponent's two bishops, thanks to the threat of ...c7-c5.

And finally, Black gets his bishop to an active square on c5 and strengthens the e5-square, without yet committing his queen's bishop!

7.a4 ♖b8

It is obvious that after 7...♗b7 there will follow 8.d3!, shutting the ♗b7 out of the game.

8.c3 d6 9.d4 ♗b6

10.a5!?

An interesting continuation, introduced into practice by GM Sergei Dolmatov. White seizes space on the queenside and drives the bishop to a7, where, as we will see, it is not entirely safe. The minus of this operation is that pressure is removed from b5, whilst the a5-pawn itself can prove vulnerable.

10...♗a7

In the stem game Dolmatov-Sikhovo, St Petersburg 2000, there occurred 10...♘xa5 11.♖xa5! ♗xa5 12.dxe5 ♘g4 13.♗g5 f6 14.exf6 gxf6 15.♗h4 with a serious initiative to White, for the sacrificed exchange.

11.h3 0-0 12.♗e3

Now, on account of the threat 13.dxe5 ♗xe3 14.exf6, Black must lose a tempo.

12...♖a8

13.♖e1

This position subsequently occurred several times in Fabiano's practice. Thus, in the game Karjakin-Caruana, Russia tt 2013, there followed 13.♘bd2 h6 14.♖e1 ♖e8 15.♘f1!? (or 15.dxe5 ♘xe5 16.♘xe5 dxe5 17.♘f1 ♕e7 18.♕f3 ♗d7 19.♗xa7 ♖xa7 20.♘e3 ♖aa8 21.♖ad1 ♖ad8 22.♘d5 ♘xd5 23.♗xd5 ♗e6 with equality, Kobalia-Caruana, Plovdiv 2012) 15...exd4 16.cxd4 ♖xe4 17.♘g3 ♖e7 18.♕d2 ♕f8 19.♖ec1 ♗d7 20.♘h4 d5 21.♘hf5 ♖e6 22.♖c2 ♖ae8 23.♖ac1 ♕b4!, and

Black successfully neutralised his opponent's initiative.

13...♗b7 14.♘bd2 exd4

Black decides to give up his pawn centre, so as then to organise piece pressure against it.

The alternative is 14...♖e8 15.♘g5 ♖e7 (Anand-Shirov, Wijk aan Zee 2010), maintaining the tension.

15.cxd4 ♘b4 16.♗g5 h6 17.♗h4 ♘d3 18.♖e3 ♘f4

Black is ready to escape from the unpleasant pin by means of 18...♘g6, and also to counterattack in the centre with ...c7-c5. Therefore White decides to break the Gordian Knot with an immediate break in the centre.

19.e5

In the game Navara-Ragger, Rijeka 2010, White tried 19.♖c1 c5! 20.e5 dxe5 21.dxc5?! (better is 21.dxe5 ♘g6 22.exf6 ♘xh4 with counterplay for Black) 21...♖c8 22.♘xe5 ♖xc5, and Black took over the initiative.

19...dxe5 20.dxe5 ♗xe3 21.fxe3 ♘g6 22.exf6 ♘xh4 23.♘xh4 ♕xf6

Beginning with the 19th move, events have developed forcingly. However, the following tempting white move proves to be inaccurate.

24.♘hf3?!

Handing the initiative to his opponent. The aggressive move 24.♕h5! leads to a whole mass of lovely and... drawn variations: 24...♕xb2 25.♖f1! ♕xd2 26.♖xf7 ♖xf7 (or 26...♕xe3+ 27.♔h2 ♕xb3 28.♖xg7+! ♔xg7 29.♕g6+ with perpetual check) 27.♕xf7+ ♔h8 28.♕f8+! (a draw also results from the more prosaic 28.♕f5! ♕e1+ (or 28...♕xe3+ 29.♔h2 ♕xb3 30.♘g6+ ♔g8 31.♘e7+ ♔h8 32.♘g6+ with perpetual check) 29.♔h2 ♕xh4 30.♗c2 ♔g8 31.♗b3+ ♔h8 32.♗c2 with a repetition of moves) 28...♖xf8 29.♘g6+ ♔h7 30.♘xf8+ ♔h8 31.♘g6+, and White again gives perpetual in a very striking way!

24...c5!

After 24...♕xb2 25.♖c1 ♖ac8 26.♖c5 the c7-pawn is blockaded.

Now the combinative fire has died down and we can assess the position. White has a microscopic material advantage. In addition, two minor pieces as a rule are stronger than a rook and pawn in the middlegame. However, in the present case, Black has some significant strategic plusses – a mobile pawn majority on the queenside, the prospect of bringing his rooks to the open files in the centre, a powerful ♗b7 and an active queen on the a1-h8 diagonal, all of which makes his chances preferable in the coming battle.

25.♕c2 c4 26.♗a2 ♖ad8 27.♖e1 ♖fe8

28.e4?!

The task of consolidating the position was better suited by 28.♗b1 ♖d3 29.b3!, which allows White to maintain approximate dynamic equality.

28...♖d3! 29.b3 ♖ed8! 30.♘f1

If 30.bxc4 Black develops an initiative by means of 30...♖c3! (nothing is given by 30...♖xd2 31.♘xd2 ♕d4+ 32.♔f1 ♕xd2 33.♕xd2 ♖xd2 34.♖e2=), for example: 31.♕b2 (31.♕b1? ♖xd2

32.♘xd2 ♕d4+) 31...♖xf3 32.e5 ♕g5 33.♘xf3 ♗xf3 34.♕f2 ♗xg2 35.♕xg2 ♕xg2+ 36.♔xg2 ♖d2+ 37.♔f3 ♖xa2 with a winning rook endgame; or 31.♕d1 b4! (no special benefit comes from 31...♖xf3 32.♕xf3 ♖xd2 33.♕xf6 gxf6 34.♗b3 b4 35.c5 f5 36.♗d5=), retaining unpleasant pressure.

30...♖c3! 31.♕b1 ♖dd3!

The black rooks break into the enemy position with surprising energy.

32.bxc4

32...♖xf3! 33.gxf3 ♖xf3

By sacrificing a piece, Black completely opens up the enemy king, which allows him to carry out his offensive practically without any risk.

34.♖e2 ♖xh3

Continuing to eat his way through to the exposed white king.

It was also worth considering 34...b4, giving the opponent problems on the queenside as well. The forcing variation winning the queen is less clear: 34...♕d4+ 35.♔g2 ♖f2+ 36.♖xf2 ♗xe4+ 37.♕xe4 ♕xe4+ 38.♖f3, and White should hold.

But another forcing line seems to be strongest of all: 34...♕g5+! 35.♖g2 ♕c5+ 36.♔h2 ♗c8! 37.♘g3 ♗xh3! 38.♖g1 (38.♔xh3 ♕h5#) 38...♗g4, and Black's attack is hardly capable of being beaten off.

35.♕e1 bxc4

The continuation 35...♕f3 36.♖h2 ♗xe4 37.♕e2 ♖g3+ 38.♘xg3 ♕xg3+ 39.♖g2 ♗xg2 40.♕xg2 ♕e1+ 41.♔h2 ♕xa5 42.cxb5 does not offer Black significant winning chances.

36.♗b1?

The final part of the game is unfortunately spoilt by time-trouble mistakes. White could quietly take the pawn by 36.♗xc4, since on 36...♕d4+ there is the reply 37.♔g2, which allows him to save himself.

36...c3 37.♖e3 ♕g5+

38.♘g3?

Losing at once. He could still battle on with 38.♖g3 ♕c5+ 39.♘e3 ♖h5 etc.

38...h5 39.♔g2 ♕g4 40.♖xc3 h4 41.♖b3 hxg3 0-1

Game 45 Ruy Lopez C78
Sergey Karjakin 2778
Fabiano Caruana 2773
Bilbao 2012 (2)

1.e4 e5 2.♘f3 ♘c6 3.♗b5 a6 4.♗a4 ♘f6 5.0-0 b5 6.♗b3 ♗c5 7.c3 d6 8.d4 ♗b6 9.♗e3 0-0 10.♘bd2 ♗b7

11.♖e1

In several variations of this system, one must reckon with the unusual pawn structure which arises after 11.d5 ♘e7 12.♗xb6 cxb6. Black's set-up is considered to be solid, but he has less space and lacks the possibility of bringing his ♗b7 to life with the aid of the break ...c7-c6.

11...exd4

Caruana adopts the same strategy of piece pressure on the centre that we saw in Game 18. More often in such positions, Black supports the centre with 11...h6.

12.cxd4 ♘b4

13.♕e2

From Game 18 we already know that after the unpleasant pin 13.♗g5 Black reacts with 13...h6 14.♗h4 ♘d3 15.♖e3 ♘f4.

With the text, White covers the d3-square against the entry of the black knight. With an analogous idea, another possibility was 13.♕b1. After 13...c5 14.a3 ♘c6 15.d5 ♘e7 16.h3 ♘g6 17.♗c2 the queen is very flexible on b1, defending e4 and supporting a possible b2-b4 advance.

13...c5

The e4-pawn is poisoned – 13...♘xe4 14.♘xe4 ♗xe4 15.♗d2 ♗xf3 16.♕xf3 c5 17.♕g3, and White firmly seizes the initiative.

14.a3 ♘c6 15.d5 ♘e7

The black knight heads to g6, keeping an eye on the e5-square.

16.h3 ♖e8 17.♗c2 ♘g6

In the resulting 'Indian' type of position, Black has decent counterplay. He has established control of e5 and prepared to carry out the advance ...c5-c4. His only headache is the passive role of the ♗b7.

18.b3

Holding up the advance ...c5-c4.

18...♗a5!

Exploiting the minus of White's last move – the black bishop heads to the square c3!

19.♖ab1 ♗c3 20.♖ec1 b4 21.a4?!

A significant inaccuracy, which allows Black to strengthen his offensive set-up on the queenside. He should have played 21.axb4 ♗xb4 22.♗d3 with an interesting, double-edged battle.

21...a5 22.♗d3 h6

Limiting the scope of the enemy pieces. The outwardly unhurried impression from the move 22...h6 is emphasised by the difficulties which White experiences in finding any sort of constructive plan. Therefore, from a psychological point of view, the Russian GM's mistake on his next move is no coincidence.

23.♕d1? ♗a6!

Activating the sleeping bishop immediately gives Black a large positional advantage.

24.♗c2

After 24.♕f1 ♗xd3 25.♕xd3 ♖a7, followed by ...♖ae7, White inevitably loses the e4-pawn.

24...♖a7 25.♔h2 ♖ae7 26.g4

This 'active' move can no longer spoil anything, since the white forces are almost totally paralysed.

26...♘xe4!

This exchange sacrifice completely destroys the white centre.

A lovely alternative way to win was pointed out by GM Mikhail Golubev: 26...♗xd2!? 27.♘xd2 ♘xd5!! 28.exd5 ♖xe3! 29.fxe3 ♖xe3, and despite his extra rook, White is unable to ward off the threats against his king, e.g. 30.♘c4 ♗xc4 31.bxc4 ♕h4 32.♕f1 ♘e5 33.♕g2 ♘f3+ 34.♔h1 ♘d4, winning.

27.♘xe4 ♖xe4 28.♗xe4 ♖xe4 29.♕c2 ♕e7 30.♖g1

30...♖xe3!

Another exchange sacrifice breaks down the last barricades on the way to the white king.

31.fxe3 ♕xe3 32.♖bf1 ♗e2

But not 32...♗xf1 – the black bishops are on fire!

33.♕f5 ♗d3 34.♕d7 ♗e5+ 35.♔h1 ♗e4 36.♕e8+ ♘f8 0-1

Game 46 English Opening A34

Fabiano Caruana	2801
Hristos Banikas	2644

Tromsø ol 2014 (9)

1.c4 c5 2.♘f3 ♘f6 3.♘c3 ♘c6 4.g3 b6

A rare move order. With his bishop on b7, Black usually puts the queen's knight on the more modest square d7.

5.d4 cxd4 6.♘xd4 ♘xd4 7.♕xd4 ♗b7 8.e4 g6 9.♗g2 ♗g7 10.0-0 d6 11.♗g5

In the game H.Olafsson-Arnason, Nordik 1992, White prepared a queenside fianchetto by means of 11.♕d2 ♖b8 (meeting the threat of 12.e5) 12.♖e1 0-0 13.b3 a6 14.♗b2 ♘d7 15.♖ad1 ♗a8, but did not achieve anything much – the position is equal.

11...0-0?!

A significant inaccuracy, which allows White to place his pieces harmoniously and secure a comfortable opening advantage. Stronger was 11...h6!, forcing the opponent to spend time on a regrouping of his forces. The game Bareev-Leko, Ubeda 1997, continued as follows: 12.♗d2 0-0 13.♕d3 ♖b8 14.♖ad1 a6 15.♖fe1 ♘d7 16.b3 ♘c5 17.♕e3 b5! 18.cxb5 axb5 19.♘xb5 ♘xe4 20.♗xe4 ♗xe4 21.♕xe4 ♖xb5 22.♕xe7 ♕a8 with sufficient compensation for the sacrificed pawn.

12.♕d2

White's plan is clear – after the traditional moves ♖ad1, ♖fe1 and b2-b3, he gets a knight outpost on d5. The aggressive action of the ♗g5 plays its part in fulfilling this programme.

12...♘g4

The start of an artificial manoeuvre in the hope of changing the unfavourable course of the game. In the game Akopian-Sorokin, Novgorod 1999, Black played the more natural 12...♖c8 13.b3 ♘d7 14.♖ac1 ♘c5, but after 15.♘d5 f6 16.♗e3 e6 17.♘c3, it turned out that the pawn on d6 faced some hard times.

13.h3 h6 14.♗f4 e5 15.♗e3

Accepting the pawn sacrifice gives Black good counterplay: 15.hxg4 exf4 16.gxf4 ♖c8 17.b3 ♕h4 etc.

15...♘xe3 16.♕xe3

So what was the Greek GM counting on, when he accepted the clear d-file weakness?

On an optimistic view, Black could perhaps convince himself of the following:
• firstly, he manages to exchange off the opponent's important dark-squared bishops;
• secondly, the remaining white bishop is restricted by its own pawns;
• thirdly, the bad bishop on g7 can come into play via h6;
• fourthly, if the knight on d5 becomes too much to stand, Black can exchange off his light-squared bishop for it and take play into an opposite-coloured bishops structure;
• and fifthly, the only weakness on d6 can perfectly well be defended against frontal attack by the white pieces.

So how come so many defensive factors did not permit Black to hold the position? The later development of the game will provide the answer to this question, but the chief drawback of the black position is its passivity.

16...♗c8

The transfer of the bishop to e6 aims to neutralise the white colleague, which is heading for h3.

17.♖fd1 ♗e6 18.b3 ♕e7 19.♖d3 ♖fd8 20.♖ad1 h5 21.h4 ♔h7 22.♔h2 ♗h6 23.♕e2 ♖ac8

24.♗h3

Creating the necessary tension in the position. Understandably, White does not take on e6 (because of 24...fxe6), but it cannot be ruled out that he might do so at the right moment.

24...♖c6 25.♔g2 a6 26.♖f3

This move does not create concrete threats, but demonstrates the great manoeuverability of the white rooks compared with their opposite numbers.

26...♔g7 27.a4

Cutting off at the roots any counterplay with ...b6-b5.

27...♕b7 28.♖fd3 ♕c8 29.♖h1! ♔h7 30.♘d5 ♕b7

31.g4!

The decisive break! The space advantage in the centre permits White easily to switch the attack to the black king.

31...hxg4 32.♗xg4 ♗xd5

Going into an opposite-coloured bishops ending no longer helps Black, as the opponent's attack on the light squares develops of its own accord!

33.exd5 ♖c5 34.h5! g5

A desperate attempt to close lines for the white rooks.

35.♕e4+ ♔g8 36.♖f3 ♔g7 37.♗e6!

The decisive blow. The crushing entry of the white queen on g6 cannot be prevented.

Black resigned.

Game 47 English Opening A34

Veselin Topalov	2772
Fabiano Caruana	2801

St Louis 2014 (1)

1.♘f3 ♘f6 2.c4 c5 3.♘c3 ♘c6 4.g3 d5 5.cxd5

The alternative is the sharp 5.d4.

5...♘xd5 6.♗g2 ♘c7

The famous Rubinstein Variation, involving the creation (after ...e7-

e5) of a knight outpost on d4. In the
1930s, Botvinnik won a number of
games with this system.

7.0-0 e5

8.a3

White's main idea in such positions
is the preparation of a break against
the c5- and e5-pawns by means of
b2-b4 or f2-f4.

The main line in this variation is
considered to be 8.d3 ♗e7 9.♘d2
♗d7 10.♘c4 f6 11.f4 b5 12.♘e3 exf4
13.♖xf4 or 13.gxf4 with mutual
chances.

8...♖b8

An accurate move, reducing the
effectiveness of the break b2-b4,
which would follow after the
naïve 8...♗e7?! 9.b4! cxb4 10.axb4
♗xb4? 11.♘xe5! ♘xe5 12.♕a4+ ♘c6
13.♗xc6+ bxc6 14.♕xb4, and Black's
position falls apart. Now the point
of 8...♖b8 becomes apparent – at the
end of the above variation, the ♗b4
is defended!

9.d3

After 9.♖b1 a possibility is 9...♗e7
10.b4 cxb4 11.axb4 b5! (Svidler-
Karjakin, Stavanger 2014),
blockading the b4-pawn and in the
future turning it into a target. Here

too we see the usefulness of the
move 8...♖b8.

9...♗e7 10.♗e3 0-0 11.♖c1 ♗d7

Sooner or later Black will have to
play ...b7-b6, so the ♘c6 should be
defended.

12.♘d2

Returning to the plan with the
break f2-f4.

If 12.♘e4 b6 13.b4 cxb4 14.axb4
Black gets a solid position after
14...♘b5! (but not 14...♗xb4?!
because of 15.d4! with a dangerous
initiative for White).

12...♘d4 13.♘c4 f6 14.f4 exf4

If 14...b5 15.♘a5 the white knight
would be actively placed on the
edge of the board.

15.♗xf4

15...♘de6!

Another accurate move, driving
the white bishop from its active
position.

16.♗d2 b6

Black has managed to consolidate
and achieve a compact arrangement
of his forces. At the same time,
the white position contains some
elements of strategic risk, since
his pawn structure (three islands
against two) is worse.

17.g4!?

This move attracted the criticism of commentators, although they made no concrete alternative recommendations. For example, the manoeuvre 17.♘e3 ♘d4 18.♘ed5 suggests itself, but it leads only to an exchange of knights which is favourable to Black.

One peculiarity of the position is that it is not easy for White to find a way of strengthening his position further, whereas it is easy for Black to find constructive ideas. For example, it is worth considering the manoeuvre ...♗d7-e8-f7, strengthening his influence in the centre. This is a typical thing with Caruana, whose strategic ideas never seem to lead to a dead end. But let us return to the move 17.g4. At the cost of a weakening of the king's protection, White gets the idea of playing ♗g3, creating a strongpoint on f5 for the knight. By way of an alternative, I can suggest 17.♖b1!?, returning to the idea of breaking with b2-b4.

17...♗e8! 18.♗e1 b5!

A subtle reaction to the change in the situation. Now the jump 19.♘a5

is impossible, as after 19...♕d4+ the pawn on g4 is lost.

19.♘e3

19...♗d6!

A brilliant combination of activity and prophylaxis! The transfer of the white bishop to g3 is now prevented.

20.♘cd5?

A serious mistake, after which the white position deteriorates rapidly. Exchanges favour Black, because they emphasise the static weaknesses in the white pawn structure.

He should have strived for consolidation with 20.♘f5 ♗e5 21.e3 g6 22.♘g3 with a complicated battle.

20...♘xd5 21.♗xd5 ♗f7 22.♘f5 ♗e5 23.♕d2

23...♘d4!

Continuing his clear line of strategy. Gradually, the active white pieces disappear from the board, whilst the numerous pawn weaknesses remain!

24.♗xf7+ ♖xf7 25.♖d1

Meeting the threat of 25...♘b3.

25...♘xf5 26.gxf5 ♕d4+ 27.♗f2 ♕g4+ 28.♔h1

28...c4!

A timely break, increasing the sphere of influence of the black rooks.

29.♕c2

After 29.dxc4 bxc4 30.♗d4 ♖d7 31.e3 ♗xd4 32.exd4 ♖db7 the pawn on b2 is lost.

29...♖e8!

All the black pieces are involved in the attack against the pawn on e2.

30.dxc4

There is already no satisfactory defence. On 30.e4 there could follow 30...♖d7 31.dxc4 (or 31.d4 ♕f3+ 32.♔g1 ♗f4 33.♖fe1 ♖de7, and the white central pawns fall) 31...♖xd1 32.♖xd1 ♕h5 33.♗xa7 ♕f3+ 34.♔g1 ♗xh2+! 35.♔xh2 ♖xe4, winning.

30...♕h5!

The attack switches from the centre to the white king.

31.h4

After 31.♗g1 Black decides things with 31...♗xh2! 32.♗xh2 ♖xe2 33.♖d8+ ♖f8 34.♖xf8+ ♔xf8.

31...♕g4 32.♕d3 bxc4 33.♕e3 ♖fe7 34.b3 ♗b2!

An elegant final move. After 35.♕f3 ♕xf3+ 36.exf3 c3 the black pawn promotes.

White resigned.

Game 48 English Opening A29

Fabiano Caruana   2794

Viswanathan Anand   2762

Moscow ct 2016 (10)

1.c4 e5 2.♘c3 ♘f6 3.♘f3 ♘c6 4.g3 ♗b4 5.♗g2 0-0 6.0-0 e4

7.♘g5

An ambitious continuation. A quiet manoeuvring game results

from 7.♘e1 ♗xc3 8.dxc3 h6 9.♘c2, transferring the knight to the blockading square e3.

7...♗xc3 8.bxc3 ♖e8 9.f3

The idea of this break is to create a mobile white pawn centre.

9...exf3

In the first game of the Kasparov-Karpov match (Seville 1987) the pawn sacrifice 9...e3!? was introduced in practice. Kasparov's reaction – 10.d3 d5 11.♕b3! – is to this day still considered the main line.

10.♘xf3 d5

11.d4

Since the game Sigurjonsson-Smyslov, Reykjavik 1974, the continuation 11.cxd5 ♕xd5! 12.♘d4 ♕h5! has been regarded as better for Black.

The text was introduced with crushing success in the game Kasparov-Ivanchuk, Moscow 1988. White develops energetically, not paying any attention to the pawn hanging on c4.

It would be noted that the variation with 7.♘g5 owes its place in modern theory largely to the researches of the 13th World Champion.

11...dxc4

The source game Kasparov-Ivanchuk, Moscow 1988, developed in very instructive fashion: 11...♘e4 12.♕c2 dxc4 13.♖b1 f5 14.g4! ♕e7 15.gxf5 ♘d6 16.♘g5 ♕xe2 17.♗d5+ ♔h8 18.♕xe2 ♖xe2 19.♗f4 ♘d8 20.♗xd6 cxd6 21.♖be1 ♖xe1 22.♖xe1 ♗d7 23.♖e7 ♗c6

analysis diagram

24.f6!, and Black resigned! Anand had already tested his move 11...dxc4 in practice. The game Aronian-Anand, St Louis 2015, continued 12.♗g5 h6 13.♗xf6 ♕xf6 14.e4 (if 14.♘e5 ♕e6 15.♗xc6 bxc6 16.♖xf7 c5 Black has good counterplay) with the following options:

A) The author notes with pleasure that the position after 14.e4 was apparently seen for the first time in the game Kalinin-I.Kuzmin, Moscow 1991, where there followed 14...♕g6 15.♕a4 ♗d7 16.♕xc4 ♕xe4 17.♕xf7+! ♔xf7 18.♘g5+ ♔g8 19.♘xe4 b6 20.g4! ♘a5 21.g5, and White seized the initiative in the endgame;

B) 14...♗g4 15.♕a4 ♕d6 16.♖ae1 ♖ab8! 17.♕xc4 b5, and the flank

break against the centre ensures
Black sufficient counterplay.

12.♕c2!

A novelty, which shocked the
Indian GM. The idea belongs
to ex-FIDE World Champion
Rustam Kasimdzhanov, who was
Caruana's second at the Candidates'
tournament.

White does not rush to force
matters and quietly completes his
mobilisation.

In its strategic picture the position
reminds one of a variation of the
Catalan Opening, in which White
sacrifices the c4-pawn to create a
powerful pawn centre, supported by
the ♗g2.

12...h6

After 12...♘e4 Black transposes
to Kasparov-Ivanchuk. The
commentators unanimously
recommended 12...♕e7!?. The
objective assessment of this move is
a task for the future.

13.♗f4 ♘e4

Trying to slow up White's intended
advance of the central pawns.

14.♖ad1 ♗f5

After 14...f5 the Kasparovian 15.g4!
shatters the centre.

15.♘e5!

This programmed knight jump
easily overcomes the black
blockade. The central avalanche is
now unstoppable.

15...♘d6

In the variation 15...♘xg3 16.e4
♘xf1 17.exf5 White's advantage is
obvious.

16.e4 ♗h7 17.♕e2

Controlling the centre, White
begins an attack on the kingside.

17...♘e7

He cannot drive the knight from its
dominating position: 17...f6 18.♘xc6
bxc6 19.e5! ♗d3 20.♖xd3 cxd3
21.♕xd3 fxe5 22.dxe5 ♘f7 23.♕c4,
and Black is in trouble.

18.♗xh6!

Caruana conducts the attack
directly and elegantly. The

commentators, after having seen the consequences of a hidden defence for Black, all agree that the strongest continuation was a gradual build-up of threats with 18.♗c1!.

It should be added that 18.♘xc4 would be a distraction from the main aim and would allow 18...♘d5!.

18...gxh6 19.♕h5

19...♘ef5?

In trying to douse the flames of the attack, Anand immediately returns the piece and forces a transition into an endgame which is difficult for Black.

Hanging onto the material would be even worse: 19...♖f8 20.♕xh6 ♘xe4 21.♗xe4 ♗xe4 22.♖f4 ♕d6 23.♖f6 ♕a3 24.♖e1 ♗h7 (24...♕xa2 25.♖f2!) 25.♕g5+ ♘g6 26.♘xg6 ♗xg6 27.♖ee6!, and White wins. However, a hidden resource was uncovered: 19...♘d5!! 20.exd5 (20.♘xf7 ♘f6! 21.♘xh6+ ♔h8) 20...♕g5. Now going into the endgame with 21.♕xg5+ hxg5, with the white pawn on d5 rather than f5, is not dangerous for Black. After 21.♕f3 White retains the advantage in the middlegame, but

there would be a considerable fight ahead.

20.exf5 ♕g5 21.♕xg5+ hxg5

22.f6!

Putting a bone in the opponent's throat! Strategically, the game is already decided.

22...♘e4

A desperate attempt to break his bonds. With quiet play, White will carry out a decisive kingside attack without difficulty.

23.♖fe1!

Much more accurate than the immediate win of a pawn after 23.♗xe4 ♗xe4 24.♘xc4.

23...♘xc3

On 23...♘d6 there follows 24.♗d5, intending the variation 24...c6 25.♗xc4 ♖xe5 26.♗xf7+ ♘xf7 27.dxe5, winning.

24.♖c1 ♘b5 25.♗xb7 ♖ad8

Equally hopeless is 25...♖ab8 26.♗c6 ♖e6 27.d5! with the idea of 27...♖xf6 28.♘d7.

26.♗c6 ♘xd4 27.♗xe8 ♖xe8 28.♔f2

Black has not a shred of compensation for the exchange.

28...♘c2 29.♖ed1 ♗e4 30.♘xc4 ♖e6 31.♖d8+ ♔h7 32.♔g1 ♖xf6 33.♖f1

Black resigned.

Game 49 Ruy Lopez C81
Fabiano Caruana 2807
Anish Giri 2769
St Louis 2016 (7)

1.e4 e5 2.♘f3 ♘c6 3.♗b5 a6 4.♗a4 ♘f6 5.0-0 ♘xe4 6.d4 b5 7.♗b3 d5 8.d4xe5 ♗e6 9.♕e2
A continuation recommended by Keres, with the idea of establishing pressure along the d-file.
9...♘c5
The main lines are 9...♗e7 or 9...♗c5.
10.♖d1 ♘xb3
And here 10...♗e7 is more common. The text has not enjoyed a reliable reputation in recent times.

11.cxb3!?
Ever since the game Smyslov-Euwe, Moscow World Championship 1948, the main white trump here has been considered to be the gambit continuation 11.axb3 ♕c8 12.c4 dxc4 13.bxc4 ♗xc4 14.♕e4 etc.
But the game Yu Yangyi-Wei Yi, Taizhou 2015, ended in a quick repetition after 11...♗e7 12.c4 b4 13.cxd5 ♗xd5 14.♕d3 ♗e4 15.♕e2 ♗d5 16.♕d3 ♗e4.
Interestingly, back in 1950 there was a game Unzicker-Blau, in which White played 14.♖xa6 (instead

of 14.♕d3) 14...♖xa6 15.♕xa6 0-0 16.♕b5 ♗c4 17.♖xd8 ♗xb5 18.♖d5 ♖d8 19.♖xd8+ ♗xd8, with equality.
Overall, it seems that this old line is still at the development stage. Understanding that his opponent has not come to the game empty-handed, Caruana chooses a rare continuation.
The capture c2xb3, of course, deprives White of the resource c2-c4, but it opens pressure on the c-file and deprives the enemy knight of a post at b4, because of the reply a2-a3.
11...♗e7 12.♘c3 0-0 13.♗e3

13...♕d7
Anish Giri sticks to classical lines, posting his pieces in the centre. One of the few games in this line continued as follows: 13...♘a5 14.♖ac1 ♘b7 15.♘e4 ♗g4 16.h3 ♗xf3 17.♕xf3 c6 18.♘g3 ♖c8 19.♘f5 g6, and here there followed the knockout blow 20.♖xd5! in Ivkov-Donner, Havana 1965.
14.h3
After the immediate 14.♖d2 there could follow 14...b4 15.♘a4 (15.♘e4 ♗g4) 15...♗g4 16.h3 ♗xf3 17.♕xf3 ♖ad8 (less accurate is 17...♘xe5 18.♕xd5 ♕b5 19.♘c5 with pressure

149

for White) 18.♗f4 ♕e6 with good play for Black.

14...♖ad8?!

Surprisingly, this move proves to be a significant error, despite being logical from all points of view. Black gets good play after the immediate 14...f6! 15.exf6 ♖xf6, and if 16.♘e4, then 16...♖g6.

15.♖d2 f6

16.♖ad1!

A brilliant decision! Instead of the expected 16.exf6, White heads for what appears to be a totally harmless endgame.

16...♘xe5 17.♘xe5 fxe5 18.♘xd5 ♗xd5 19.♖xd5 ♕xd5 20.♖xd5 ♖xd5

21.♕c2!

A subtle move. After the immediate 21.g3 ♗c5! Black achieves the exchange of bishops.

21...c5 22.g3 ♔h8 23.h4 ♖fd8 24.♕e4

On closer examination, it transpires that the resulting endgame is extremely unpleasant for Black. The centralised white pieces control the whole board, depriving the opponent of any counterplay. At the same time, the threat of an advance of the white pawns hangs over Black like the Sword of Damocles.

24...h6 25.♔g2 ♗f6 26.♔h3

The pawns on g3 and h4 are ready to advance to the 5th rank, which provokes the opponent's rash response, which only exacerbates the situation.

26...h5

27.a4!

More accurate than the immediate 27.♕f5 e4 28.♕xe4 ♗xb2. White prepares a favourable situation on the queenside.

27...♖d3

Black is in an unusual kind of zugzwang. For example: 27...♔g8 28.♕f5 e4 29.♕e6+ ♔h8 30.♕xa6; 27...♖8d7 28.♕g6 e4 29.axb5 axb5 30.♗xc5; 27...♖8d6 28.♕c2 etc.

28.axb5 axb5 29.♕g6 e4

Or 29...♖xb3 30.♕xh5+ ♔g8 31.g4 with a decisive attack.

**30.♕xh5+ ♔g8 31.♕f5 ♗xb2
32.♕xe4 c4 33.bxc4 bxc4 34.♕xc4+
♖3d5 35.g4**

The further advance of the white pawns crushes the position of the black king. There followed:
**35...♔h8 36.g5 ♗d4 37.♗xd4
♖xd4 38.♕f7 ♖8d7 39.♕e8+ ♔h7
40.♕h5+ ♔g8 41.g6 ♖e4 42.♕h7+
♔f8 43.♕h8+ ♔e7 44.♕xg7+ ♔e6
45.♕h8 ♖d3+ 46.♔h2**
Black resigned.

USA $12.99   Europe €9.95   UK £8.30   2012#8   www.newinchess.com

NEW IN CHESS

Trio tops London Grand Prix

The rich career of Borislav Ivkov

Grand Slam Final Magnus Carlsen plays catch-up (again)

**INTERVIEW
GARRY KASPAROV**

'The winds of history are no longer blowing in Kirsan's sails'

Number 5
in the world

Fabiano Caruana fears no one

ISBN 978-90-5691-390-8
9 789056 913908
5 1299

ALEXANDER ALEKHINE AS A SCHOOL BOY   **KINGS' TOURNAMENT REVIVED IN BUCHAREST**   **JUST CHECKING BORIS AVRUKH**

CHAPTER 7

Attacking on the queenside

Queenside attacks are not usually as immediately decisive as attacks on the king. Therefore, in such situations, a manoeuvring game usually ensues, aiming at obtaining small positional advantages.

In Game 50 we see an example of exploiting a queenside pawn majority. One extra subtlety here is the presence of opposite-coloured bishops.

A typical positional piece sacrifice, for the sake of obtaining mobile passed pawns on the queenside, is carried out in Game 51.

Lovers of the Catalan will undoubtedly be very interested in Game 52. Here the main battle revolves around the backward black pawn on the c-file.

Game 50 Sicilian Defence B43

Fabiano Caruana 2646

Srdjan Cvetkovic 2407

Budva 2009 (10)

This modest game has gone unnoticed in the chess world, but I could not resist including it in this collection. The reason is the surprisingly similar middlegame positions, arising from two completely different openings. I hope the reader will permit a small preamble, since we seem to be in the presence of the establishment of a new type of typical position...

Thirty-six years ago, at a junior event in Moscow, the following game was played, in which my opponent was the Kharkov player Boris Alterman, now a well-known GM.

Kalinin-Alterman, Yaroslavl 1983

1.e4 c5 2.♘f3 ♘c6 3.d4 cxd4 4.♘xd4 g6 5.c4 ♗g7 6.♗e3 ♘f6 7.♘c3 ♘g4 8.♕xg4 ♘xd4 9.♕d1 e5

10.♗e2

In ECO at the time, GM Miroslav Filip gave the variation 10.♗xd4 exd4 11.♘d5 0-0 12.♗d3 d6 13.0-0 ♗e6 14.♕d2 ♗xd5 15.exd5 ♕d7 with the assessment ?(!). Luckily, in my childhood, I never read opening books, else it would not have entered my head to go for the position in the next diagram.

10...a6 11.0-0 0-0 12.♘d5 d6
13.♗xd4 exd4 14.♗d3 ♗e6 15.♕d2
♗xd5 16.exd5 ♕d7

The difference between this position and the one given in Filip's variation seems insignificant – the black pawn is on a6, rather than a7. This nuance allows White to carry out a pawn advance on the queenside, exploiting the a6-pawn as a target to 'bite on'.

17.a4 ♖ae8

If 17...a5, the plan was 18.♖a3 with the idea of ♖a3-b3-b5, ♖b1 and then b2-b4!.

18.a5 ♖e5 19.b4

Black's queenside is in a bind and White will develop his attack by preparing the break b4-b5. However, in the game, things did not get this far.

**19...♖h5 20.♖ae1 ♗h6 21.f4 ♗g7
22.♖e4 ♗f6 23.♖fe1 ♔g7 24.♖b1 g5
25.♕e2 ♖h6 26.fxg5 ♗xg5 27.♖g4
f6 28.h4 ♖e8 29.hxg5 ♖xe2 30.gxh6+
♔xh6 31.♗xe2 ♕e7 32.♖b3**

Black resigned.

After this small excursion into last century, events in our hero's present game will be more understandable...

1.e4 c5 2.♘f3 e6 3.d4 cxd4 4.♘xd4
a6 5.♘c3 ♕c7 6.♗d3 g6

A perfectly possible continuation, although a rare one. David Bronstein once observed of a similar pawn structure in the Paulsen, 'It is surprising that the black ship can float, with so many holes!'

7.0-0 ♗g7 8.♘f3

In this position, 8.♘de2, 8.♘b3 and 8.♗e3 have also been seen – in any case, White will follow up with f2-f4. In view of the weakness on d6, Caruana instead keeps the f4-square free for his bishop.

**8...♘c6 9.♗e3 ♘f6 10.♕d2 0-0
11.♗f4 d6 12.♗e2**

12...e5

Black has to create a backward pawn on d6 and weaken d5,

obtaining in return the possibility of a free piece set-up. Such a formation in the Sicilian has long ceased to bother anyone.

13.♗g5 ♗e6 14.♖fd1 ♖ad8

15.♘d5!

Transforming his advantage – little can be squeezed out of the d-file weakness.

15...♗xd5 16.exd5 ♘e7 17.♗xf6 ♗xf6 18.c4

White's plan is clear – to activate his queenside pawn majority and carry out the break c4-c5. Black's prospects of advancing with ...f7-f5 are less clear, and in addition, he still needs the preparatory moves ...♗g7 and ...h7-h6 (so as not to allow the manoeuvre ♘f3-g5-e6). The Serbian GM decides to change the structure, by putting his knight on d4.

18...♘f5 19.♗d3 ♘d4 20.♘xd4 exd4

We have an absolute 'body double' of the position in the diagram from the inserted game! We should note that if the pawn were on a7, the position would be completely equal, since White would not be able to open lines on the queenside.

21.b4!?

As we recall, in the 'stem game' White played 21.a4 with the idea after 21...a5 of playing ♖b5. Caruana plays directly and everything works out perfectly.

21...b6

It was worth seriously considering 21...♖a8!? 22.♖db1 ♖fb8 23.a4 a5, with counterplay against the a4-pawn.

22.a4 a5 23.bxa5 bxa5 24.♖ab1 ♖b8 25.♖b5!

The rook outpost on an open file will inevitably be transformed into a protected passed pawn.

25...♖xb5 26.cxb5 ♖c8 27.g3 ♕c3 28.♕e2 ♕c5

Black has established control of the c-file, but this does not being him any special dividends. The passed pawn on b5 is very strong and plays a serious deflecting role.

29.h4!

Opening a second front on the kingside.

With some delay, we will see the effect of opposite-coloured bishops in the middlegame. Whereas the black bishop is blocked by the d4-pawn, its white colleague plays on both flanks.

29...♔g7

The attempt to hold up the h4-pawn with 29...h5 leads to a weakening of the black king's protection. A possible development of events is illustrated by the following variations: 29...h5 (taking the d5-pawn only increases the strength of the light-squared bishop – 29...♕xd5 30.♖b1) 30.♖b1 ♗d8 (30...♕b6 31.♗xg6! fxg6 32.♕e6+) 31.♕e4 ♔f8

analysis diagram

32.b6!? ♗xb6 33.g4 ♖e8 (the point of the pawn sacrifice is revealed in the line 33...hxg4 34.h5 gxh5 35.♕h7, and Black has no defence against 36.♗f6) 34.♕f4 ♖e5 35.g5 ♗d8 (35...♔g8 36.♖c1!; 35...♕c7 36.♗xg6) 36.♖b8 ♖e8 37.♗b5, and White wins.

30.♖b1 ♕b6 31.h5 ♖c3 32.♔g2

Freeing the back rank for the manoeuvres of the white rooks.

32...♖a3 33.♖h1 ♕b8 34.h6+

Establishing a wedge in the black king position, which will serve as the source of mating threats on the back rank.

In Megabase, the game is shown as continuing 34.hxg6 hxg6 35.♖b1 etc. One can only note with regret that many of the games of modern masters will be passed down to our descendants in distorted form.

34...♔f8

35.♖b1!

White pursues his opponent over the entire board!

35...♖xa4

Other replies do not help Black: 35...♗g5 36.b6 ♗xh6 37.b7 ♖c3 38.♕g4 ♗g7 39.♗a6 f5 40.♕h4 h6 41.♖e1 ♖c7 42.♖e6 d3 43.♕f4 ♔f7 44.♕e3, winning, or 35...♕b7 36.b6 or 35...♕b6 36.♖e1 ♕d8 37.b6 ♖b3 38.♗b5, and the b6-pawn promotes.

36.♖c1!

The c-file was only recently in the opponent's hands, but now decides the game in White's favour!

36...♖a3 37.♖c6 ♖c3 38.♗c4 d3 39.♕g4 1-0

Game 51 Slav Defence D15
Fabiano Caruana   2736
Anish Giri   2714
Wijk aan Zee 2012 (11)

1.d4 d5 2.c4 c6 3.♘f3 ♘f6 4.e3 a6
The Chebanenko Variation is
popular in modern practice. By
carrying out the advance ...b7-b5,
Black establishes a decent queenside
set-up.
5.♘c3 b5 6.c5
The principled continuation –
White seizes space on the left flank.
6...g6
Also seen are 6...♗g4 and 6...♘bd7.
The main idea of all three
continuations is to prepare the
break ...e7-e5. In this context, the
bishop's ideal square is g7.

7.♘e5
Underlining the downside of 7...g6 –
insufficient control at this moment
of the square e5.
7...♗g7 8.f4 a5
An idea of GM Volkov. The usual
continuation here is 8...0-0 9.♗e2
♘fd7 10.♘d3 (exchanges follow
10.0-0 ♘xe5 11.fxe5 f6) 10...a5
(10...f5? 11.a4) 11.0-0 f5, with a
solid position for Black, in which,

however, the initiative remains
with White, in connection with the
possibility of breaking with g2-g4.
The text involves an altogether
different idea – Black keeps his
king in the centre for the moment,
which reduces the effectiveness of a
white kingside pawn advance.
9.♗e2
On 9.♗d3 there follows 9...♗f5!.
9...♕c7 10.0-0

10...h5!
Consistently following his general
line of play. Black prepares to bring
the bishop out to f5, establishing
control over e4.
In the game Gelfand-Wang Yue,
Bazna 2010, events developed in
more traditional fashion: 10...0-0
11.a3 ♗e6 12.♗f3 ♘bd7 13.♘d3!,
and Black was condemned to a long
defence.
11.h3 ♗f5 12.♗d2
The sharp 12.g4 hxg4 13.hxg4 ♗e4
14.g5 ♕c8 brings White nothing
except weaknesses.
12...♘bd7 13.♗f3
The tension around the square e4
increases notably.
13...h4?!
A committal move. Black does not
wish any longer to have to reckon

with the possibility of g2-g4, but the vulnerability of the h4-pawn pretty much rules out kingside castling. As we will see, the text also uses up an important tempo. In Caruana's opinion, the continuation 13...♘e4 14.♘xe4 dxe4 15.♗e2 f6! 16.♘xd7 ♗xd7 17.a4 b4 18.♗c4 e6 19.♕b3 ♔e7, followed by ...f6-f5, leads to equal chances.

14.♕e1

A move full of poison. The threat of the break e3-e4 forces matters.

14...♘e4 15.♘xe4 dxe4 16.♗e2 f6?

Consistent, but bad! It was essential to play 16...♘xe5, after which Caruana planned to reply 17.dxe5 f6 18.exf6 ♗xf6 19.♗c3, and White's chances are preferable.

17.♗xa5!

An unexpected blow, completely destroying the black queenside (now we see the idea of the move 14.♕e1 ! – see the variation after Black's 13th move). For the sacrificed piece, White gets three connected passed pawns.

17...♖xa5?

Black hopes that with queens on, he will have more chances to muddy the waters. However, in Caruana's

opinion, the best chance of resistance was offered by 17...♕xa5! 18.♕xa5 ♖xa5 19.♘xc6 ♖a8 20.♗b5 e5! (an important resource – Black wants at any cost to bring the ♗g7 into the game) 21.b4 exf4 22.exf4 ♗e6 23.d5! ♗xd5 24.♖fd1 f5 25.♖ac1 ♗e6 26.♖d6 ♘f8 27.♖cd1 ♗d7 28.a4, and White's initiative grows.

18.♘xc6 ♖a8

The subtlety of the combination consists in the variation 18...♖a6 19.♘b4 ♖a5 20.♘d5 ♕a7 21.a4! ♖xa4 (after 21...bxa4 22.b4! the black rook is trapped) 22.♗xb5 ♖xa1 23.♕xa1 ♕xa1 24.♖xa1 ♔f7 25.♖a7 ♖d8 26.c6, and Black is in a bad way.

19.♗xb5

Now the advanced white pawn mass cannot be stopped. An especially depressing aspect of the position for Black is that his ♗g7 is out of play.

19...♗e6 20.a4 f5 21.♕d2 ♗f6 22.d5 ♗f7 23.♖ac1 ♔f8

Black cannot even castle – 23...0-0 24.d6 exd6 25.cxd6 ♕b7 26.♘e7+, winning a piece.

24.b4 ♕c8

25.d6

The ideal moment to open the game – the black pieces are completely incapable of resistance.

**25...exd6 26.cxd6 ♕e8 27.♘e7 ♗e6
28.♖c7 ♖h7 29.♘d5**

The simplest way to win was
29.♗xd7 ♗xd7 30.♖xd7 ♕xd7
31.♕d5, with a double attack on the
squares a8 and g8.

29...♗d8 30.♖b7 ♖c8

31.a5

Black has nothing at all to do,
whilst the a-pawn simply marches
on to queen.

**31...♔g7 32.a6 ♔h6 33.a7 ♕f8
34.♘e7 ♘b6 35.♕f2 ♖f7**

On 35...♕f6 Caruana had prepared
the blow 36.♗d7!.

**36.♕xh4+ ♔g7 37.♕g5 ♗d5
38.♕xg6+ ♔h8 39.♕h5+ ♔g7
40.♘xf5+ ♔g8 41.♘e7+**

Black resigned.

Game 52 Catalan Opening E05
Fabiano Caruana   2782
Sergey Karjakin   2750
Wijk aan Zee 2014 (3)

**1.d4 ♘f6 2.c4 e6 3.g3 d5 4.♘f3 ♗e7
5.♗g2 0-0 6.0-0 dxc4**

A closed game results from 6...♘bd7
7.♕c2 c6 followed by ...b7-b6.

7.♕a4 a6 8.♕xc4 b5 9.♕c2 ♗b7

Black has solved the problem of
his queen's bishop, but he has a
backward pawn on the c-file. The
main battle in this Catalan line
revolves around that pawn.

10.♗d2 ♗d6

With the idea of putting the queen
on e7 and playing ...c7-c5.
After 10...♘bd7 11.♗a5! ♖c8 12.♘bd2
the advance ...c7-c5 is stopped.
Ever since the Karpov-Kasparov
matches, the main line has been
10...♗e4 11.♕c1 ♗b7. Later the text
became popular, and even 10...♖a7!?.

11.a3

Preparing a bind with b2-b4.
GM Victor Bologan, in his book on
the Catalan, considered the most
promising continuation for White
to be 11.♖e1 (with the idea of e2-e4)
11...♗e4 12.♕c1 ♗b7 13.♗g5 ♘bd7
14.e4 ♗e7 15.♘bd2 c5 16.♗xf6 ♗xf6
17.dxc5 ♖c8 18.b4! ♗xa1 19.♕xa1,
with good compensation for the
sacrificed exchange, Harikrishna-
Pashikian, Kallithea 2008. The
choice is a matter of taste.

11...♘bd7 12.b4 ♖a7

Freeing the queen's path to a8,
which allows Black to take control
of the long diagonal a8-h1 and the

square e4. The c7-pawn remains where it is for the moment. Black's task consists in breaking the enemy's bind with the pawn pushes ...a6-a5 and ...e6-e5.

13.♗c3!?

A novelty by Caruana and a highly logical one. From c3, the bishop holds back ...e6-e5, whilst the ♘b1 is ready to come via b3, establishing control of the squares a5 and c5. The drawback of the manoeuvre is just its slowness.

GM Marin, who annotated this game, pointed out that the computer, working at a depth of 23/56, still does not list the move 13.♗c3 even among its 8 (!) strongest continuations! Such a fact must stroke the vanity of the carbon-based chess player!

The usual continuation in this position is 13.♘c3. In Carlsen-Aronian, London 2013, there followed 13...♕a8 14.♘h4 ♗xg2 15.♘xg2 c6, and Black regrouped to carry out the break ...a6-a5.

13...♗e4 14.♕c1

The best retreat – on b2, the queen would be attacked after ...♘a4.

14...♕a8 15.♘bd2 ♗d5 16.♕c2 ♘b6 17.♘e1!

An important manoeuvre, allowing him to challenge the opponent's control of e4. The threat is e2-e4.

17...♘a4

Here Marin suggested an interesting continuation, which appears to allow Black to maintain the dynamic balance: 17...♗xg2 18.♘xg2 ♘fd5 19.♗b2 (19.e4 ♘xc3 20.♕xc3 a5! or 19.♘b3 ♘c4 20.♗d2 e5 with counterplay) 19...a5! (19...♘a4 20.♘b3!) 20.e4 axb4! 21.exd5 bxa3 22.dxe6 (after 22.♗c1 ♘xd5 Black gets three strong passed pawns for the knight) 22...axb2 23.♖xa7 ♕xa7 24.♕xb2, and the chances are roughly equal.

18.♘b3 ♗e4

After 18...♗xg2 19.♘xg2 ♕e4 20.♖a2! ♘xc3 21.♕xc3 e5 22.♖d1! (22.♘e3 a5!) 22...♖aa8 23.♘e3 White again has a positional advantage.

19.♗xe4 ♕xe4

20.♖a2!!

It turns out that White's entire strategy hangs on this modest square! Now he manages to keep control of the a5-square and obtain the advantage.

On the other hand, after 20.♕xe4 ♘xe4 21.♗d2 a5! 22.bxa5 ♘xd2 23.♘xd2 ♖xa5 Black manages to maintain a blockade.

20...♘xc3 21.♕xc3 e5

Black succeeds in undermining the d4-square, but he still does not free his c7-pawn, as it is kept there by the foot-soldier on b4!

22.♘f3 exd4 23.♘fxd4 ♖aa8 24.♖c2 ♘d5 25.♕f3 ♕xf3 26.♘xf3

The middlegame fires die down, and in the ending, White has a clear advantage. The c7-pawn is useless and the white kingside pawn majority will announce its presence with an ever-louder voice.

Caruana plays the technical phase unhurriedly and confidently.

26...♖fe8 27.♖d1 ♘b6 28.♘a5 g6 29.e3 ♔g7 30.♖d3 ♖ac8 31.♖c6 ♖b8 32.♔f1 h5 33.h3 ♔f6 34.♘d2 ♔g7 35.♘db3 ♖e6 36.♔g2 ♔f8 37.f4 ♖ee8 38.♔f3 ♖ed8 39.♖c2 ♖d7 40.e4 ♔e8 41.e5

The events on the board follow a general strategical idea and are comprehensible without words. White's spatial expansion is assuming threatening proportions.

41...♗e7 42.♖xd7 ♔xd7 43.♖d2+ ♔e8 44.♘c6 ♖a8 45.♘ba5 f5

46.g4 hxg4+ 47.hxg4 fxg4+ 48.♔xg4 ♔f7 49.♖h2 ♗f8 50.f5 ♘d5

It is completely hopeless after 50...gxf5+ 51.♔xf5 followed by e5-e6.

51.f6 ♘xf6+ 52.exf6 ♔xf6

Black has given up a piece for the powerful enemy passed pawns, but this does not bring him any chances of saving himself. For the complete picture, we give the remaining moves:

53.♖f2+ ♔e6 54.♖e2+ ♔d5 55.♖d2+ ♔e4 56.♘b7 ♔e3 57.♖d7 ♖e8 58.♖xc7 ♗h6 59.♘c5 ♖f8 60.♖e7+ ♔d2 61.♖e6 ♖f1 62.♘a7 ♗e3 63.♖xa6 ♔e2 64.♖xg6 ♖f4+ 65.♔h3 ♖f3+ 66.♖g3 ♖f7 67.♘xb5 ♗f2 68.♖b3 ♖f4 69.♘c3+ ♔f1 70.♖b1+ ♗e1 71.♖xe1+

And Black resigned.

A game with few outward highlights, but a complete and beautiful effort.

Tal Memorial,
Moscow 2012

CHAPTER 8

Playing on two flanks

Play using the entire board always creates a great aesthetic impression.

In Game 53 we see an example of the typical strategy in closed positions with a space advantage. Black's position looks fairly solid. However, exploiting the closed nature of the position, White gradually increases the pressure on both flanks. Unable to withstand the pressure, Black's defences start to creak.

The battle in Game 54 assumes a different character. Here the position is more open and the play is more dynamic. An effective blow on the queenside at move 29 leads to a decisive attack on the opposite side of the board.

Game 53 Slav Defence D94
Fabiano Caruana 2786
Gata Kamsky 2762
Tashkent 2012 (3)

1.d4 d5 2.c4 c6 3.♘f3 ♘f6 4.♘c3 a6 5.e3 g6
A hybrid of the Chebanenko and Schlechter variations. Black delays the advance ...b7-b5 until he has completed his development.
6.♗d3 ♗g7 7.0-0 0-0

8.h3

Preventing the move ...♗g4, which would allow Black to offload his inactive bishop.
8...b5 9.b3
After the immediate 9.c5 ♘bd7, White does not manage to keep control of the square e5 and so he retains the tension instead.
9...♘bd7 10.♕c2 ♗b7 11.c5!
A timely advance, shutting the ♗b7 out of play.
11...♘e8
In the variation 11...a5 12.a3 e5 13.dxe5 ♘e8 14.e4! the position opens up to White's advantage.
12.♗b2 ♘c7 13.b4 a5 14.a3 ♘e6
Black refrains from the freeing advance 14...e5, not wishing to allow the ♗b2 to come alive. After 15.dxe5 ♘xe5 16.♘xe5 ♗xe5 17.♘e2 or 17.♘xb5!? ♗xb2 18.♘xc7 ♗xa1 19.♘xa8 ♗e5 20.♘b6 axb4 21.axb4, White's chances are preferable.

The transfer of the knight to e6 aims to hold up the move e3-e4, which would be effective because of the passive ♗b7.

15.♘d2!
The standard manoeuvre. By playing f2-f4 and ♘f3, White intends to increase his space advantage.
15...♛c7 16.f4

16...axb4
Simplifying the position by an exchange of rooks. There is no sense in closing the position further with the move 16...a4, because the white rooks will be good on the kingside. Nor can the queenside be considered completely blocked in that case, because in the future one cannot rule out possible sacrifices on the squares a4 or b5.
17.axb4 ♖xa1 18.♖xa1 ♖a8
19.♖xa8+

In principle, the rooks could be retained, but Caruana decides to draw the enemy bishop further from the square c8. In addition, he may later exploit the a-file with his queen.
19...♗xa8 20.♘f3

20...♗b7
This move was widely criticised. For example, GM Konstantin Sakaev wrote: 'Up to now, Black has defended patiently and had he played 20...f5, he would have had good chances to establish a fortress, because after 21.g4 there is the strong 21...fxg4 22.hxg4 ♘xf4 23.exf4 ♛xf4 24.♛e2 ♛xg4+ with counterplay'.
In my opinion, it is somewhat premature to speak of 'fortresses'. White is strong on both wings and Black must constantly watch the a-file and the possibility of sacrifices on b5. White will gradually prepare the advance g2-g4.
One illustrative possible variation is 21.♗c1!? (with the idea of g2-g4) 21...♘f6 22.♛a2 ♗b7 23.♘e5 ♘d7 24.♘xc6! ♗xc6 (or 24...♛xc6 25.♗xb5 ♛c8 26.♘xd5) 25.♘xd5,

and the black position is very dangerous.

21.g4!

Sakaev: 'White seizes space over the whole board and Black has no further chance to escape the bind.'

21...♗c8 22.♗c1 ♘f6 23.♕a2 h6 24.♘e5 g5

Running on the spot is psychologically difficult, and Black tries to obtain some sort of counterplay.

25.♗f5 ♘d8 26.♗d3 gxf4

After the repetition 26...♘e6 one possibility is 27.♕a8 ♘d8 28.♔g2, gradually strengthening the position.

27.exf4 ♘d7

28.♘f3!

Avoiding exchanges which would favour Black, who lacks space.

28...♘e6 29.♘e2

Now, under cover of the aggressive pawn mass, White needs to regroup his forces for the decisive assault on the weakened position of the black king.

29...♕b7

Or 29...♘f6 30.f5 ♘f8 31.♗f4.

30.♗e3 ♕a6 31.♕b2 ♘ef8 32.♘g3 e6 33.♘h5 ♗h8 34.f5 ♘f6 35.♗xh6 ♘e4

36.f6!

A nice positional pawn sacrifice, keeping the ♗c8 shut in.

36...♘xf6 37.♘e5 ♘e4 38.♗xe4 dxe4 39.♕f2 ♗xe5 40.dxe5 ♕a1+ 41.♔g2 f5

He also loses after 41...♕xe5 42.♘f6+ ♔h8 43.♗xf8.

42.exf6 ♔f7 43.♗xf8 ♔xf8 44.♕d2 ♔f7 45.♕d8 ♕b2+ 46.♔g3 ♕c3+ 47.♔h4 ♕e1+ 48.♘g3 1-0

Game 54 Ruy Lopez C77

Fabiano Caruana   2801

Levon Aronian   2805

St Louis 2014 (4)

1.e4 e5 2.♘f3 ♘c6 3.♗b5 a6 4.♗a4 ♘f6 5.0-0 ♗e7 6.d3

An old method of play, which has suddenly become beloved of contemporary GMs.

6...b5 7.♗b3 0-0 8.♘c3 d6 9.a3 ♘a5

On the immediate 9...♗e6 there follows 10.♘d5.

10.♗a2 ♗e6 11.♗xe6 fxe6 12.b4

If 12.♘e2 c5 13.b4 ♘c6 Black achieves a more harmonious set-up.

12...♘c6 13.♗d2

The position looks absolutely equal. In addition, the pawn's having moved from f7 to e6 looks favourable for Black, as he controls the squares d5 and f5 and has the open f-file for his rooks. Even so, things are not quite so simple, because of the differing prospects of the bishops remaining on the board. Whereas the black bishop is currently passive, its white colleague harmonises splendidly with the pawn trio c2/d3/e4 and is ready to support operations on the queenside, involving the advance a3-a4.

13...d5

For the reasons outlined above, Black's desire to change the pawn structure is understandable. He has also tried 13...♘d4 14.♘xd4

exd4 15.♘e2 c5 with a complicated battle, Topalov-Kasimdzhanov, Thessaloniki 2013.

14.♖e1

Immediately drawing attention to the undefended e5-pawn.

14...♕d6

15.♘a2!?

In the game Dominguez-Karjakin, Beijing 2013, White tried 15.h3 ♘d7 16.♘e2 a5 17.♖b1 axb4 18.axb4 ♖fb8 with a solid position for Black. Caruana's original text move is associated with the idea of transferring the knight via c1 to b3. If this plan succeeds, then the black queenside weaknesses on a5 and c5 will be fixed.

15...♘d7

The start of a similar manoeuvre – the black knight aims for a4. The attempt to solve the queenside problems immediately with 15...a5 fails to 16.♘c3! ♖fb8 17.exd5 exd5 18.♘xe5! ♘xe5 19.♗f4 ♕c6 (less accurate is 19...♕d7 20.♗xe5 axb4 21.axb4 ♖xa1 (21...♗xb4? 22.♖xa8 ♖xa8 23.♗xf6 gxf6 24.♘xd5!) 22.♕xa1 ♗xb4 23.♖b1 with pressure for White) 20.♗xe5 axb4 21.axb4 ♗xb4 22.♖xa8 ♖xa8 23.♗xf6 ♗xc3

24.♗xc3 ♕xc3 25.g3 h6 26.♔g2, and in the resulting major-piece endgame White's chances are preferable, thanks to his control of the e-file and the open position of the black king.

16.♕e2 d4

Giving the ♘d7 the possibility of continuing its journey to a4.

It was worth giving serious attention to 16...♗f6!?, maintaining the tension in the centre. It would then be harder for White to plan his actions, because in several variations, he has to reckon with the move ...♘d4. For example: 17.♖eb1 (17.♘c1 a5 or 17.♖ab1 ♖fb8 with the idea of ...a6-a5) 17...♘d4 18.♘xd4 exd4 etc.

17.♖eb1!

Preventing the freeing advance ...a6-a5 and preparing the manoeuvre ♘b3.

The subtlety of having the king's rook on b1 is demonstrated in the variation 17...♖fb8 18.♕e1!, and the move ...a6-a5 is again 'frozen'.

17...♘b6

The continuation 17...a5 18.bxa5 ♘xa5 19.♖xb5 ♕xa3 20.♕d1 ♘c6

21.♖bb1 ♕d6 22.♘c1 leads to a white initiative on the kingside.

18.♘c1! ♘a4 19.♘b3

19...♖f7

Up to now, the two sides have played very purposefully. However, Black's 19th move was condemned by Aronian directly after the game. The Armenian GM recommended the energetic 19...♘c3!? 20.♗xc3 dxc3, with the idea of stabilising the position with the aid of the move ...♘d4. The variations prove the solidity of the black position: 21.♕e1 ♘d4 22.♘fxd4 exd4 23.e5 ♕d5 24.♕e4 ♖ad8 25.♖e1 c5 or 21.♕e3 ♖ad8 (21...♗f6? 22.♕e1!, and already there is not 22...♘d4 because of the fork at the end of the variation) 22.♘c5 ♖b8!? (re-establishing the idea of ...♘d4, since on 23.♘xa6?! there follows 23...♖xf3! 24.gxf3 ♖a8 25.♘c5 ♘d4, and Black seizes the initiative) 23.♘b3 ♖bd8, maintaining the dynamic balance.

20.♖c1!

Forcing the opponent to reckon with the break c2-c3 and preparing the knight jump to g5 (20.♘g5? ♗xg5 21.♗xg5 ♘c3).

20...♖d8

21.♘g5!

Switching attention to the kingside.
Now it is clearly seen that the ♗d2
directs play over the whole board!

21...♖f6?!

After the game, Caruana pointed to
this move as a serious inaccuracy.
His recommendation was 21...♗xg5!
22.♗xg5 ♖df8 23.f3 ♘e7! 24.♗d2
♘g6, holding back the break c2-c3
by the threat of ...♘f4, and leading
to a long manoeuvring struggle.

22.♕h5! h6 23.♘f3 ♖df8

24.♖f1

The appearance of the queen on
h5 allows the enemy pieces to be
restricted to the maximum (the
♘c6 is tied to the defence of the
e5-pawn and the ♘a4 needs to
guard the squares c3 and c5), and

now White gradually transfers play
to the kingside.

24...♖8f7 25.♖ae1 ♗f8

Preparing to drive the enemy queen
from her active position.

26.h3!

This 'little' move has great
consequences – the threat of ♘g4
hangs over Black.

26...g6 27.♕h4 ♕e7 28.♕g3

28.♗xh6?? would be a grievous
error because of 28...♗xh6 29.♕xh6
♖xf3! 30.gxf3 ♖h7, and White is
mated.

28...♗g7

29.♘a5!

A spectacular widening of the
front. All the black weaknesses are
attacked.

A slower building of the pressure,
as both players showed, would
have achieved nothing: 29.♘h2 ♖f8
30.♘g4 ♖f4! 31.♗xf4 exf4 32.♕f3 e5,
and in this closed position, White's
extra exchange is not of great
significance.

29...♘xa5 30.♘xe5!

This positional sacrifice is the point
of White's idea! After 30.bxa5 ♖xf3!
31.gxf3 ♕f6 he gets nowhere.

30...♘b7 31.♘xg6!

The relative strength of the pieces in action! The stingy 31.♘xf7 ♕xf7 loses all White's advantage.

31...♕d8 32.e5 ♖f5 33.f4!

White has two pawns for the knight, and an attack with his kingside pawns. It is hard for Black to overcome the poor position of his pieces.

33...c5

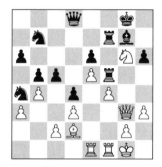

34.♘h4 ♖h5 35.♘f3

This consolidating knight transfer to f3 is the last preparatory step before the advance of the white infantry.

35...♔h7?

Hastening defeat. The most tenacious was 35...♕e8, but even

in this case, after 36.♕g6 ♖e7 37.♕xe8+ ♖xe8 38.bxc5 ♘bxc5 39.♘xd4, Black is in a bad way.

36.♕g4 ♖hf5

37.♘h4

Now White will have a material advantage as well.

37...♔h8 38.♘xf5 ♖xf5 39.♕g6 ♕e7 40.g4 ♖f8 41.f5 ♕e8 42.♕xe8 ♖xe8 43.f6 ♗f8 44.f7 ♖e7 45.♖f6 ♘b6

If 45...♔h7 decisive is 46.♗xh6 ♗xh6 47.♖xh6+ ♔g7 48.♖h7+ ♔f8 49.♖f1!.

46.♗xh6 ♘d7 47.♖ef1 cxb4 48.axb4 ♗xh6 49.♖xh6+ ♔g7 50.♖h5

And on account of 50...♖xf7 51.♖h7+, Black resigned.

Carlsen-Caruana, Wijk aan Zee 2010

Carlsen-Caruana, Zurich 2014

CHAPTER 9

Defence and counterattack

The art of defence is one of the most important components of chess mastery, requiring tenacity, character and subtle judgement of the position.

In Game 55, the World Champion carries out a spectacular, but entirely well-founded attack on the king. With enviable calmness, Caruana goes down the main line of the opponent's combination, refuting it with an energetic counterattack.

Game 56 is a complicated one. For a long time, Black was under unpleasant pressure from one of the best positional players in the world. It is instructive to follow how, despite an absence of counterplay, Caruana patiently improves the position of his pieces, preparing for the inevitable opening of the position. Whilst dominating the position, White at some moment relaxes his attention and the picture changes rapidly! Caruana carries out the counterattack faultlessly.

Game 55 Bishop's Opening C24
Magnus Carlsen   2877
Fabiano Caruana   2801
St Louis 2014 (3)

1.e4 e5 2.♗c4 ♘f6 3.d3
The World Champion's repertoire usually involves stepping aside from well-known continuations at the first opportunity.
3...c6 4.♘f3 d5 5.♗b3

5...♗b4+!?
Subtle provocation – by luring the pawn to c3, Black deprives the enemy knight of its natural development square.
In the event of the immediate 5...♗d6 6.exd5 cxd5 7.♗g5 ♗e6 8.♘c3, the black centre comes under piece pressure.
6.c3 ♗d6 7.♗g5 dxe4
Aiming to stabilise the pawn structure. After 7...♗e6 8.d4!? complications arise in the centre.
8.dxe4 h6
A useful inclusion. In the game Karjakin-Efimenko, Poikovsky 2011, play went 8...0-0 9.0-0 ♕e7?! (9...h6 10.♗h4! ♕e7=) 10.♗h4! ♘a6 11.♘d2 ♘c5 12.♕f3 ♘xb3 13.axb3, and White seized the initiative.
9.♗h4 ♕e7

Caruana has played the opening stage subtly, not yet committing his king.

10.♘bd2 ♘bd7

11.♗g3

The commentators unanimously condemned this voluntary bishop retreat as being indecisive. Maybe Carlsen's improvisation in this game was not the most successful, but the move 11.♗g3 does not lack sense – after 11...0-0 there follows the familiar 12.♘h4!; and if the ♘d7 quits its post, then the knight jump to c4 becomes unpleasant.

11...♗c7

Neutralising the move ♘c4.

12.0-0

On 12.♘h4 there could follow 12...♘c5 13.♗c2 g6, limiting the agility of the white knight.

12...♘h5 13.h3?!

Continuing along the same original lines. By provoking the exchange on g3, Carlsen has dreamed up an interesting tactical operation...

13...♘xg3 14.fxg3 ♘c5

The computer recommends the straightforward 14...♘f6. But Caruana wants to place the knight more flexibly. After 14...0-0 15.♘h4

the move 15...♘c5? is impossible because of 16.♘g6.

15.♗xf7+?!

One can only be amazed by the World Champion's imagination! Objectively, of course, he should have refrained from this blow, but it arises logically from his previous few moves.

Now a whole mass of threats surrounds the black king, but Caruana goes calmly towards the danger.

15...♔xf7

A serious mistake would be 15...♕xf7? 16.♘xe5 ♗xe5 17.♖xf7 ♔xf7 18.♕h5+ ♔e6 19.♕f5+ ♔d6 20.♘c4+, winning.

16.♘xe5++

There are interesting subtleties after 16.♘h4+!? ♔g8 17.♘g6.

analysis diagram

Now 17...♕g5 18.♖f8+ ♔h7 19.♖xh8+
(19.♘xh8 loses to 19...♗g4! 20.♕f1
♗e2! 21.♕f2 ♖xf8 22.♕xf8 ♕xd2)
19...♔xg6 20.♕f1! (20.♕f3? ♗g4!)
20...♕xg3 (similar consequences
follow 20...♕xd2 21.♖xc8 ♘xe4
22.♖xc7 ♕e3+) 21.♖xc8 ♕e3+
22.♔h2 ♘xe4 23.♖xc7 ♕g3+ 24.♔g1
♕e3+ 25.♔h2 ♕g3+ leads to
perpetual check.

Black has to give up the queen
after 17...♕e8! 18.♖f8+ ♕xf8
19.♘xf8 ♔xf8 20.♕h5 ♗e6 21.♘f3
♘d7 22.♖f1 ♔e7 23.♘h4 ♖he8
24.♘g6+ ♔d8, obtaining more than
sufficient material compensation
and successfully evacuating his
king from the danger zone.

16...♔g8 17.♘g6 ♕g5

Now 17...♕e8? 18.♖f8+ ♕xf8
19.♘xf8 ♔xf8 20.♕h5 leads to an
advantage for White.

18.♖f8+ ♔h7 19.♘xh8

The forcing attack has reached its
apotheosis – White has an extra
exchange and two pawns. But now
it is Black's move...

19...♗g4! 20.♕f1 ♘d3!!

A brilliant resource – the black
knight takes part in an energetic
counterattack by his army. Now
three black pieces are attacked.

The emotionless computer shows
two other promising lines for Black:

A) 20...♖xf8 21.♕xf8 ♗e6!! 22.♘f1
♕f6 23.♕xf6 (23.♕xc5 ♗b6 or
23.♕e8 ♘xe4) 23...gxf6, and the two
bishops should gradually overcome
White's rook and two pawns;

B) 20...♗e2 21.♕f5+ ♕xf5 22.♖xf5
♗b6!! 23.♔h2 ♔xh8, and with an
analogous material balance, Black's
advantage is again not in doubt.

21.♕xd3

Let us examine other captures:
21.♖xa8 ♕e3+ 22.♔h1 ♘f2+ 23.♕xf2
♕xf2 24.hxg4 ♕xd2 or 21.hxg4
♕e3+ 22.♔h1 ♖xf8 23.♕xf8 ♘f2+
24.♔g1 ♘xe4+ etc. – both variations
end in disaster for White.

There is also the ingenious
resource 21.♘g6!. I can only
offer the computer variation:
21...♕e3+ (21...♔xg6? 22.♕f7+ ♔h7
23.♕g8+=) 22.♔h1 ♕xg3 23.e5 ♖xf8
24.♘xf8+ ♔g8 25.♘g6 ♘f2+ 26.♔g1
♘xh3+ 27.♔h1 ♘f2+ 28.♔g1 ♗e6!
(28...♗b6 29.♕c4+ ♔h7 30.♘f8+
♔h8 31.♘g6+=) 29.♘e7+ (29.♕xf2?
♗b6−+) 29...♔h8 (29...♔h7 30.♕b1+
♘d3 31.♘f3) 30.♘g6+ (30.♘f3 ♘g4)
30...♕xg6 31.♔xf2 ♕c2 32.♕e2
(32.♕c1 ♗b6+) 32...♕xb2 33.♖b1
♕xc3, and Black should win.

21...♖xf8 22.hxg4 ♕xg4 23.♘f3 ♕xg3 24.e5+ ♔xh8

So, material equality is re-established, but the open position of the white king signifies a clear advantage for Black.

25.e6

Trying to change the unfavourable course of events, the World Champion throws forward his passed pawn. 25.♖e1?? ♖xf3! would be a terrible mistake.

25...♗b6+ 26.♔h1 ♕g4!

Transferring the queen to a better position with tempo.

27.♕d6

Again 27.♖e1 is bad because of 27...♖xf3! 28.♕xf3 ♕h4+, whilst 27.e7 is met by 27...♖e8 28.♖e1 ♕h5+ 29.♘h2 ♗c7 30.g3 ♕f7 31.♕e3 ♗d6, winning the pawn on e7.

27...♖d8!

Including in the attack the rook, which could have a passive role after 27...♖e8 28.♖e1. The course of events now develops by force.

28.♕e5 ♖d5! 29.♕b8+ ♔h7 30.e7 ♕h5+ 31.♘h2?

An oversight in time-trouble. The only way to prolong resistance was 31.♕h2 ♕e8! 32.g4! (32.♖e1? ♗f2 33.♖f1 ♖h5) 32...♕xe7 33.♖e1 ♕f6 34.♕e2, although Black's extra pawn and the poor white king position leave no doubt as to the outcome.

31...♖d1+ 32.♖xd1 ♕xd1+ 33.♘f1 ♕xf1+ 34.♔h2 ♕g1+

After 35.♔h3 ♕e3+ the e7-pawn falls, so White resigned.

Game 56 Queen's Pawn Game D03
Vladimir Kramnik 2788
Fabiano Caruana 2802
Shamkir 2015 (6)

1.d4 ♘f6 2.♘f3 g6 3.♗g5 ♗g7 4.c3

A solid system of play, aiming to restrict the activity of the ♗g7.

4...0-0 5.♘bd2

5...d5

Caruana is a Grünfeld player. King's Indian devotees would probably prefer 5...d6, allowing 6.e4.

6.e3 ♘bd7 7.♗e2 c5

A move enjoing great popularity is
7...♖e8 followed by ...e7-e5.

8.0-0 b6 9.a4 a6 10.b4

Typical strategy for such positions.
White keeps the pawn triangle c3/
d4/e3 intact and seizes space on the
queenside, advancing the a- and
b-pawns into the battle.

Another active white idea would
be to establish an outpost for the
knight on e5.

10...♗b7

Caruana considers 10...c4 more
active, avoiding the opening of lines
on the queenside. However, both
moves have been met in practice.

11.a5!

But this is a novelty, if one believes
the database. White forces a
favourable change in the pawn
structure.

11...cxb4 12.cxb4 b5

The structure has mutual holes
on c4 and c5, which the knights,
in particular, will aim for. The
difference, however, is that the
white knight, when it reaches c5,
will also attack the a6-pawn. This
motif means a clear advantage for
White.

**13.♖c1 ♘e8 14.♘b3 ♘d6 15.♘e1!
♘c4 16.♘d3**

16...♖a7

'Black has nothing to do and must
limit himself to passive waiting. My
task is to arrange my pieces on the
most harmonious squares possible
and see what plan White will adopt.
A stage of long manoeuvring starts'
– Caruana on ChessBase.

17.♗h4

'Many players would have played
17.♘bc5 ♘xc5 18.♘xc5 here, but this
would significantly simplify my
task. Kramnik correctly decides to
keep more pieces on the board' –
Caruana.

17...♗a8 18.♗f3 ♘f6 19.♕e2 ♘e8!

20.g4!?

This looks very sensible. White
increases his space on the kingside

and harmoniously places his bishops on g2 and g3.

20...♘ed6 21.♗g2 ♕c8 22.♘bc5 ♖e8 23.♗g3 ♕d8

24.♖cd1

'Maybe somewhere around here Kramnik lost the initiative. I would suggest by way of an improvement 24.♗e5!? – the exchange of dark-squared bishops favours White, whilst avoiding it is not good for Black: 24...♗f8 (24...f6? 25.♘e6 ♕c8 26.♘xg7; 24...♗h6 25.h4; 24...♘xe5 25.dxe5 ♘c4 26.e6) 25.g5, with the initiative on the kingside' – recommendation on the website Chess Pro.

24...e6 25.f3

'Kramnik prepares the advance e3-e4, but possibly his play is a little too direct. The move 25.h4!? was worth serious attention' – Caruana.

25...♕e7 26.♔h1 ♗h6 27.♘f4?!

Manoeuvring in a comfortable position has slightly weakened White's attention and, as we will see, his pieces lose coordination for a moment.

After 27.♗f2 (with the idea of e3-e4) 27...f5 Black achieves a solid position, but in Caruana's opinion,

his opponent would have retained some pressure.

27...♘b7! 28.♘cd3 ♘d8!

It suddenly transpires that after ...♘c6 White has problems defending the b4-pawn, because of the inconvenient placing of his knights.

29.e4?

'Mistakes rarely come in singles'. Upset at having squandered his advantage, White opens the game at the most inappropriate moment. After the quiet 29.♘c5, Caruana planned to repeat the position with 29...♘b7.

29...♘c6 30.exd5 ♘xb4 31.dxe6

After the game, Kramnik explained that from afar, he had intended the move 31.d6!?, but then noticed the positional queen sacrifice 31...♘xd3!? 32.dxe7 ♘xf4 33.♗xf4 ♗xf4 or 33.♕f2 ♘xg2 34.♔xg2 ♘e3+ 35.♔g1 ♖axe7, and the black pieces dominate.

The computer, in reply to 31.d6, recommends the calm 31...♕xd6 32.♘xg6 ♕d8!, giving a clear preference to Black.

31...♘xd3 32.♖xd3 fxe6?!

An automatic reply. The players both missed the zwischenzug

32...♕f6!, which immediately gives Black an enormous positional advantage. This is the only blemish on Caruana's strong play in this game.

33.♕e1 ♕d8

The a5-pawn, previously the pride of the white position, is now doomed. The text also opens the path for the ♖a7 to the kingside.

34.h4 ♖f7 35.g5 ♗g7 36.♗h3

36...♖xf4!

An elegant exchange sacrifice, allowing the e6-pawn to burst into the white position.

37.♗xf4 e5! 38.♗g3 e4! 39.♖d1 ♗d5!

Completely blocking the enemy pieces. A grave mistake would have been 39...exf3? 40.♗e6+ ♔h8 41.d5, and White frees himself.

40.♗e5 exf3 41.♕f2

More tenacious was 41.♔g1, although here too, after 41...♘xa5, the white position is strategically lost.

41...♕xa5

The black queen comes into the game with great strength from the square a5.

42.♗g4

White's only chance is to surround and eliminate the f3-pawn.

42...♖f8 43.♖d3 ♕b4!

An accurate move. Unexpectedly, the ♗g4 is hanging along the fourth rank.

Taking the f3-pawn was also impossible: 44.♗xf3 ♖xf3 45.♖xf3 ♘d2 46.♕e1 ♕c4 or 44.♗xg7 ♔xg7 45.♗xf3 ♗e4! 46.♗xe4 ♖xf2 47.♖xf2 ♕e1+, and White suffers material losses.

44.♗g3

44...h5!

The decisive blow! Black secures the h6-square for his bishop, which makes possible the knight transfer to e4 via d2.

45.gxh6

Or 45.♗xf3 ♖xf3 46.♖xf3 ♘d2, winning.

45...♗xh6 46.♔h2 ♘d2 47.♖a1 ♘e4

Now the white position finally collapses. There followed:

48.♕c2 ♘xg3 49.♖xa6 ♗e4 50.♗xf3 ♕e1 51.♕b3+ ♔h8 52.♗xe4 ♖f2+ 53.♔h3 ♕f1+ 54.♔g4 ♖f4+

White resigned.

Stavanger 2018 (Photo: Lennart Ootes)

CHAPTER 10

The Berlin endgame

Savielly Tartakower once described the Ruy Lopez as 'a cow that can be milked to infinity'. For Fabiano, the Berlin endgame has become just such a beast.

The games given here show his subtle understanding of this complicated endgame which contains many middlegame ideas.

Game 57 Ruy Lopez C67

Fabiano Caruana 2801
Parimarjan Negi 2645

Tromsø ol 2014 (3)

1.e4 e5 2.♘f3 ♘c6 3.♗b5 ♘f6 4.0-0 ♘xe4 5.d4 ♘d6 6.♗xc6 dxc6 7.dxe5 ♘f5 8.♕xd8+ ♔xd8

The famous Berlin endgame, which became such a big thing after the Kasparov-Kramnik match (London 2000). The position turns out to be extremely unusual and difficult to get to grips with. I know many grandmasters who do not wish to play the position with either colour. I can understand them, because to play the position really well, one needs to feel its nuances to the tips of one's fingers.

Back in my schooldays, I remember seeing in Andrei Malchev's classic Soviet work on the Spanish a game Maroczy-Pillsbury, Munich 1900. It made a great impression on me. I simply could not believe that after the moves 9.♖d1+ ♔e8 10.♘c3 h6 11.b3 ♗b4 12.♗b2 ♗xc3! 13.♗xc3 ♗e6 14.♘d4 ♘xd4 15.♖xd4 c5 16.♖d2 ♖d8 17.♖ad1 ♔e7 18.♔f1 ♖xd2 19.♖xd2 b6 20.♔e2 a5 21.♔e3 ♖a8!,

White has to fight for a draw in an endgame with opposite-coloured bishops and doubled black pawns on the queenside! Even so, that is the case. It is all about the difference in bishop activity – White's bishop is obstructed by its own pawns, whilst its opposite

179

number has targets to attack. This small historical excursion can serve as the introduction for the reader to one of the secrets of the Berlin – Black strives for an opposite-coloured bishops position, in which it is easier for him to establish a light-square blockade.

9.h3

For the moment, White does not reveal the fate of his queen's knight, but makes a useful move with the h-pawn, preparing a later advance g2-g4.

9...♗d7 10.♖d1 ♗e7

11.g4

This move is usually played at a moment when the black knight does not have the square e7 at its disposal. I would add that the advance g2-g4 is one of Fabiano's favourite ideas in this position. In the game Anand-Carlsen (World Championship match, Chennai 2013) play continued 11.♘c3 ♔c8 12.♗g5 h6 13.♗xe7 ♘xe7 14.♖d2 c5 15.♖ad1 ♗e6 16.♘e1 ♘g6 17.♘d3 b6, and Black successfully solved his opening problems.

11...♘h4 12.♘xh4 ♗xh4

The exchange of a pair of knights in such positions, as a rule, favours

White, because it is easier for him to play f2-f4 and reduce to a minimum Black's aggressive possibilities.

13.♘d2!

Only now does the knight declare its intended route, heading for f3. In this case the agenda will include the exchange of the dark-squared bishops on g5.

13...♔c8 14.♘f3 ♗e7 15.♖d3

For the moment, 15.♗g5 is insufficient because of 15...♗c5!.

15...c5?!

In the game Caruana-Grischuk, Warsaw 2013, Black played the prophylactic 15...h6 16.♘d4 ♖e8 17.♗f4 c5 18.♘f5 ♗f8 19.c4 a6 20.♘e3 b5 21.b3 g5 22.♗g3 ♗e6 23.♖ad1 ♔b7 24.h4 ♔c6 25.h5 ♖eb8 26.f3 a5, retaining counterchances on the queenside. It is also worth considering 15...b6!? (a recommendation of Marin), for the moment keeping c5 free for the bishop.

16.♗g5!

The exchange of the dark-squared bishops deprives Black of any compensation for his doubled pawns and White's pawn majority on the kingside, but the Indian GM had counted on a forcing variation, leading the game into an opposite-coloured bishops position.

16...c4 17.♖d4 ♗c6 18.♗xe7 ♗xf3 19.♔h2 ♖e8 20.♗h4 c6 21.♖e1 ♗d5 22.f4

This time, unlike in Maroczy-Pillsbury, going into the opposite-coloured bishops ending has brought Black no benefits. The white kingside pawns have developed some mobility, which makes the black position difficult.

22...a5 23.c3 b5

The doubled pawns prevent Black developing real counterplay on the queenside, and the advance ...b7-b5 leads only to a weakening of the dark squares in his camp.

24.♖d2 b4

25.♗f2!

The weakness of the c5-square allows the white bishop to reach a dominating position on d6.

25...bxc3 26.bxc3 ♖b8 27.f5 a4

If 27...♖b5 White strengthens his position with 28.♔g3 and a later ♔f4.

28.♗c5 ♖b7 29.♔g3 ♔d7 30.♗a3 ♖b5 31.♔f4 ♖bb8 32.h4

It is clear that Black has nothing with which to oppose the advance of White's kingside pawns.

32...♖b5 33.h5 h6 34.♖dd1 f6

Black is afraid of the break f5-f6, but the medicine is here worse than the disease.

35.e6+ ♔c7 36.♖b1 ♖eb8 37.♖b4 ♖a8 38.♖eb1 ♖ab8 39.♔e3 ♔b6 40.♖d1 ♖xb4 41.♗xb4 ♔c7

42.♖e1!

Black is in zugzwang! He cannot simultaneously control the e6-pawn and prevent an invasion along the b-file.

42...♔d8

Or 42...♗g2 (42...♖e8 43.♖b1 ♖b8? 44.♗d6+!) 43.♖b1! ♔c8 44.♖g1! ♗d5 45.♗f8, winning.

43.♗f8 ♖b7 44.e7+ ♔e8 45.♖e2

At the realisation stage, White's advantage is aided by unhurried manoeuvring, aiming to eliminate the slightest enemy counterplay.

45...Rb1 46.Bxg7 Kxe7 47.Bf2+ Kf7 48.Bxh6 a3 49.Bf4 Rd1 50.Bd6

White exploits his extra pawns on the right flank for an attack on the black king.

50...Rd3 51.Re7+ Kg8 52.h6 Rh3 53.Rg7+ Kh8 54.Rg6 Rxc3 55.Be7 Kh7 56.Bxf6

With the decisive threat 57.g5 and then 58.Rg7+.

56...Rc2+ 57.Kg3

Black resigned.

Game 58 Ruy Lopez C67

Fabiano Caruana   2805

Magnus Carlsen   2876

Stavanger 2015 (2)

1.e4 e5 2.Nf3 Nc6 3.Bb5 Nf6 4.0-0 Nxe4 5.d4 Nd6 6.Bxc6 dxc6 7.dxe5 Nf5 8.Qxd8+ Kxd8 9.h3

Again we have the main *tabiya* of the Berlin endgame. Fabiano and Magnus have played a whole series of games from this position, always with Fabiano as White.

9...h6

A useful move, limiting the scope of the white pieces.

In recent times, the more popular plan has been that with ...h7-h5. In conceding control of g5 to his opponent, Black counts on strengthening the light squares. At a recent US Championship (St Louis, 2017), Caruana, as Black, played this line against Wesley So: 9...Ke8 10.Nc3 h5 11.Bg5 Be6 12.Rad1 Be7 etc.

10.Rd1+

Forcing the black king to remain in the centre, since 10...Bd7? (with the idea of ...Kc8) is impossible because of 11.g4 Ne7 12.e6!, and White wins.

10...Ke8 11.Nc3

11...Ne7

This flexible retreat was introduced into practice by GM Zoltan Almasi. Black is worried by the possibility of g2-g4, and so he transfers the knight to a more stable position. In the game Caruana-Karjakin, Shamkir 2014, Black tried 11...Bd7 12.Bf4 Rd8 13.Ne4 (a novelty at that moment. In the game Caruana-Ponomariov, Paris 2013, there followed the immediate 13.e6 Bxe6

14.♗xc7 ♖xd1+ 15.♖xd1 ♗e7 16.g4
♘h4 17.♘d4 ♗d7 18.♖e1 ♔f8 19.♗g3
g5 20.♗xh4 gxh4 21.♘e4 ♔g7, but
Black was not posed any serious
problems) 13...♗e7 ('I was pleased to
see this move. After the exchange
of knights, White's position
becomes very comfortable. More
principled is 13...c5!?, after which I
planned to play 14.e6 ♗xe6 15.♗xc7
♖c8 16.♗h2 with a small advantage
to White' – Caruana on ChessBase)
14.g4 ♘h4 15.♘xh4 ♗xh4 16.♔g2
♗e6 17.f3 b6 18.b3 c5?! ('A strategic
mistake. After the game, Sergey
said that he wanted to exploit the
square d4, but underestimated the
importance of d5' – Caruana) 19.c4
♖d7 20.♗g3 ♗e7 21.♖xd7 ♗xd7
22.♘c3 ♔d8 23.♘d5 ♖e8 24.♖d1
♔c8? (a blunder. It was essential to
play 24...c6 25.♘xe7 ♖xe7 26.♗h4
g5 27.♗g3 with a clear advantage to
White) 25.♘xc7!, and after winning
an important pawn, White easily
conducted the game to victory.

12.b3
Several months before the present
game, the same opponents played
the following encounter: 12.♗f4
♘g6 13.♗h2 ♗b4 14.♘e2 ♗e7
15.♘fd4 ♘f8 16.g4 h5 17.♘f5 ♘e6
18.♔g2 b6 19.f3 c5 20.♗g3 ♗g5 21.h4
hxg4 22.hxg5 gxf3+ 23.♔xf3 ♘xg5+
24.♔f4 ♘h3+ 25.♔e4 ♘g5+ 26.♔f4
♘h3+, and the game ended in
perpetual check (Caruana-Carlsen,
Baden-Baden 2015).

12...♗f5
Carlsen immediately activates
his light-squared bishop. More

common is the flexible 12...♘g6
13.♗b2 ♗e7 etc.

13.♘d4 ♗h7 14.♗b2 ♖d8

15.♘ce2!
An excellent manoeuvre. From
e2, the knight has a wide range of
possibilities.
In the game J.Polgar-Howell,
Warsaw 2013, the energetic 15.e6
was tried, but it did not bring White
any special benefit.

15...♘d5 16.c4
Denying the black knight a path to
f4.

16...♘b4
The knight's appearance on
b4 involves developing active
possibilities for the ♗h7.

17.♘f4 ♖g8

This mysterious moves aims to
defend the g7-square in advance.

18.g4!

A typical idea. The white knight is ready to jump to f5 and shut off the ♗h7. It is not so easy to get at the centralised black king – after the 'attacking' 18.e6?! ♗d6 19.exf7+ ♚xf7 White is simply worse!

18...♘a6?!

Black continues to seek the best post for his knight, but it seems he should have immediately burst the Gordian Knot with 18...♘c2! 19.♘xc2 ♖xd1+ 20.♖xd1 ♗xc2 21.♖d2 ♗b1 22.♗c3 ♗e7, and Black should gradually consolidate the position.

19.♘f5 ♘c5 20.♖xd8+ ♚xd8

21.♖d1+ ♚c8

By retreating the king to c8, Black hopes to be able to bring into action the ♖g8.

22.♗a3!

A subtle move, limiting the activity of the black pieces and containing quite a lot of poison.

22...♘e6?

The World Champion plays the move he has planned, but falls into a trap!

However, Black is already in difficulties. It seems he should have simplified the position with 22...♗xf5 23.gxf5 g6 24.fxg6 fxg6,

but here too, White's chances are superior thanks to his passed pawn in the centre and the fact that the black king is cut off from the kingside along the d-file.

23.♘xe6 ♗xa3

It transpires that after 23...fxe6 there follows the unexpected blow 24.♗e7!!, and the game ends immediately.

24.♘exg7 ♗f8

It may seem as though the knight is cut off in enemy territory, but White has a convincing retort.

25.e6! ♗xf5

The variations are obvious: 25...♗xg7 26.♘e7+ or 25...fxe6 26.♘xe6 ♗xf5 27.♖d8#.

26.♘xf5 fxe6 27.♘g3

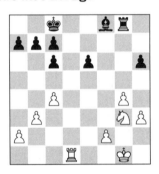

As a result of the tactical crossfire, White has obtained a strategically winning endgame. Black has absolutely nothing to do against the advance of the kingside pawn majority.

27...♗e7 28.♚g2 ♖f8

At attempt to hold up the advance f2-f4.

29.♖d3!

The third rank is an excellent highway for the white rook.

After its transfer to f3, the white expansion on the kingside continues.

29...♖f7 30.♘h5 ♗d6 31.♖f3 ♖h7

The minor piece ending arising after 31...♖xf3 32.♔xf3 ♔d7 33.♔e4 is also hopeless for Black.

32.♖e3 ♖e7 33.f4

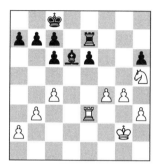

The white pawns start moving forward, which signifies the end for Black. The game concluded:

33...♗a3 34.♔f3 ♗b2 35.♖e2 ♗c3 36.g5 ♔d7 37.♔g4 ♖e8 38.♘g3 ♖h8 39.h4 b6 40.h5 c5 41.g6 ♖e8 42.f5 exf5+ 43.♔f4 ♖h8 44.♘xf5 ♗f6 45.♖g2

Black resigned.

Dortmund 2014

CHAPTER 11

The Dortmund pearls

The two most famous combinations by Caruana, which can without exaggeration be described as his calling cards, were played at the Dortmund tournaments in 2014 and 2015.

In Game 59, White's subtle work, aimed at preserving the tension in the position, is crowned with an explosive combination with successive sacrifices of rook and bishop. The combination is spectacular but not that difficult. Even so, together with the subtle positional build-up, it remains long in the memory.

The combination from Game 60 was often compared with the famous Ortueta-Sanz masterpiece (Madrid, 1934). In general, the original is more artistic (see page 193), but in this case, Caruana's beauty is characterised by the logical way it flows from the preceding positional play!

Game 59 Petroff Defence C42
Fabiano Caruana   2789
Ruslan Ponomariov   2728
Dortmund 2014 (2)

___

**1.e4 e5 2.♘f3 ♘f6 3.♘xe5 d6 4.♘f3
♘xe4 5.♘c3 ♘xc3 6.dxc3**

An exceptionally popular line against the Russian/Petroff Defence in modern practice.

The outwardly harmless position conceals a great deal of internal tension, assuming of course that White castles queenside.

6...♗e7 7.♗e3 ♘c6 8.♕d2 ♗e6

In a game played between the same opponents a year earlier, there followed 8...0-0 9.0-0-0 ♘e5 10.♘xe5 dxe5 11.♗d3 ♗e6 12.♕e2 ♕e8 13.♔b1 f5 14.♗c4 ♗f6 15.g4! ♗xc4 16.♕xc4+ ♕f7 17.♕b4 f4 18.♗c5 ♖fb8 19.f3, and White achieved some advantage, Caruana-Ponomariov, Bucharest 2013.

This time, Ponomariov avoids a position with opposite-side castling by sending his own king to the queenside, which leads to quieter play.

9.0-0-0 ♕d7 10.♔b1 ♗f6

Black hesitates with queenside castling for the moment, not wanting to allow the enemy bishop to b5. All the while the black king is in the centre, 11.♗b5 can be met by 11...a6 12.♗a4 b5!.

11.h3!?

Preparing g2-g4 followed by ♗g2. In the game Caruana-Landa, Reggio Emilia 2010, White was successful with the energetic 11.h4 h6 (11...0-0-0) 12.♘d4 ♘xd4 13.♗xd4 ♗xd4 14.♕xd4 0-0 15.♖g1 ♖ae8 16.g4 ♕c6 17.♗g2 ♕a6 18.b3 (a characteristic moment – the doubled pawns on the queenside significantly influence the safety of the white king) 18...♗d7 19.g5 h5 20.g6 ♖e7 21.♗d5 ♗e6 22.♖de1 c5 23.♕d1 ♖fe8 24.♕xh5 fxg6 25.♖xe6, and Black resigned. Of course, his play can be improved.

11...h6 12.b3

An interesting prophylactic/waiting move. I cannot say precisely what the idea is. I will only point out that on 12...0-0-0 there could follow 13.♘d4!? with the idea of 13...♘xd4 14.♗xd4, with a nice double attack on a7 and f6.

12...a6 13.g4 0-0-0 14.♗g2

The position looks absolutely equal. Even so, White's piece and pawn configuration on the kingside is more aggressive.

Now a tempting line for Black is the gradual improvement of his position with 14...♔b8 and then ♖he8. Fabiano intended in this case the original manoeuvre 15.♘g1!? with the idea of ♘f4 or f4-f5.

14...g5?!

This move, leading to a weakening of the kingside, was unanimously condemned by the commentators. Black intends to correct the situation with ...♗g7 and ...f7-f5, but the opponent shoots first...

15.♘d4! ♘xd4 16.cxd4 d5 17.f4!

Destroying the opponent's pawn structure.

17...gxf4 18.♗xf4 h5!

A good reply, giving Black counterchances.

19.g5 ♗g7

Black has two constructive ideas – to play ...f7-f6, getting rid of the weak pawn on f7, or ...h5-h4, giving White a weakness on h3. Caruana decides that his main task is to stop ...f7-f6.

20.♖de1 h4! 21.♗e5

White's achievements are obvious – he has established control over the dark squares. Even so, it is too early to speak of a clear advantage,

in view of the weaknesses on g5 and
h3. Undoubtedly, these factors were
in the Ukrainian GM's mind when
he played 14...g5.

21...♖dg8 22.♕f4 ♕d8 23.♗f1!

The transfer of the bishop to d3
creates the threat of g5-g6.

23...♔b8 24.♗d3 ♗c8!

An excellent defensive resource –
the black bishop leaves its unstable
position. The tactical justification is
the variation 25.♕xf7 ♗xe5 26.dxe5
♖f8!, and Black equalises.

25.♔b2 ♗xe5 26.♖xe5 ♖g7

'At this point I realized that I have
no constructive ideas to improve
my position. On the other hand,
Black also doesn't want to spoil his
ideal setup, so I decided to give him
a move' – Caruana in New In Chess
2014/6.

An instructive decision by the
professional player!

27.a4 a5

'Not entirely ideal, as this weakens
the b5-square. I could see Pono
was hesitant to play this, but it's
difficult to find an other move' –
Caruana.

28.♔a2

White simply continues to wait!

28...♔a7

Black adopts the same tactics! The
attempt to transform the position
by means of 28...♖hg8 29.♕xh4
♖xg5 30.♖xg5 ♕xg5 31.♕xg5 ♖xg5
32.h4 ♖h5 33.♗e2 ♖h6 34.h5 looks
suspicious.

29.♕d2

Provoking the opponent into new
pawn moves, but Black finds a way
to keep waiting, for the moment.

29...♔b8 30.♕f4 ♔a7 31.♖he1

'Finally doing something, now
that the king is misplaced on a7' –
Caruana.

31...♗xh3 32.♖h1 ♗c8

A mistake would be 32...♕d7?
33.♕f6 ♖hg8 34.♖e7 ♕c8 35.g6!, and
Black's defences break down.

33.♖xh4 ♖xh4 34.♕xh4

34...b6?

The desire to place all his pawns
'according to the rules' (i.e. on
squares of the opposite colour
to that of his bishop) plays an
evil trick on the ex-FIDE World
Champion. By playing 34...c6!, Black
reliably defends the d5-pawn, and
his position would not be easy to
break down.

35.♕h6 ♖g8 36.♕c6!

An effective queen transfer along the 6th rank, which allows him to drive the black bishop to a bad position.

36...♗e6

It would be hard to find volunteers to defend the position a pawn down after 36...♖xg5 37.♖xg5 ♕xg5 38.♕xc7+ ♗b7 39.♕xf7.
Equally, the variation 36...♗b7 37.♕f6 ♕xf6 38.gxf6 ♔b8 (the black bishop cannot get from b7 to e6, which allows the white rook into e7) 39.♖e7 ♖f8 40.♗b5! leads to an extremely passive position for Black in the endgame.

37.g6 ♖g7

Allowing a surprising end. Caruana had also prepared a beautiful combination in the variation 37...♖f8 38.g7 ♖g8 39.♖g5!!, and White wins.
Black's best chance was 37...♗d7 38.♕xd5 fxg6 39.♗e4 ♕c8 40.♖e7 ♖d8 41.♕f7 ♔b8 42.♕xg6, but he is hardly likely to save the position, a pawn down and with a bad king.

38.gxf7 ♗xf7

39.♖e7!!

Lightning from a clear sky! This double-piece sacrifice combination will be rememberd for a long time.

39...♕xe7 40.♗a6!!

There is no defence against mate. Ponomariov decides to play to the gallery and allow the mate.

40...♔xa6 41.♕a8#

After the game Caruana revealed his happiness: 'One of the most satisfying combinations I have ever played!'

Game 60 Evans Gambit C52
Liviu Dieter Nisipeanu　　　2654
Fabiano Caruana　　　　　　2805
Dortmund 2015 (7)

1.e4 e5 2.♘f3 ♘c6 3.♗c4 ♗c5 4.b4

The Evans Gambit – a romantic 19th century opening!
Even in our day, GMs occasionally resurrect this old opening, counting largely on the element of surprise.

4...♗xb4 5.c3 ♗a5 6.d4 d6

Emanuel Lasker's defence. Black is ready to return the gambit pawn, but to get a solid position in the centre. In the days of the genius of combinations, Adolf Anderssen, many sharp battles arose after 6...exd4 7.0-0!.

7.♕b3

Regaining the pawn with 7.dxe5 dxe5 8.♕xd8+ ♘xd8 9.♘xe5 ♗e6 leads to a comfortable endgame for Black.

7...♕d7

This strange-looking move is largely forced, since after 7...♕e7 8.d5 ♘d4 9.♘xd4 exd4 10.♕a4+ ♗d7 (10...♔f8 11.♗d3!) 11.♕xa5 ♕xe4+ 12.♔d1 Black has to sacrifice a piece for unclear compensation.

8.dxe5 ♗b6!

The classical theoretical recommendation. Black prepares ...♘a5, and beats off the attack. Black has also tried 8...dxe5 9.0-0 ♗b6 10.♖d1 ♕e7 11.a4!?, in which White has more chances of sharpening the game.

9.a4

Rather more frequently, White plays 9.♘bd2, so as after 9...♘a5 10.♕c2 ♘xc4 11.♘xc4 to bring the ♘b1 into play quickly.

9...♘a5 10.♕a2 ♘xc4 11.♕xc4 ♘e7

12.♗a3

The stem game Nakamura-Anand (London rapid 2014) went 12.exd6 cxd6 13.0-0 0-0 14.♕d3 ♘g6 15.a5 ♗c5 16.♗e3 ♖e8 17.♘bd2 ♗xe3

18.♕xe3 d5, and Black did not have any problems.

Nisipeanu's novelty also causes Black no real difficulty.

12...0-0

A typical practical decision – in an open position, completing development is the most important thing!

The computer is more taken with 12...d5!? 13.exd5 ♕xd5, which is also good.

13.0-0 ♖e8

Here the computer sees the following trick: 13...♘g6 14.exd6 cxd6 15.♖d1 ♕g4! 16.h3 (16.♗xd6? ♘h4!) 16...♘e5! with good play for Black. With the subtle text move, Caruana liquidates the pin on the a3-f8 diagonal and favourably ratchets up the tension in the centre.

14.exd6 cxd6 15.♖d1 ♕c6 16.♘bd2

16...♗e6!

This positional pawn sacrifice allows Black to seize the initiative. The continuation 16...d5 17.♕xc6 bxc6 18.c4! leads to rough equality.

17.♕xc6 ♘xc6 18.♗xd6 ♖ad8

For the pawn, Black has excellently placed pieces and the two bishops.

In addition, the pawns on a4 and c3 will become a permanent headache for White.

19.♗b4

After 19.e5 f6! the position opens up, to Black's obvious advantage.

19...♖d3 20.a5 ♗c7 21.♘f1

Possibly White should have preferred 21.♖db1, retaining a minimal material advantage of the exchange as compensation for his strategic weaknesses.

21...♖xd1 22.♖xd1 ♘xa5 23.♘d4

By returning the pawn, White has somewhat activated his pieces, although from a positional point of view, things do not look very good for him.

23...♘c4!

Striving to transform the advantage, a Caruana characteristic. Refusing the two bishops, Black quickly damps down the opponent's temporary initiative (23...♗c8 24.♘b5; 23...♗c4 24.♘e3).

24.♘xe6 ♖xe6 25.♖d7

White should aim for a counter-attack – with quiet play, the enemy outside passed pawn can easily decide the outcome of the game.

25...♖c6 26.♘g3 g6 27.♘e2

There are only a few checks after 27.♖e7 a5 28.♖e8+ ♔g7 29.♗f8+ ♔f6 30.♗e7+ ♔e6, and Black should win.

It seems that the unstoppable knight jump to d4 will solve all White's defensive problems. However, Caruana has prepared a surprising combinational trap.

27...a5! 28.♘d4?

Falling into the trap. It was essential to play 28.♗e7, retaining chances of defence.

28...axb4! 29.♘xc6 b3! 30.♖xc7

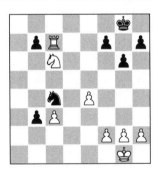

30...♘d6!!

A brilliant finish! The black knight proves quicker than the white rook (there is no help even from 31.♘e7+ ♔f8), and the b3-pawn cannot be stopped from promoting.

White resigned.

After the game, Caruana declared on Twitter: 'This game is my Ortueta-Sanz!'

For the sake of comparison, we will show you this famous fragment too:

(see fragment on the right)

Martin Ortueta Esteban
José Sanz Aguado
Madrid 1934

31...♖xb2! 32.♘xb2 c3 33.♖xb6 c4!!
34.♖b4 a5 35.♘xc4 c2 0-1

Stavanger 2018 (Photo: Lennart Ootes)

CHAPTER 12

Queen sacrifices

We conclude our exposition with two artistic productions on the theme of queen sacrifices. Here we are concerned with 'real sacrifices', as Rudolf Spielmann called them, made for long-term positional compensation.

There is one small correction – in both cases, the queen sacrifice was prepared by Caruana in his home laboratory and therefore the risk involved was reduced to a minimum.

Does the shine of the games below get diminished by the circumstances of the sacrifices being prepared? From a purely emotional viewpoint, they certainly do. But from the point of view of 'positional compensation', the reader will be interested to hear that, according to an interview with Caruana, the computer does not see the idea of the queen sacrifice in Game 62!

Game 61 Grünfeld Indian Defence D76
Rafael Leitao 2624
Fabiano Caruana 2700
Khanty-Mansiysk ol 2010 (9)

1.d4 ♘f6 2.c4 g6 3.♘f3 ♗g7 4.g3
Grünfeld players now have a choice between two continuations – the symmetrical 4...c6 5.♗g2 d5 and the text, which is more consistent with the idea of piece pressure against the enemy pawn centre.
4...d5 5.cxd5 ♘xd5 6.♗g2 ♘b6 7.♘c3 ♘c6 8.e3 0-0 9.0-0 ♖e8 10.♖e1
Practice has also seen 10.d5 ♘a5 11.♘d4 ♗d7 followed by ...c7-c6.
10...a5
This position was something of a Grünfeld *tabiya* at the 39th Olympiad in Khanty-Mansiysk, being met more than ten times in the course of the event!

The main line in the 20th century was 10...e5 11.d5 ♘a5 12.e4 c6, but later White began to achieve good results with the restraining move 13.b3.

In playing 10...a5, Black tries to seize space on the queenside, preparing the best conditions for the key break ...e7-e5.
11.♕e2
Now 11.d5 involves a pawn sacrifice – 11...♗xc3 12.bxc3 ♕xd5 etc. With the text, White prepares to meet the advance 11...e5 with

12.dxe5 ♘xe5 13.♘xe5 ♗xe5 14.e4, activating his pawn phalanx in the centre.

11...♗e6 12.♖d1

Alternative moves are 12.♘d2 and 12.b3.

12...♗c4 13.♕c2 ♘b4 14.♕b1

We have reached one of the critical positions of the line. Black's active moves have run out and now his pieces can be restrained with b2-b3. In the event of 14...a4 White plays 15.e4 ♕d7 16.♗e3 ♖ed8 17.♕c1!, achieving a comfortable position in the centre.

14...e5!

'The move 14...e5 was first played in this Olympiad, only two days before the present encounter. But because every day I looked at all the games from the event, I did not miss this important theoretical idea! I analysed the move 14...e5 thoroughly and got the chance to use it, whereas my opponent possibly was unaware of it' – Caruana on ChessBase.

15.a3

In the stem game there followed 15.b3 exd4! (the key idea behind the move 14...e5) 16.exd4 (16.♘xd4

♗d3!) 16...♗e6 17.♗f4 ♗f5 18.♕b2 ♘d3 19.♕d2 ♘xf4 20.♕xf4 a4 with advantage to Black, McNab-Duric, Khanty-Mansiysk 2010.

In preparing for the game, Caruana had analysed the following principal variations:

A) 15.b3 exd4! 16.bxc4 dxc3 17.♖xd8 ♖axd8 18.♘d4 ♖xd4! 19.exd4 ♖e1+ 20.♗f1 ♗xd4, and despite the fact that Black has only a knight for the queen, it is White who must fight for a draw!;

B) 15.♘xe5 ♗xe5 16.b3! ♗d3 17.♖xd3 ♘xd3 18.♕xd3, and White has good compensation for the exchange, but only sufficient to hold the balance.

15...exd4!

Black has no way back!

16.axb4

The continuations 16.exd4?! ♘4d5 or 16.♘xd4 ♗d3! 17.♖xd3 ♘xd3 18.♕xd3 c5 favour Black.

16...dxc3!

This positional queen sacrifice is the key resource for Black in the resulting complications.

Fabiano had also analysed 16... axb4!? 17.♖xa8 ♕xa8 18.♘e4, coming to the conclusion that it was more risky for Black. Here are several of the variations pointed out by him, which testify to the depth of his preparation: 18...♕a4 19.b3! (19.♖e1 ♗a2 20.♕d3 ♗c4=) 19...♕xb3 20.♗b2 dxe3? (better is 20...♕a2 or 20...♗e2) 21.♗xg7 ♖xe4 (or 21...exf2+ 22.♔xf2 ♔xg7 23.♕a1+ ♔h6 24.♘fd2 ♕a2 25.♕d4 with a strong attack for White) 22.♖d8+ ♔xg7 23.♕xe4 e2 24.♕d4+ (unclear is 24.♕e5+ ♔h6) 24...f6 25.♘e1 ♕b1 26.♕d2 b3 27.h4! (27.♕b4? c5) 27...b2 28.♕b4 c5 29.♕xc5 ♕xe1+ 30.♔h2, and Black has no defence against mate.

17.♖xd8 ♖axd8

18.♕c2?!

'A natural move, but it leads to problems. White could make a draw by means of 18.bxc3 ♖d1+ 19.♗f1, but I was not convinced that my opponent would look at such a line. At first glance, White's position looks extremely dangerous, but Black has no advantage: 19...♗xf1 (nothing changes after 19...♗xc3 20.♖xa5 ♗xf1 21.♕c2 ♗e2+ (21...♖ed8 22.♘d4) 22.♔g2 ♗f1+=) 20.♕c2, and Black has nothing better than perpetual check –

20...♗e2+ (20...♖ed8 21.♘d4) 21.♔g2 ♗f1+' – Caruana.

18...axb4

A surprising position! Black has only a rook for the queen, but his pieces are so well placed that the opponent, in order to avoid an immediate catastrophe, is obliged to give back part of the 'loot'.

19.♘d2!

He loses after 19.bxc3? b3 20.♕b2 ♖d1+.

19...cxd2 20.♗xd2

20...♖a8!

This unexpected switch of the attack to the a-file is the prologue to a mass attack on b2.

21.♖xa8

If 21.♖b1 b3 22.♕d1 c6! Black's advantage is not in doubt, since White's pieces are too passive.

21...♖xa8

22.♗xb7?

The decisive mistake. The outcome of the battle would have remained unclear after 22.h4!, trying to create counterplay against the black king. Then Caruana gives the following possible scenario: 22...♖a2 (or 22...♖a1+ 23.♔h2 b3 24.♕e4 ♗xb2 25.♕e8+ ♔g7 26.h5) 23.♗c1 b3 24.♕d2 h5 (24...♗f6!?) 25.g4! hxg4 26.h5! with chances of a draw.

22...♖a1+ 23.♗c1

Black achieves a surprising domination after 23.♔g2 ♗f1+ 24.♔f3 ♘c4! 25.♗xb4 (25.b3 ♗d3–+) 25...♘e5+ 26.♔f4 ♖c1 27.♕a4 ♖c4+ 28.e4 ♘d3+ 29.♔f3 ♘xb4, winning.

23...b3 24.♕d1?

Losing at once, but White was already unable to save himself. After 24.♕d2 ♗e6 White cannot save the ♗c1: 25.♔g2 (25.♕d8+ ♗f8 26.♕xc7 ♘c4–+) 25...♘c4 26.♕d1 ♘d6, and Black wins.

24...♗xb2

White resigned.

Fabiano spent no more than five minutes on the entire game! A miracle of opening preparation!

Game 62 Sicilian Defence B96

Fabiano Caruana   2828
Hikaru Nakamura   2779

London 2016 (6)

1.e4 c5 2.♘f3 d6 3.d4 cxd4 4.♘xd4 ♘f6 5.♘c3 a6 6.♗g5 e6 7.f4

One of the sharpest variations of the Sicilian, foreshadowing a real chess battle.

7...h6 8.♗h4 ♕b6

Including the moves ...h7-h6 and ♗h4 brings certain subtleties to the Poisoned Pawn Variation 9.♕d2 ♕xb2 10.♖b1 ♕a3.

For example, after 11.f5 the reply 11...♗e7 (which is not good with the white bishop on g5) is now possible: 12.fxe6 fxe6 13.♗c4 ♘xe4! 14.♘xe4 ♗xh4+ 15.g3 ♗g5 16.♘xg5 hxg5 17.♘xe6 ♗xe6 18.♗xe6 ♕xg3+! 19.hxg3 ♖xh1+ 20.♔e2 ♖h2+ 21.♔e1 ♖xd2 22.♔xd2 ♖a7 23.♗d5 ♘d7 24.♖xb7 ♖xb7 25.♗xb7 ♘c5, and the battle ended in a mutual elimination of material in Vallejo Pons-Morozevich, Reggio Emilia 2010.

9.a3

But this is one of the advantages for White of ...h7-h6 and ♗h4 –

after 9...♘c6 (9...♕xb2?? 10.♘a4) he can consolidate his position with 10.♗f2.

9...♗e7 10.♗f2 ♕c7 11.♕f3 ♘bd7 12.0-0-0 b5 13.g4

White's plan is obvious – to advance his kingside pawns into the attack. Note that the white ♗f2 does not get under the feet of its own pawns.

13...g5

Meeting the attack head on! The idea of this standard counterattack is to secure control of the e5-square. A quieter alternative is 13...♗b7.

14.h4 gxf4 15.♗e2

Preparing the break g4-g5 and defending the g4-pawn in the event of 15...♘e5 16.♕xf4.

This position has already been seen in practice. Black gets nothing good from 15...♘e5 16.♕xf4 ♘exg4 17.♗xg4 e5 18.♘d5! ♘xd5 19.♕f3 ♘f6 20.♗xc8 ♖xc8 21.c3, with a clear advantage to White.

In the game Giri-Vachier-Lagrave, Stavanger 2015, Black successfully played 15...♖g8, but later analysis showed that by 16.g5! (in the game 16.♖dg1? was played) he would have faced definite problems.

15...b4

A novelty, which was probably not a secret to his opponent, as the move 15...b4 was recommended by the computer!

The idea of the pawn sacrifice consists in the fact that in the variation 16.axb4 ♘e5 17.♕xf4 ♘exg4 18.♗xg4 e5 19.♘d5 ♘xd5 20.♕f3 Black has the move 20...♘xb4!.

16.axb4 ♘e5 17.♕xf4 ♘exg4 18.♗xg4 e5

19.♕xf6!!

A brilliant counter-novelty! However, the innovation itself comes later – the move 19.♕xf6 is within the computer's vision.

19...♗xf6 20.♘d5 ♕d8

21.♘f5!!

This is the whole point – White goes for a positional queen sacrifice for two minor pieces!

Caruana admitted that he'd had this position in his preparation and the inventor of the queen sacrifice idea was his second, Rustam Kasimdzhanov.

The computer considers the strongest line to be the regaining of the material by 21.♘c6 ♗xg4 22.♘xd8 ♗xd8, which leads to an endgame that is completely safe for Black.

The plusses of the move 21.♘f5!! are not seen by modern-day computers, which advise the reply 21...♗xf5, a move that looks suicidal to a human player – after 22.♗xf5 ♖b8 23.♖d3 (with the idea of ♖a3) Black has nothing with which to oppose the enemy's complete domination of the light squares. 'Whatever the engines may say, White's position is close to winning' confirmed Caruana.

Caissa's art gallery contains some even less obvious queen sacrifices. We can remember the game Nezhmetdinov-Chernikov (Rostov-on-Don, 1962) or Bronstein's idea in the King's Indian: 1.d4 ♘f6 2.c4 g6 3.♘c3 ♗g7 4.e4 d6 5.f3 e5 6.d5 ♘h5 7.♗e3 ♘a6 8.♕d2

8...♕h4+ 9.g3 ♘xg3 10.♕f2 ♘xf1 11.♕xh4 ♘xe3 12.♔f2 ♘xc4, played in the game Spassky-Bronstein, Amsterdam 1956.

So why did Nakamura underestimate the sacrifice here? Undoubtedly, it was a misjudgement of the position – the American GM believed too much in his 'silicon friend' and did not pay attention to the move 21.♘f5!!.

21...♖b8

Black decides against exchanging off his 'cementing' light-squared bishop and just meets the threat of 22.♗b6.

22.♘xf6+

Transformation – the exchange of the 'beautiful' knight for the 'bad' bishop allows the white pieces to break into the square d6.

22...♕xf6

23.♖xd6

In the computer's opinion, here White could have decided things with 23.♘xd6+ ♔e7 (or 23...♔f8 24.♗f5 with the irresistible threat of 25.♗c5) 24.♗c5 ♕f4+ (24...♗xg4 25.♘b5+ ♔e8 26.♘c7#) 25.♔b1 ♕xg4 (25...♗xg4 26.♘f5+ ♔e8 27.♘g7#) 26.♘xc8+ ♔e8 (26...♔f6

27.♖hf1+ ♔g7 28.♖g1) 27.♘d6+ ♔d7 (27...♔e7 28.♘f5+ ♔e8 29.♖hg1) 28.♘xf7+ ♔c7 (28...♔e6 29.♘xh8 ♖xh8 30.♖hf1) 29.♗d6+ ♔b7 30.♗xb8 ♖xb8 31.♘xe5 (31...♕xe4? 32.♘d7!), and White has a material advantage that is sufficient for victory.

The line chosen by Caruana is also good, though.

23...♗e6 24.♖hd1 0-0

25.h5!

The appearance of the bishop on h4 will significantly strengthen White's attack and 'stalemate' the enemy queen on h8.

25...♕g5+ 26.♗e3 ♕f6 27.♘xh6+ ♔h8

28.♗f5!

Here the blow 28.♘xf7+!? was possible, but the gradual

strengthening of the position better underlines the true difficulty facing Black.

The possibilities of the position can be demonstrated by a few short variations:

A) 28...♖xb4 29.♘xf7+; or

B) 28...♖fd8 29.♖xd8+ ♖xd8 30.♖xd8+ ♕xd8 31.♗xe6 ♕h4 32.♘xf7+ ♔h7 33.♔b1, and White wins;

C) 28...♖fe8 29.c3, and it is not clear what Black's next move will be.

28...♕e7

29.b5!?

A subtle, but not obligatory pawn sacrifice.

The computer shows a direct way to win: 29.♘xf7+! ♖xf7 (29...♗xf7 30.♖h6+ ♔g8 31.♖g1+) 30.♖xe6 ♕xb4 (striving for counterplay by attacking b2) 31.♖h6+ ♔g8 32.♖g1+ ♖g7 (32...♔f8 33.♖h8+ ♔e7 34.♖xb8 ♕xb8 35.♗c5+ ♔f6 36.♖g6#) 33.♗e6+ ♔f8 34.♗c5+!! (evidently this unexpected sacrifice had escaped Caruana's attention in his preliminary calculations, whereas the tempting 34.♖h8+ ♔e7 35.♖xg7+ ♔d6 36.♖d7+ ♔xe6

37.♖xb8 ♕xb8 allows Black to resist further) 34...♕xc5 35.♖h8+ ♔e7 36.♖xg7+ ♔xe6 37.♖h6#!.

In playing 29.b5!?, Caruana strives to blockade the b-file, depriving the opponent of counterplay.

29...♕e8

Losing quickly.

The idea of White's last move is revealed in the variation 29...♖xb5 30.♘xf7+ ♖xf7 31.♖xe6 ♕b4 32.♖h6+ ♔g8 33.♖d8+ ♖f8 (33...♔g7 34.♖g6+ ♔h7 35.♖c6+ ♖xf5 36.♖c7+) 34.♗e6+ ♔g7 35.♖d7+ with mate.

He should be able to hold on for the moment with 29...♖be8, but after 30.bxa6 White's position is winning, of course.

30.♘xf7+!

Now this thematic blow leads to the goal without any trouble – at the end of a forcing variation, the black queen on b5 doesn't threaten mate.

30...♖xf7 31.♖xe6 ♕xb5 32.♖h6+

And Black resigned because of 32...♔g8 33.♖g1+ ♖g7 34.♗e6+ ♔f8 35.♖h8+ ♔e7 36.♖xg7+ ♔d6 37.♖h6 with unavoidable mate.

Index of openings

(numbers refer to pages)

Index of names

(numbers refer to pages)